FIRST 50 SO

YOU SHOULD PLAY ON MANDOLIN

Arrangements by Fred Sokolow
Edited by Ronny Schiff

ISBN 978-1-4950-5663-5

HAL•LEONARD®
CORPORATION

7777 W. Bluemound Rd. P.O. Box 13819 Milwaukee, WI 53213

Visit Hal Leonard Online at
www.halleonard.com

CONTENTS

Amazing Grace

Words by John Newton
from a Collection of Sacred Ballads
Traditional American Melody
from Carrell and Clayton's Virginia Harmony
Arranged by Edwin O. Excell

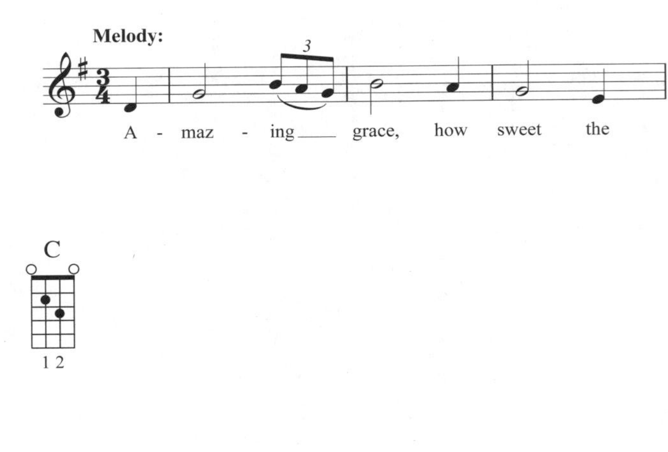

Melody:
A - maz - ing grace, how sweet the
G
D
C

Key of G
Intro
Slowly

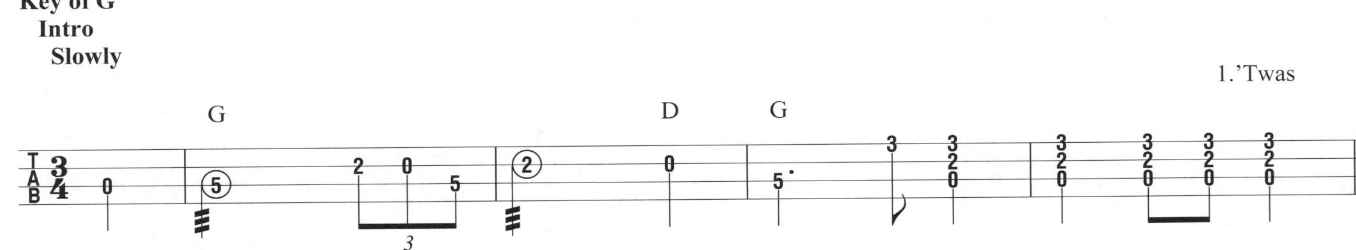

G
D
G
1.'Twas

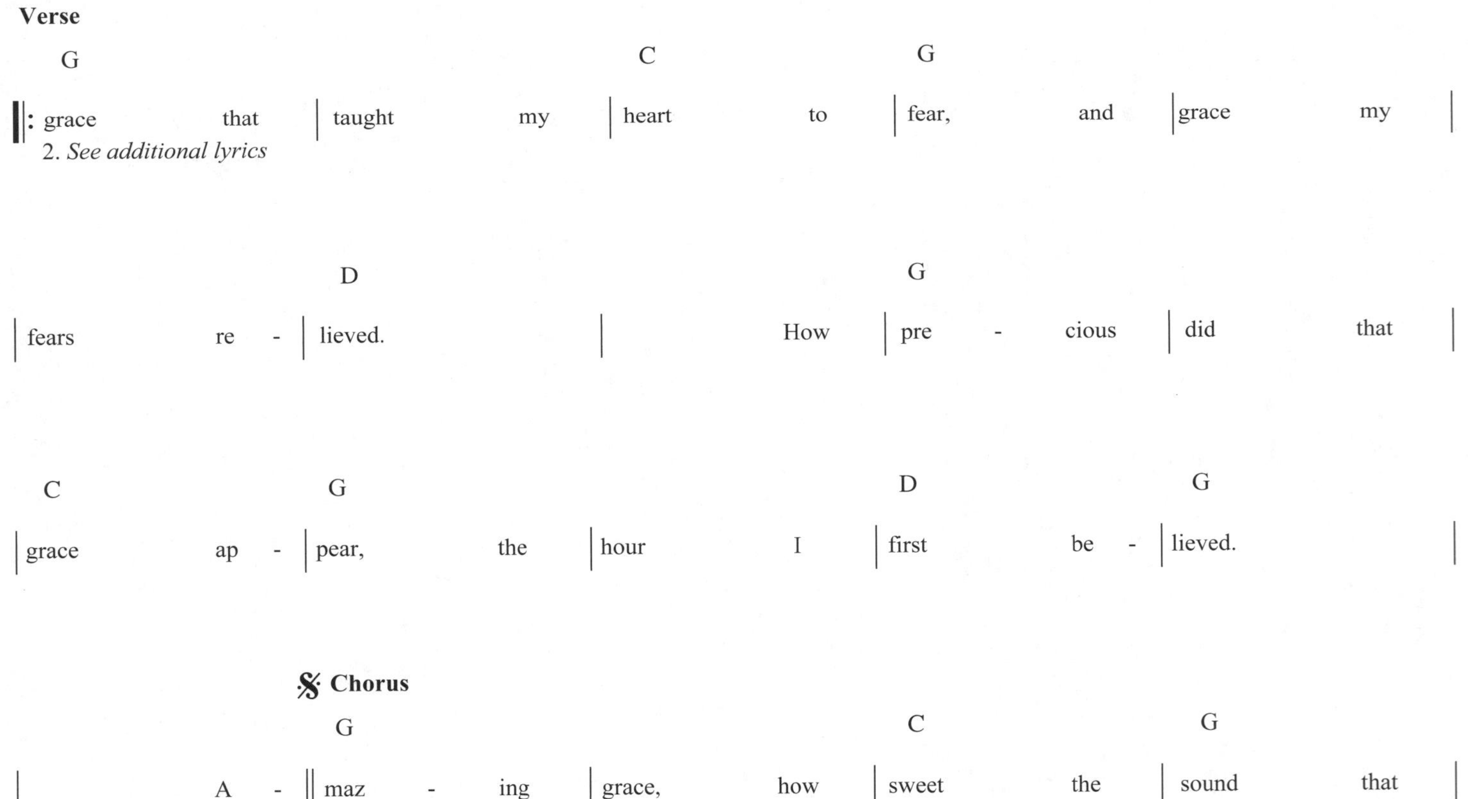

Verse
G C G
grace that taught my heart to fear, and grace my
2. See additional lyrics
D G
fears re - lieved. How pre - cious did that
C G D G
grace ap - pear, the hour I first be - lieved.
Chorus
G C G
A - maz - ing grace, how sweet the sound that

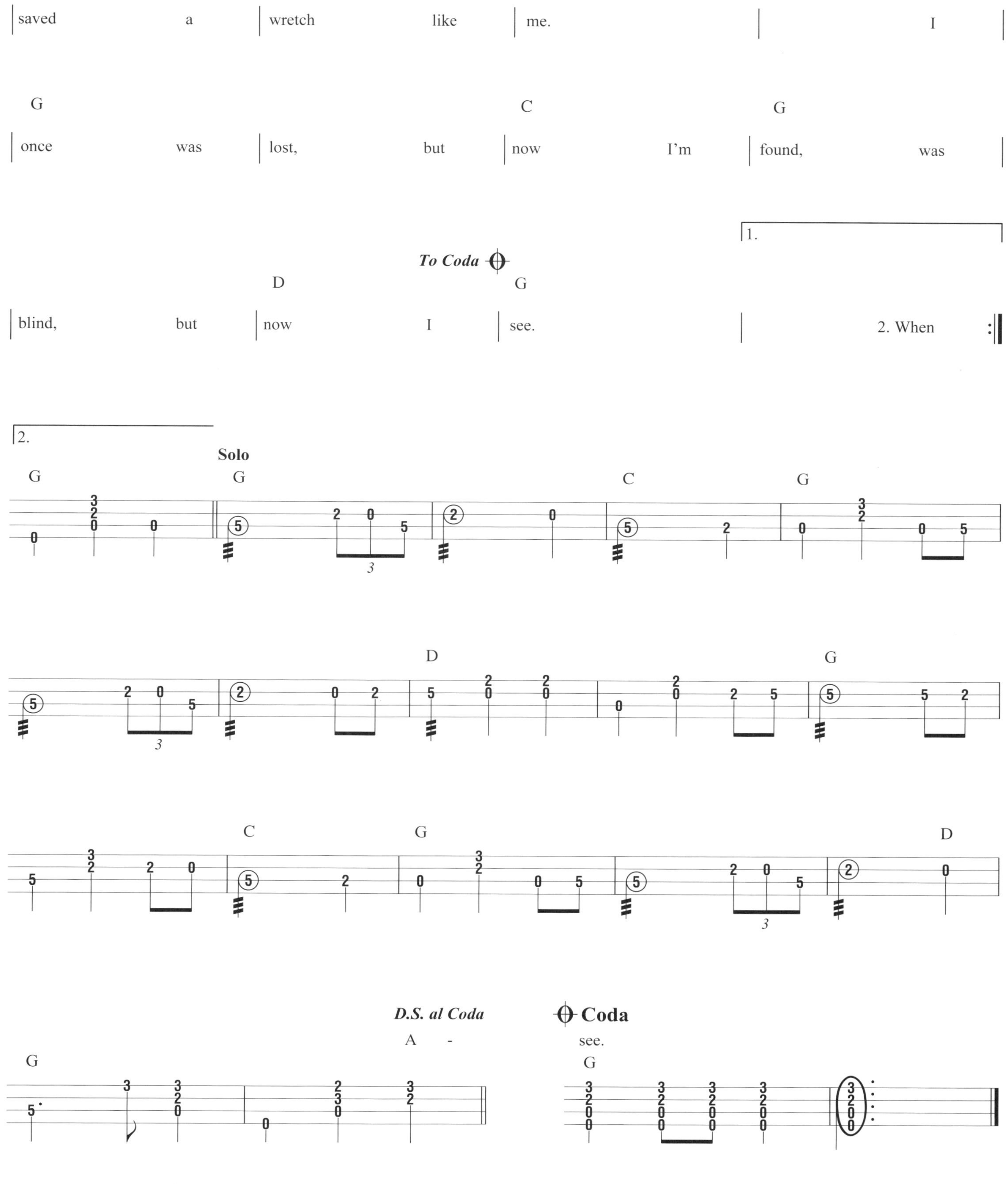
D
saved a wretch like me. I
G C G
once was lost, but now I'm found, was
To Coda
D G
1.
blind, but now I see. 2. When
2.
Solo
G G C G
D G
C G D
D.S. al Coda
A -
Coda
see.
G G

Additional Lyrics

2. When we've been there ten thousand years, bright shining as the sun,
We've no less days to sing God's praise than when we first begun.

Arkansas Traveler

Southern American Folksong

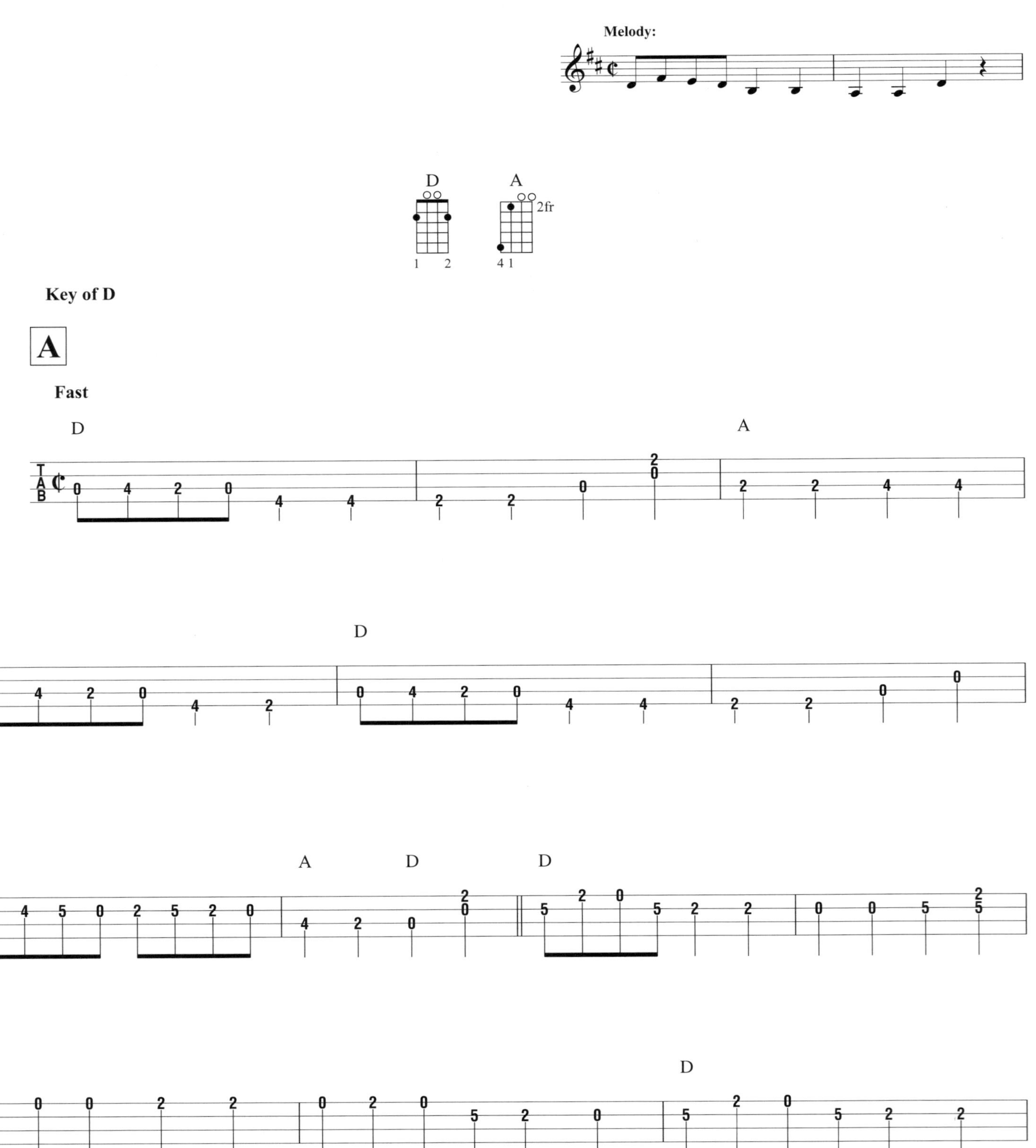
Melody:
D
A
2fr
1 2
4 1
Key of D
A
Fast
D
A
D
A
D
D
A
D

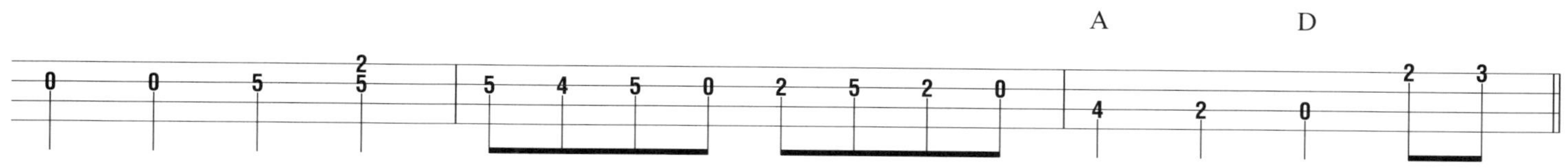
A D

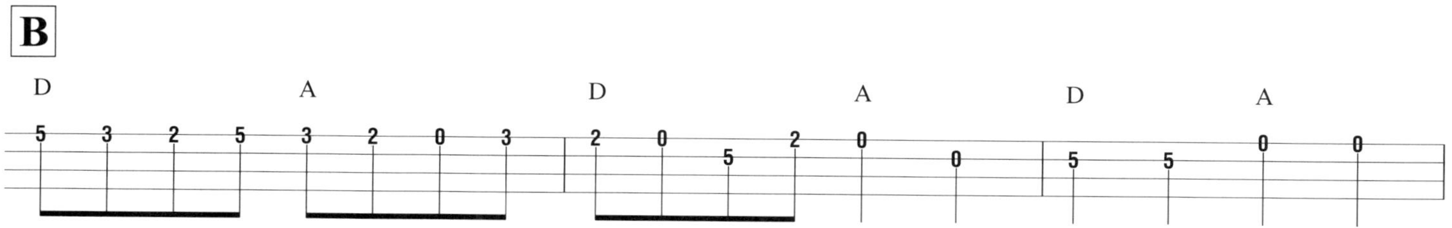
B
D A D A D A

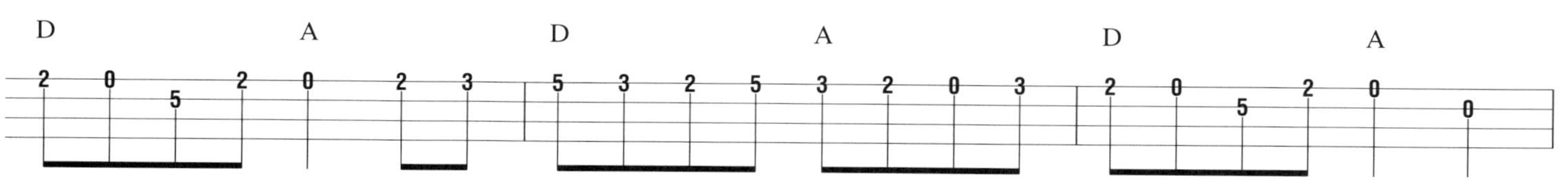
D A D A D A

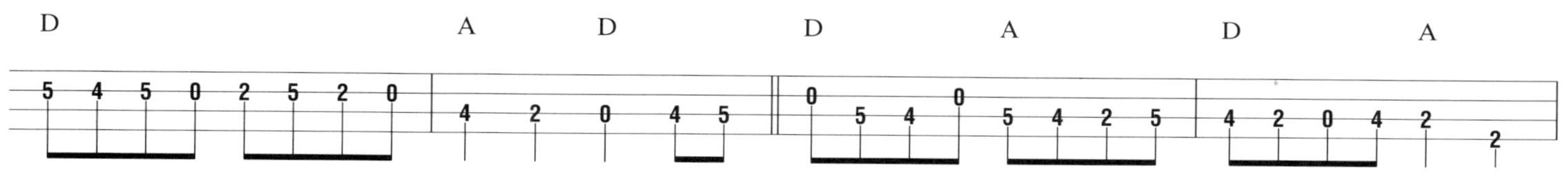
D A D D A D A

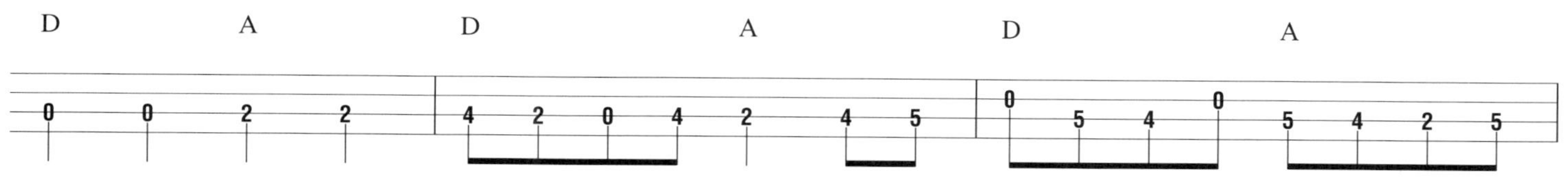
D A D A D A

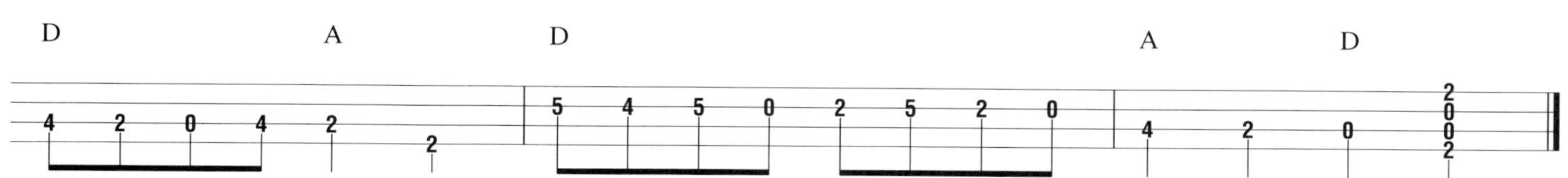
D A D A D

Arrivederci Roma
(Goodbye to Rome)

from the Motion Picture SEVEN HILLS OF ROME

Words and Music by Carl Sigman, Ranucci Renato, Sandro Giovanni and Peidro Garinei

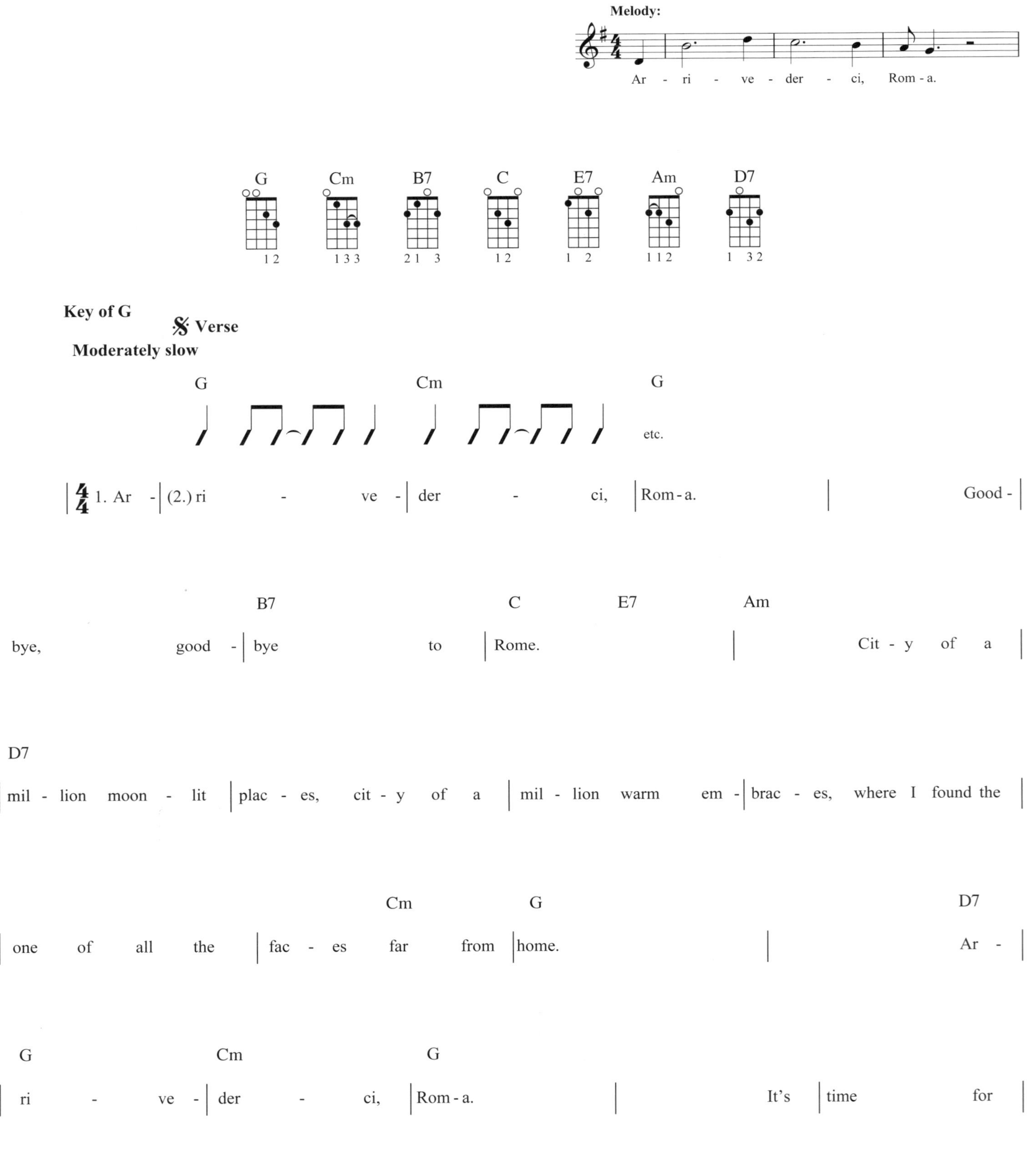
Melody:
Ar - ri - ve - der - ci, Rom - a.
G Cm B7 C E7 Am D7
1 2
1 3 3
2 1 3
1 2
1 2
1 1 2
1 3 2
Key of G
Verse
Moderately slow
G Cm G
etc.
1. Ar - (2.) ri - ve - der - ci, Rom - a. Good -
B7 C E7 Am
bye, good - bye to Rome. Cit - y of a
D7
mil - lion moon - lit plac - es, cit - y of a mil - lion warm em - brac - es, where I found the
Cm G D7
one of all the fac - es far from home. Ar -
G Cm G
ri - ve - der - ci, Rom - a. It's time for

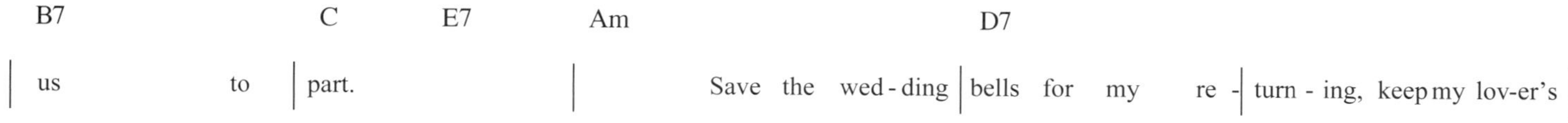
B7
C
E7
Am
D7
us to part.
Save the wed-ding bells for my re-turn-ing, keep my lov-er's

To Coda
G
arms out-stretched and yearn-ing. Please be sure the flame of love keeps burn-ing in her heart.

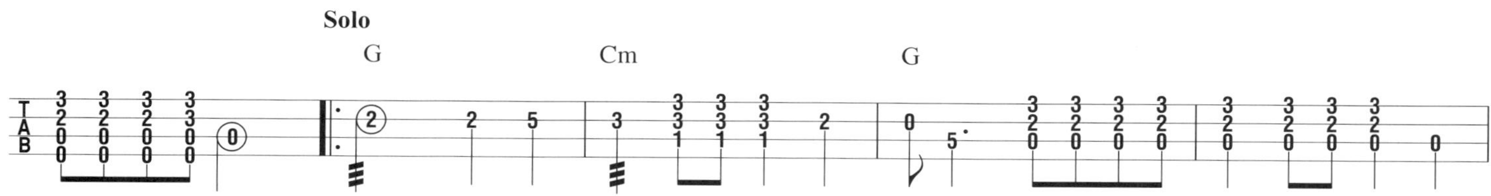
Solo
G
Cm
G
T
A
B

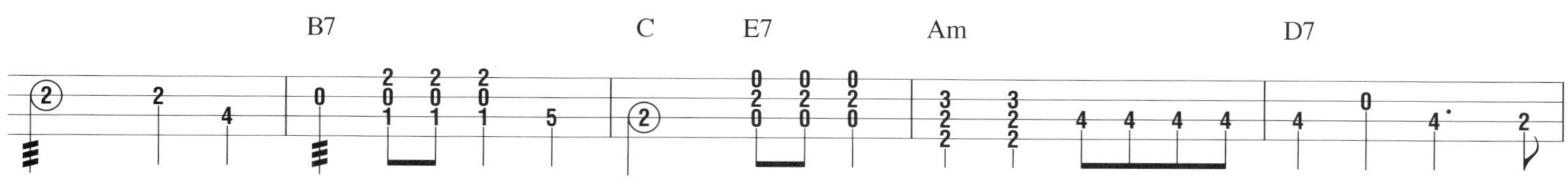
B7
C
E7
Am
D7

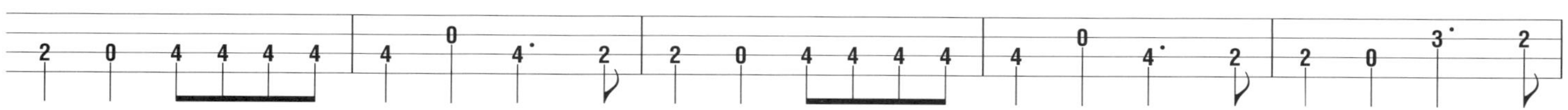

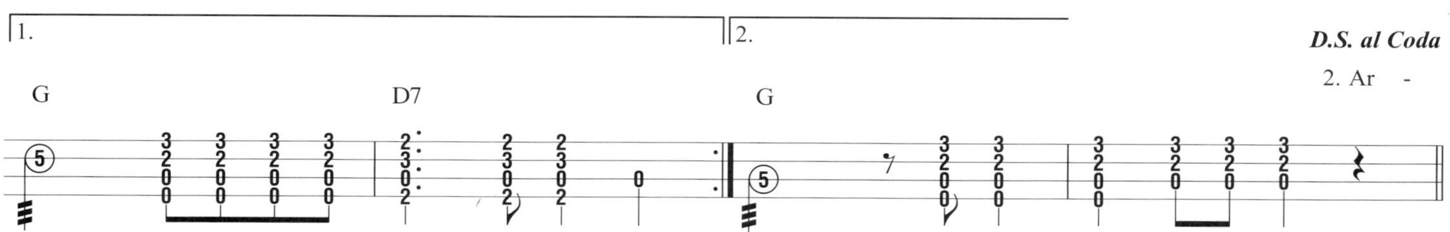
1.
2.
D.S. al Coda
2. Ar -
G
D7
G

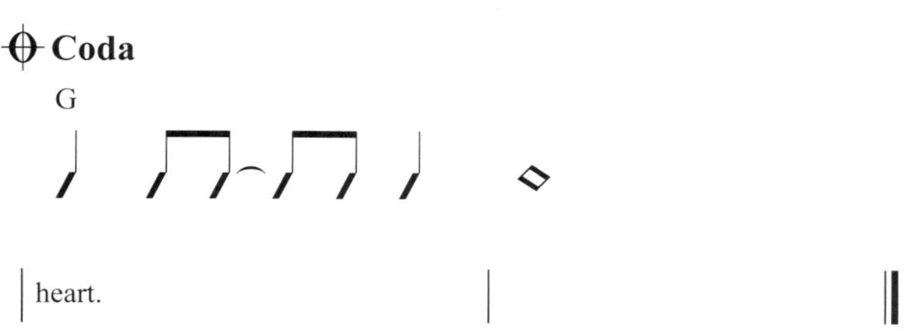
Coda
G
heart.

The Battle of Evermore

Words and Music by Jimmy Page and Robert Plant

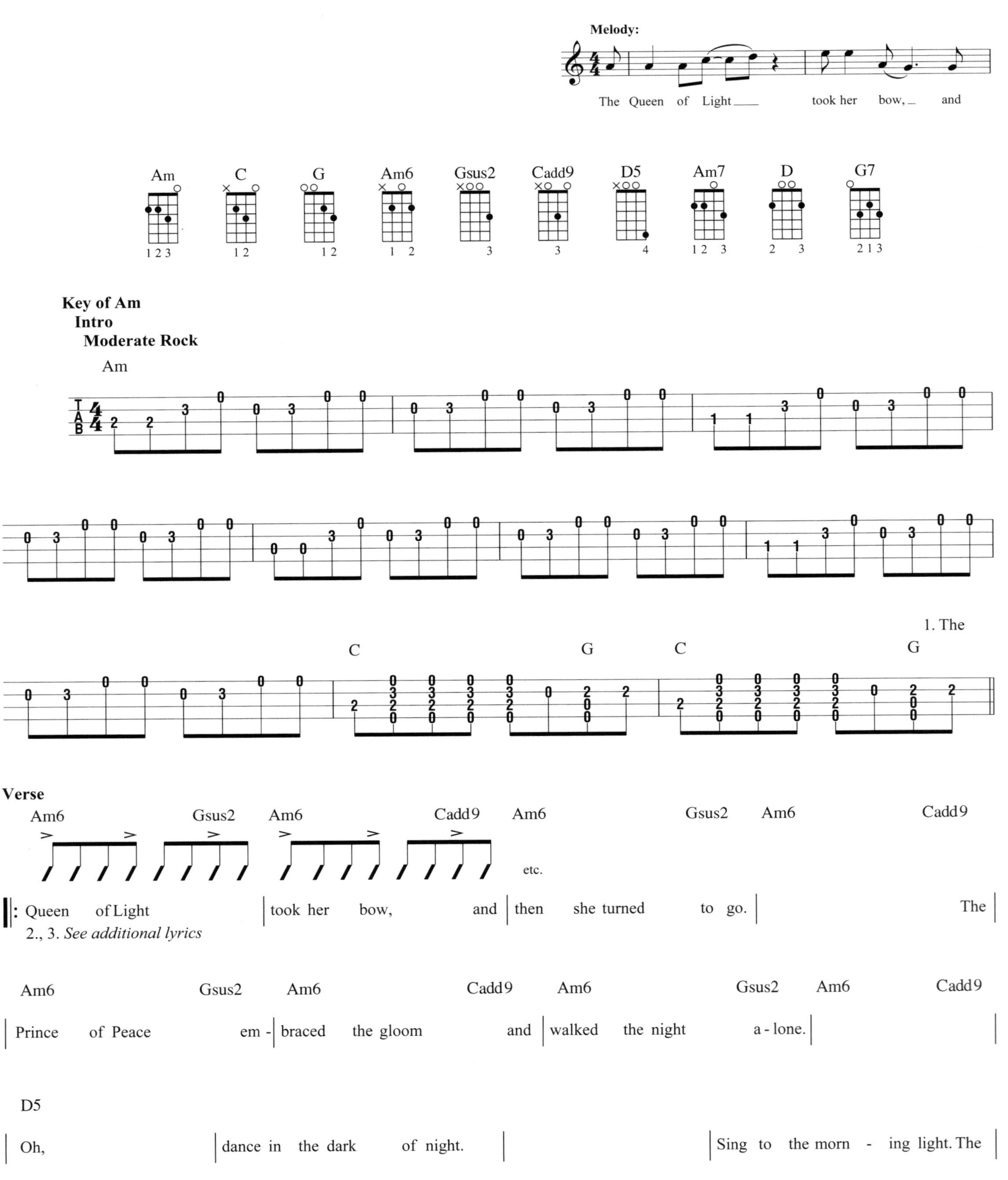
Melody:
The Queen of Light took her bow, and
Am C G Am6 Gsus2 Cadd9 D5 Am7 D G7
Key of Am
Intro
Moderate Rock
Am
C G C G
1. The
Verse
Am6 Gsus2 Am6 Cadd9 Am6 Gsus2 Am6 Cadd9
etc.
Queen of Light took her bow, and then she turned to go. The
2., 3. See additional lyrics
Am6 Gsus2 Am6 Cadd9 Am6 Gsus2 Am6 Cadd9
Prince of Peace em - braced the gloom and walked the night a - lone.
D5
Oh, dance in the dark of night. Sing to the morn - ing light. The

Am6 Gsus2 Am6 Cadd9 Am6 Gsus2 Am6 Cadd9
| dark Lord rides in | force to-night and | time will tell us | all. |

D5
| Oh, | throw down your plow and | hoe, | rest not to lock your home. |

Am6 Gsus2 Am6 Cadd9 Am6 Gsus2 Am6 Cadd9
| Side by side we | wait the might of the | dark - est of them | all. ||

Interlude

Oh...
D5

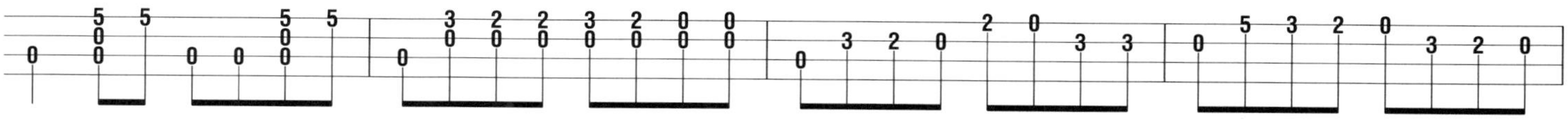

Am6 Gsus2 Am6 Cadd9 Am6 Gsus2 Am6 Cadd9

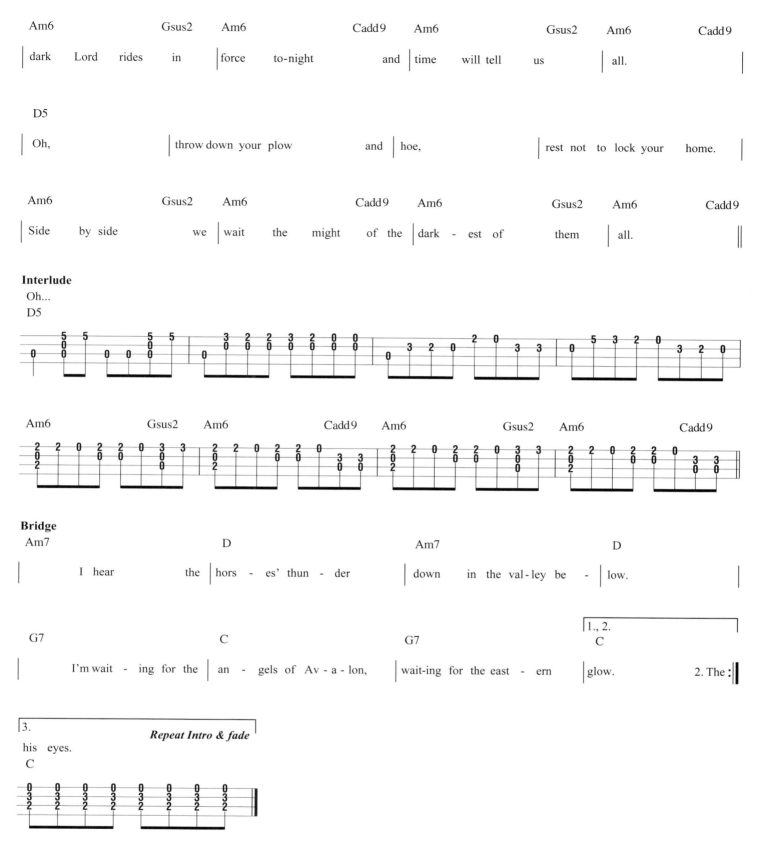

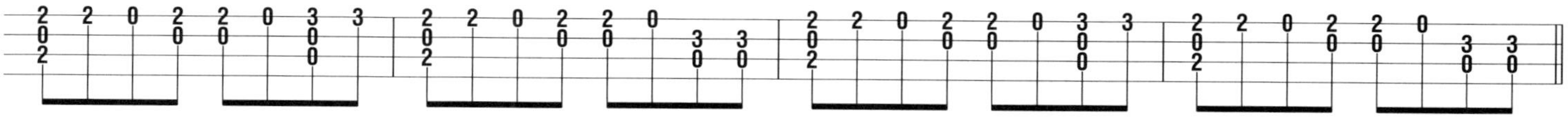

Bridge

Am7 D Am7 D
| I hear the | hors - es' thun - der | down in the val-ley be - | low. |

G7 C G7 1., 2. C
| I'm wait - ing for the | an - gels of Av - a - lon, | wait-ing for the east - ern | glow. 2. The :||

3.
Repeat Intro & fade

his eyes.
C

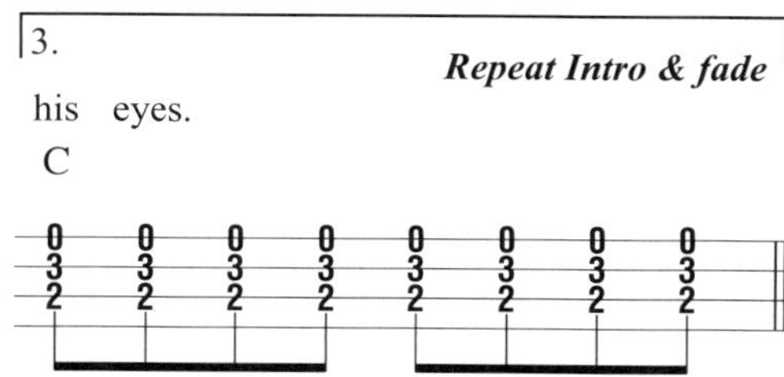

Additional Lyrics

2. The apples of the valley hold the seeds of happiness.
The ground is rich from tender care. Repay, do not forget, no, no.
Dance in the dark of night, sing till the morning light.
The apples turn to brown and black. The tyrant's face is red.
Oh, war is the common cry. Pick up your swords and fly.
The sky is filled with good and bad that mortals never know.
Oh, well, the night is long, the beads of time pass slow.
Tired eyes on the sunrise, waiting for the eastern glow.

3. The pain of war cannot exceed the woe of aftermath.
The drums will shake the castle wall, the ring wraiths ride in black, ride on.
Sing as you raise your bow, shoot straighter than before.
No comfort has the fire at night that lights the face so cold.
Oh, dance in the dark of night, sing till the morning light.
The magic runes are writ in gold to bring the balance back. Bring it back.
At last the sun is shining. The clouds of blue roll by,
With flames from the dragon of darkness, the sunlight blinds his eyes.

Blue Eyes Crying in the Rain

Words and Music by Fred Rose

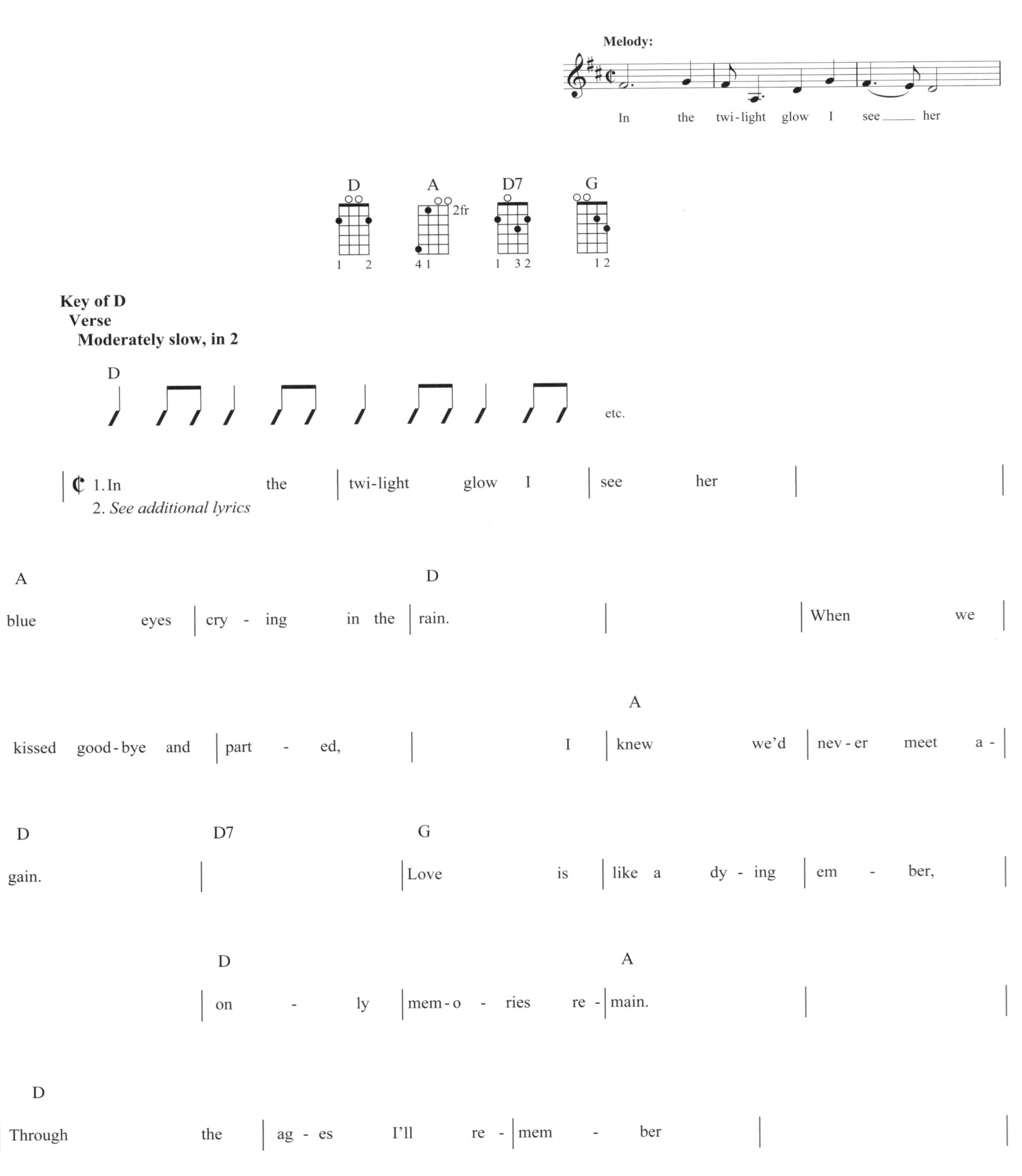

Melody:
In the twi-light glow I see her
D
A
2fr
D7
G
1 2
4 1
1 3 2
1 2
Key of D
Verse
Moderately slow, in 2
D
etc.
1. In the twi-light glow I see her
2. See additional lyrics
A
D
blue eyes cry - ing in the rain. When we
A
kissed good-bye and part - ed, I knew we'd nev-er meet a -
D
D7
G
gain. Love is like a dy - ing em - ber,
D
A
on - ly mem-o - ries re - main.
D
Through the ag - es I'll re - mem - ber

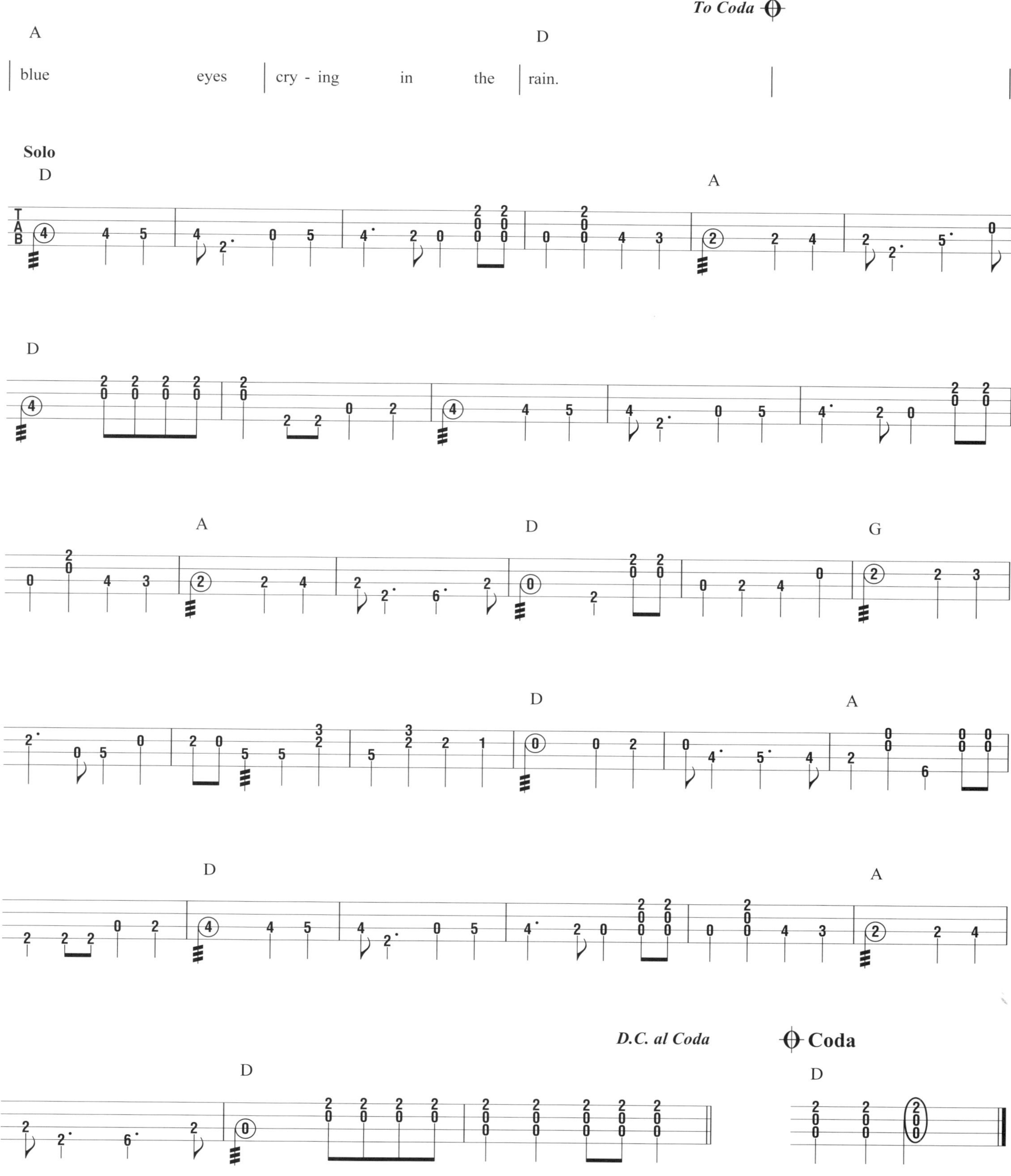
To Coda
A
D
blue
eyes
cry - ing
in
the
rain.
Solo
D
A
D
A
D
G
D
A
D
A
D.C. al Coda
Coda
D
D

Additional Lyrics

2. Now my hair has turned to silver, all my life I've loved in vain.
   I can see her star in heaven, blue eyes crying in the rain.
   Someday when we meet up yonder, we'll stroll hand in hand again,
   In a land that knows no parting, blue eyes crying in the rain.

Blue Moon of Kentucky

Words and Music by Bill Monroe

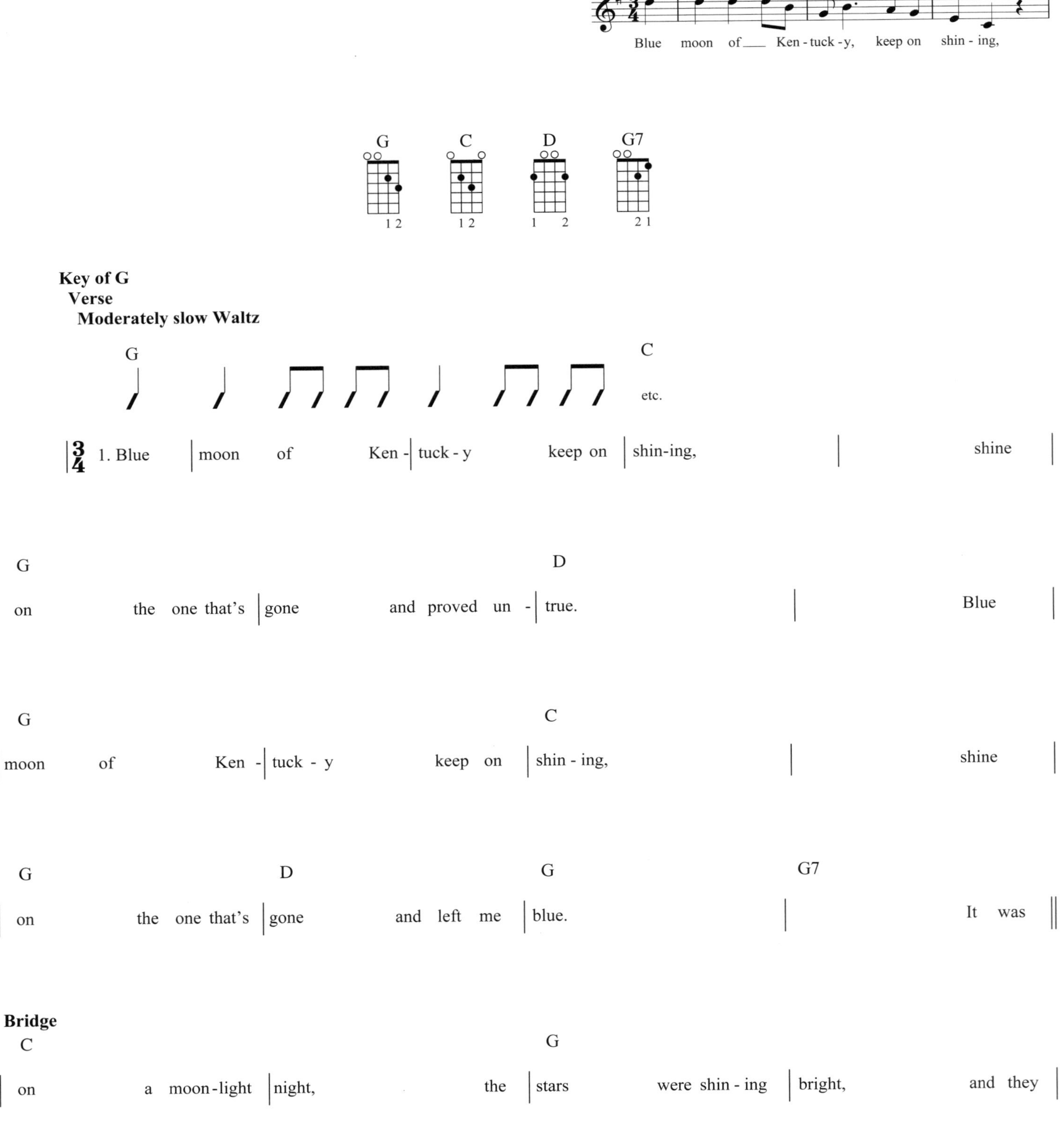

Melody:
Blue moon of Ken - tuck - y, keep on shin - ing,
G
C
D
G7
Key of G
Verse
Moderately slow Waltz
G
C
etc.
1. Blue moon of Ken - tuck - y keep on shin-ing, shine
G
D
on the one that's gone and proved un - true. Blue
G
C
moon of Ken - tuck - y keep on shin - ing, shine
G
D
G
G7
on the one that's gone and left me blue. It was
Bridge
C
G
on a moon-light night, the stars were shin - ing bright, and they

C
G
D
whis - pered from on high your love has said good - bye. 2. Blue
Verse
G
C
moon of Ken - tuck - y keep on shin - ing, shine
To Coda
G
D
G
on the one that's gone and said good - bye.
Solo
G
C
G
1.
D
2.
D
G
G7
C
G
D.S. al Coda
3. Blue
C
G
D
Coda
G
bye.

Careless Love

Anonymous

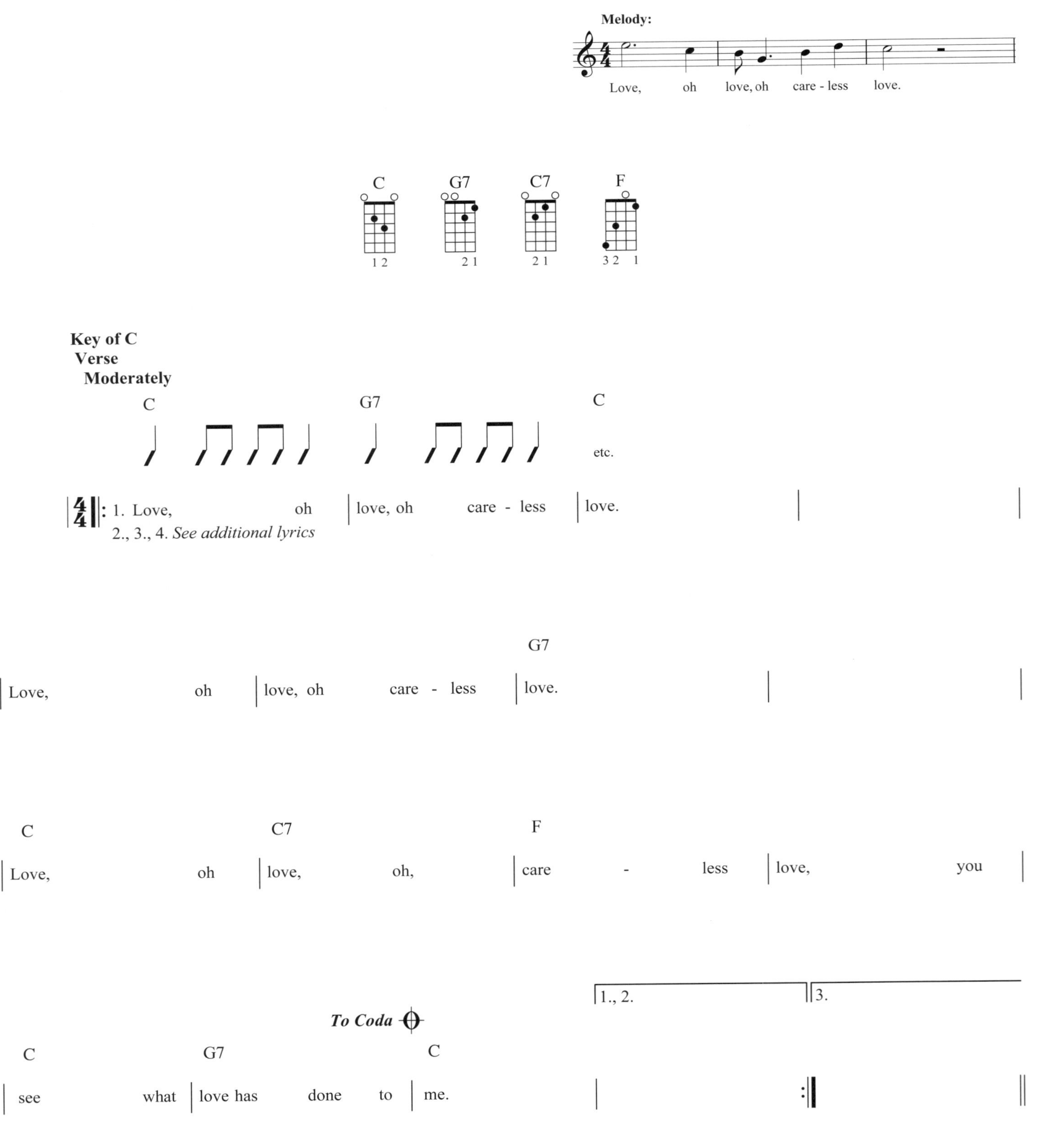
Melody:
Love, oh love, oh care - less love.
C
G7
C7
F
Key of C
Verse
Moderately
C
G7
C
etc.
1. Love, oh love, oh care - less love.
2., 3., 4. See additional lyrics
G7
Love, oh love, oh care - less love.
C
C7
F
Love, oh love, oh, care - less love, you
To Coda
1., 2.
3.
C
G7
C
see what love has done to me.

Solo

C G7 C

C G7

C C7 F

D.C. al Coda

C G7 C

𝄌 Coda

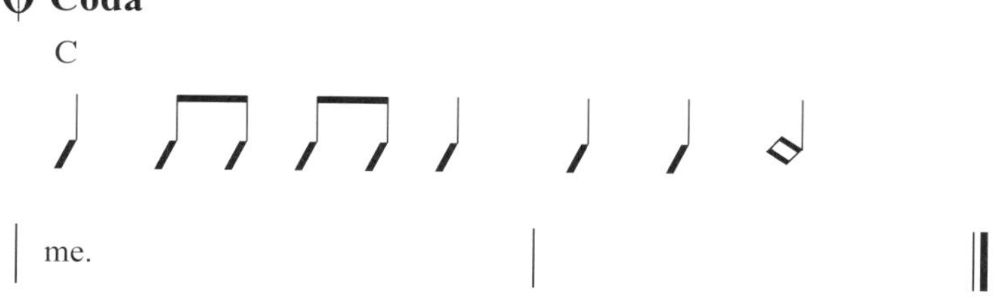
C
me.

Additional Lyrics

2. When I wore my apron low,
   When I wore my apron low,
   When I wore my apron low,
   You followed me through ice and snow.

3. Now my apron strings won't pin.
   Now my apron strings won't pin.
   Now my apron strings won't pin.
   You pass my door and won't come in.

4. I cried last night and the night before.
   I cried last night and the night before.
   I cried last night and the night before.
   Gonna cry tonight and cry no more.

Come Back to Sorrento

By Ernesto de Curtis

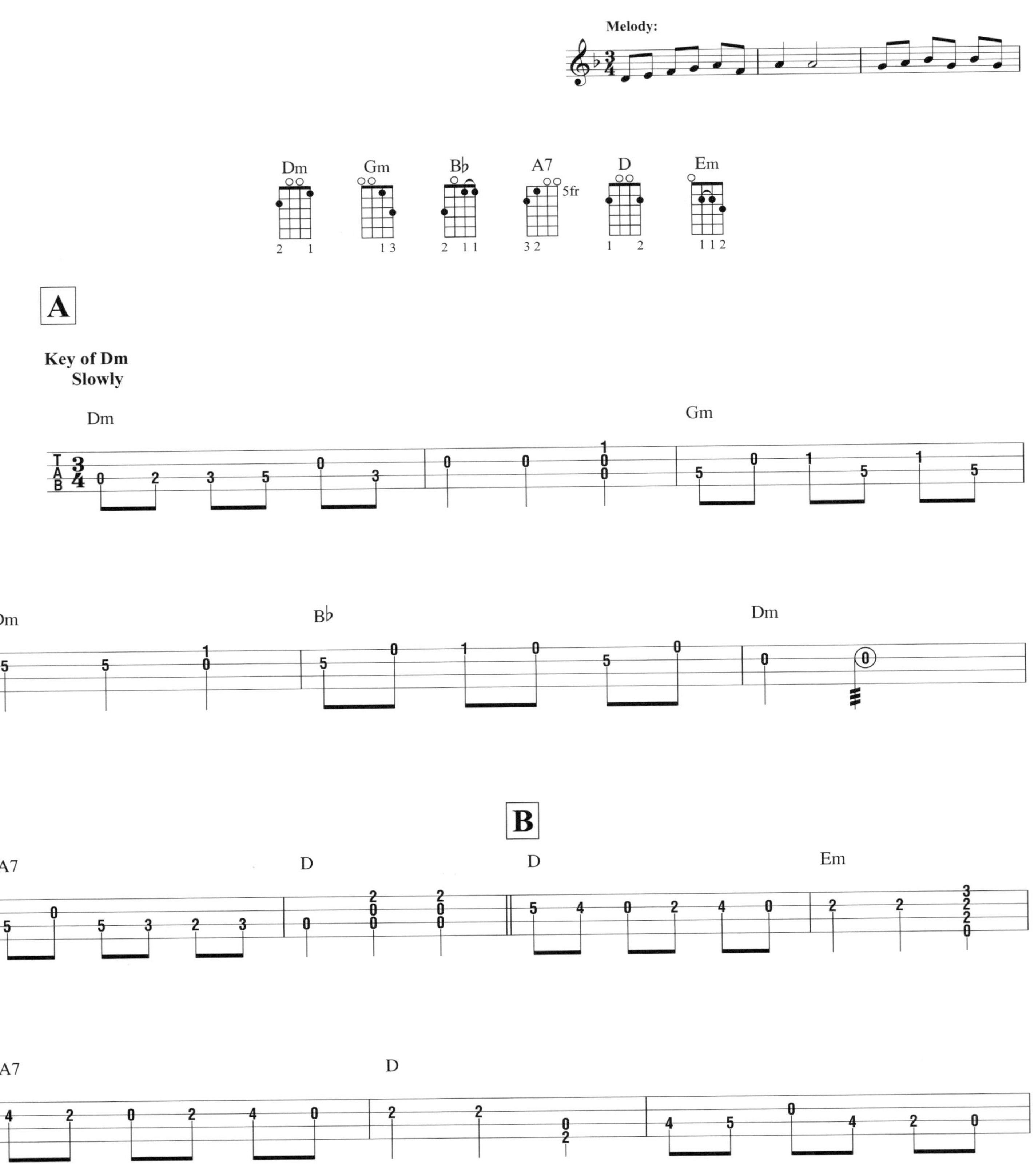

Melody:
Dm
Gm
B♭
A7
5fr
D
Em
A
Key of Dm
Slowly
T
A
B
B

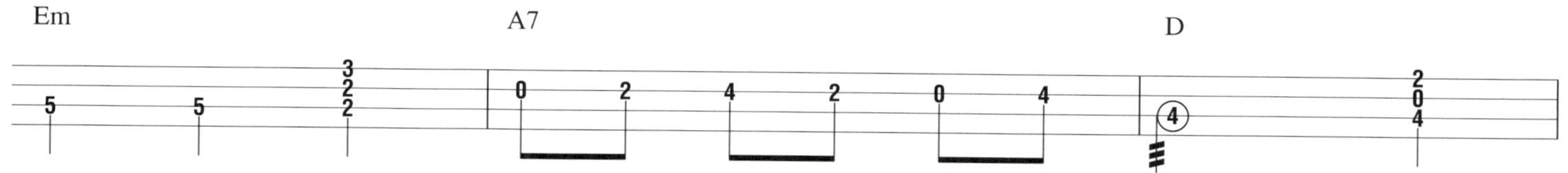
Em
A7
D

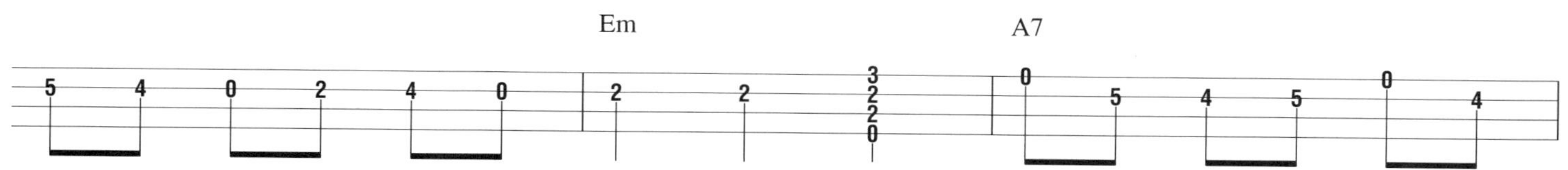
Em
A7

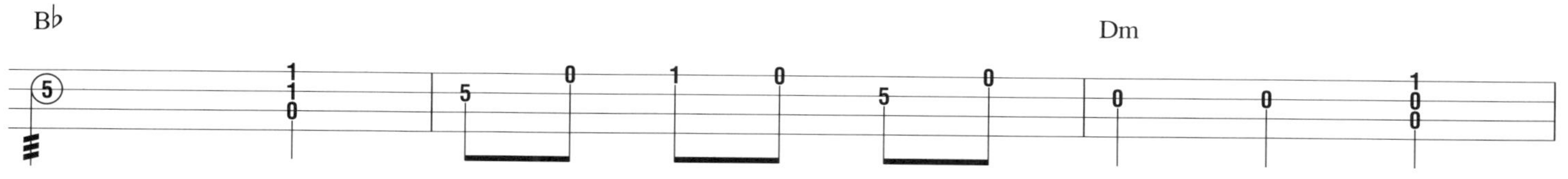
B♭
Dm

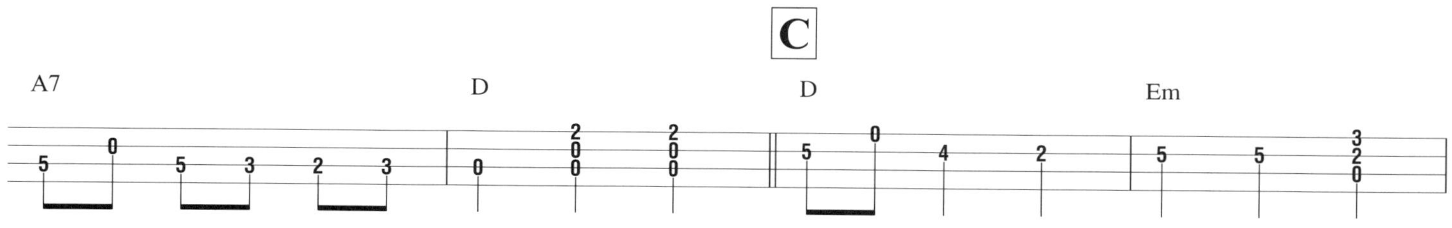
C
A7
D
D
Em

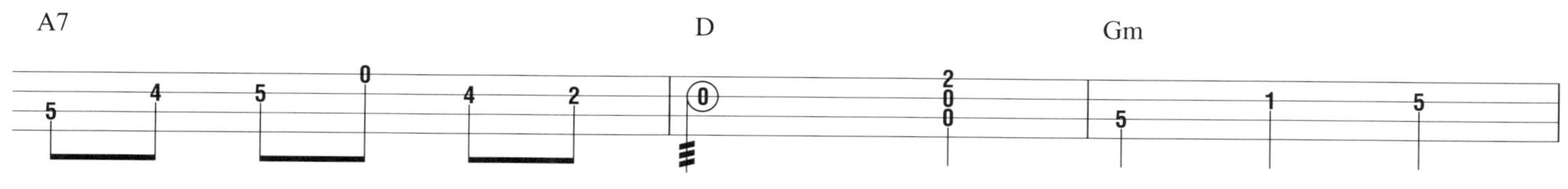
A7
D
Gm

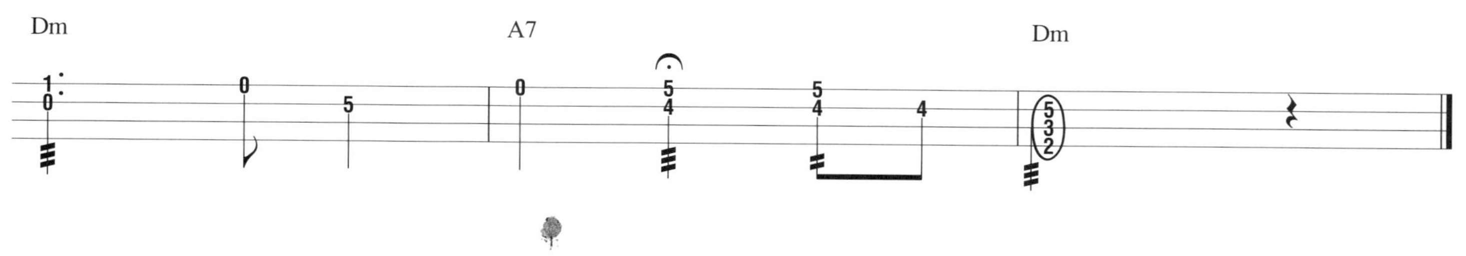
Dm
A7
Dm

Crazy

Words and Music by Willie Nelson

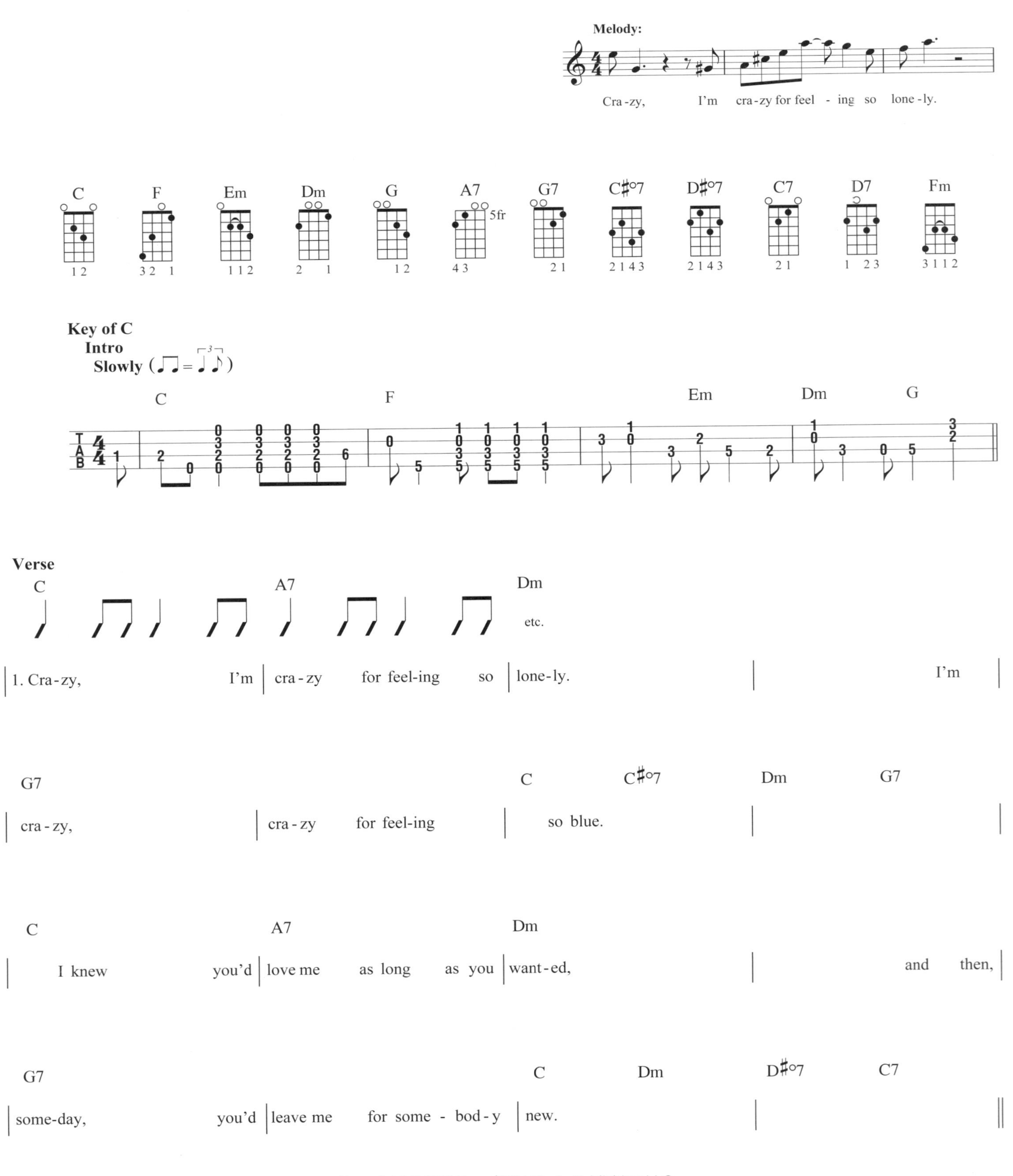

Melody:
Cra-zy, I'm cra-zy for feel - ing so lone-ly.
C F Em Dm G A7 G7 C♯°7 D♯°7 C7 D7 Fm
Key of C
Intro
Slowly
Verse
C A7 Dm
etc.
1. Cra-zy, I'm cra-zy for feel-ing so lone-ly. I'm
G7 C C♯°7 Dm G7
cra-zy, cra-zy for feel-ing so blue.
C A7 Dm
I knew you'd love me as long as you want-ed, and then,
G7 C Dm D♯°7 C7
some-day, you'd leave me for some - bod-y new.

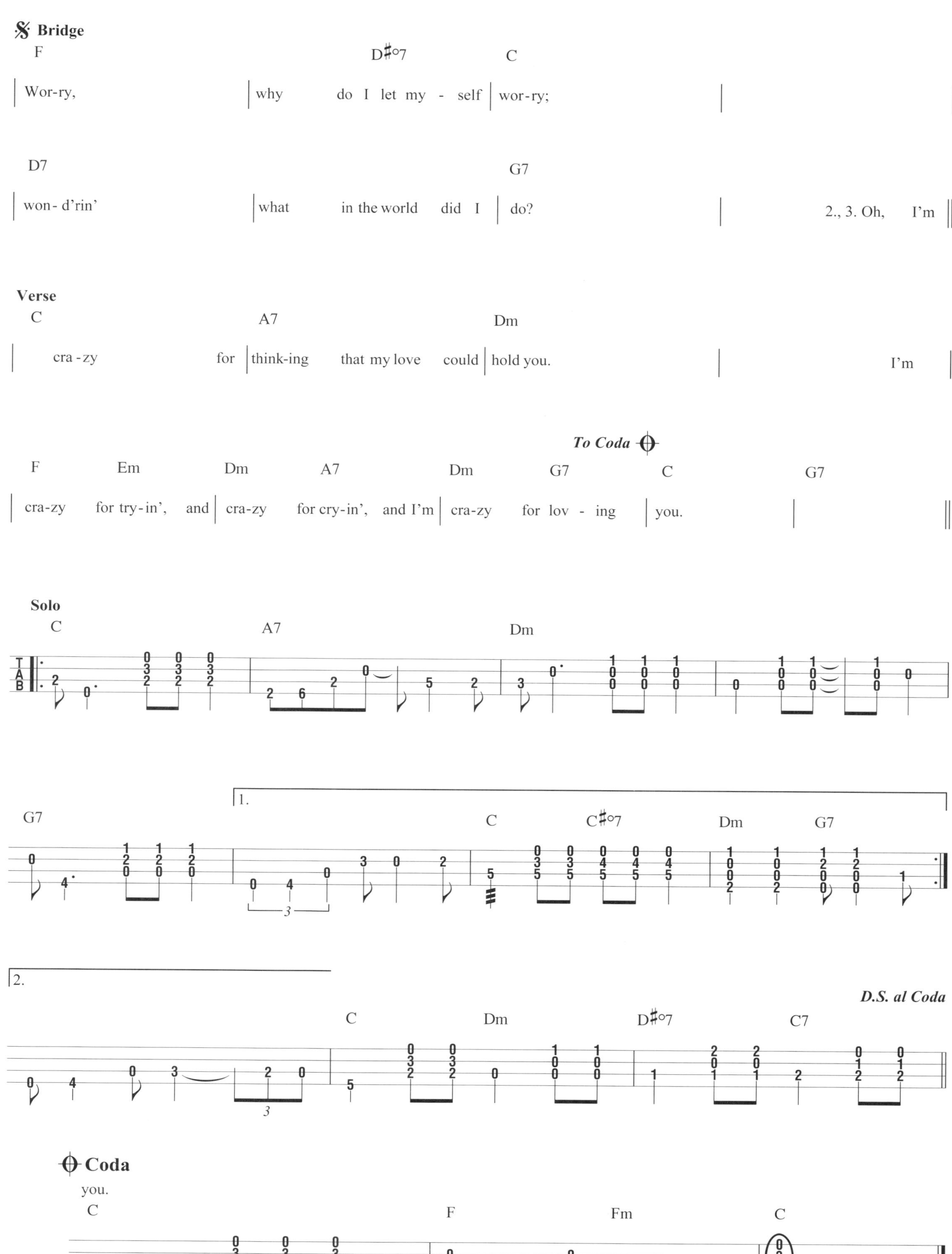
Bridge
F D♯°7 C
Wor-ry, why do I let my - self wor-ry;
D7 G7
won- d'rin' what in the world did I do?
2., 3. Oh, I'm
Verse
C A7 Dm
cra - zy for think-ing that my love could hold you.
I'm
To Coda
F Em Dm A7 Dm G7 C G7
cra-zy for try-in', and cra-zy for cry-in', and I'm cra-zy for lov - ing you.
Solo
C A7 Dm
G7
1.
C C♯°7 Dm G7
2.
D.S. al Coda
C Dm D♯°7 C7
Coda
you.
C F Fm C

Cripple Creek

American Fiddle Tune

Melody

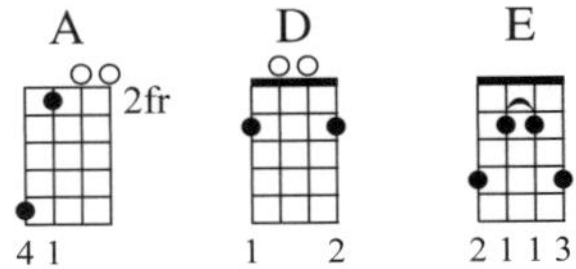
A
D
E
2fr
4 1
1 2
2 1 1 3

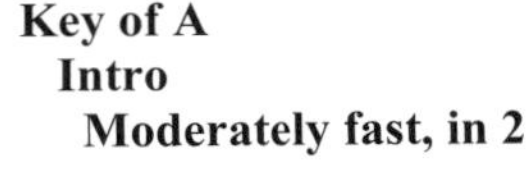
Key of A
Intro
Moderately fast, in 2

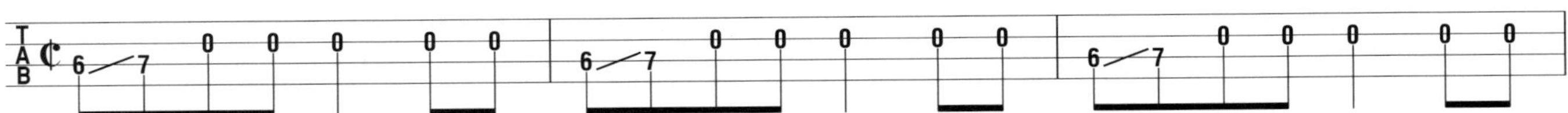
A

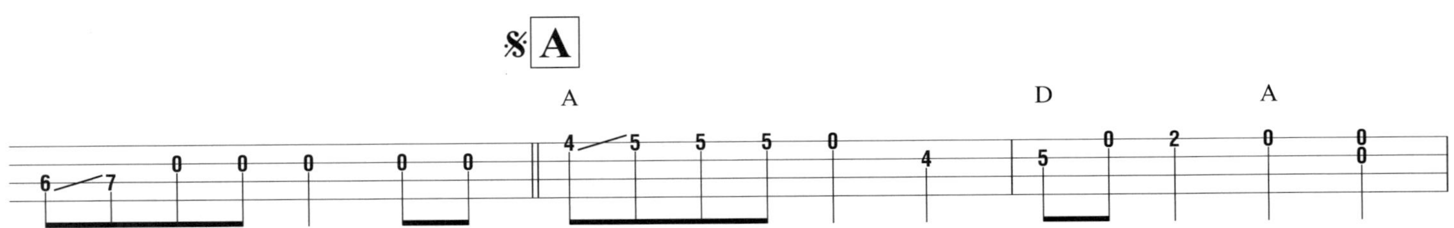
A
A
D
A

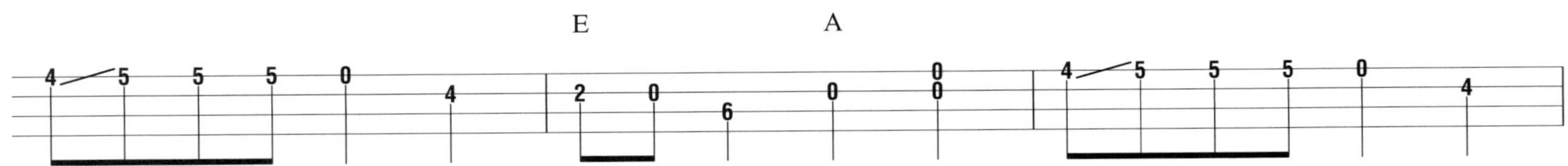
E
A

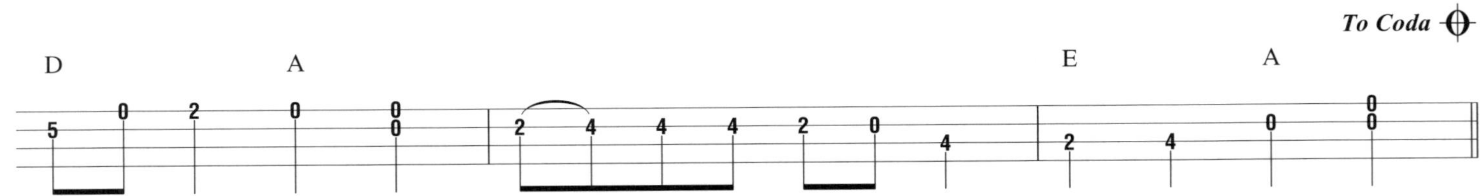
To Coda
D
A
E
A

B
A
E
A

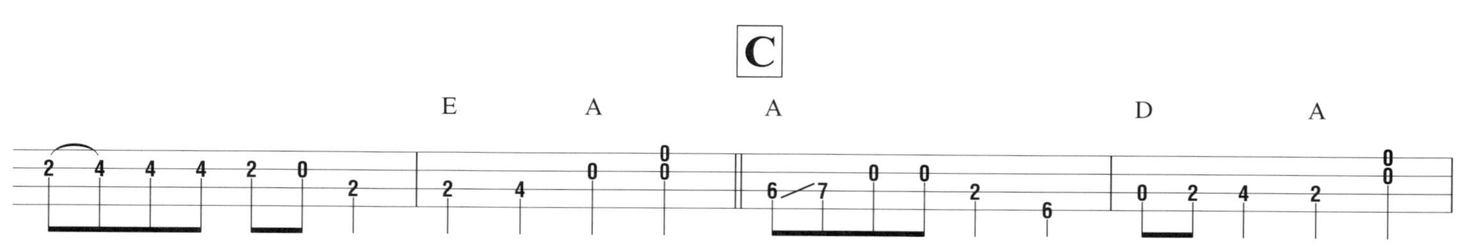
C
E
A
A
D
A

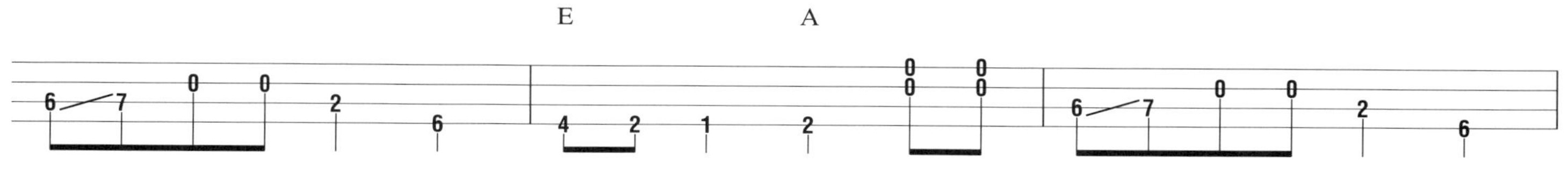
E
A

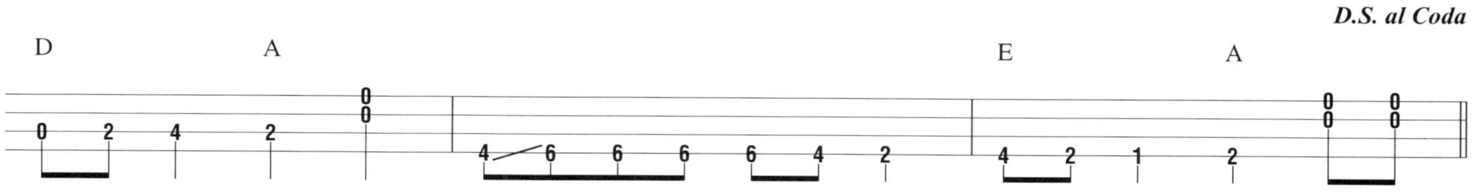
D.S. al Coda
D
A
E
A

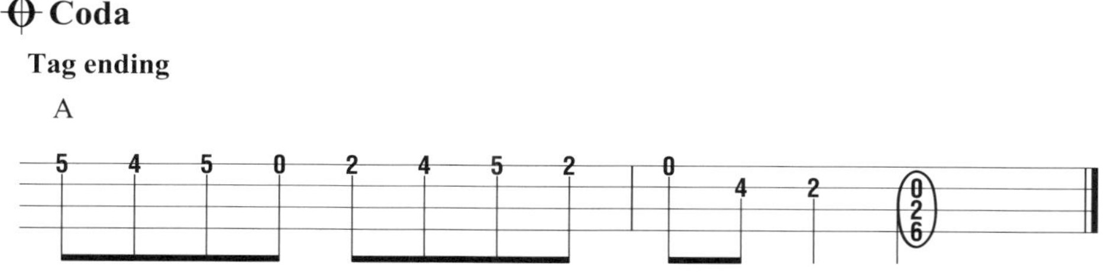
Coda
Tag ending
A

Folsom Prison Blues

Words and Music by John R. Cash

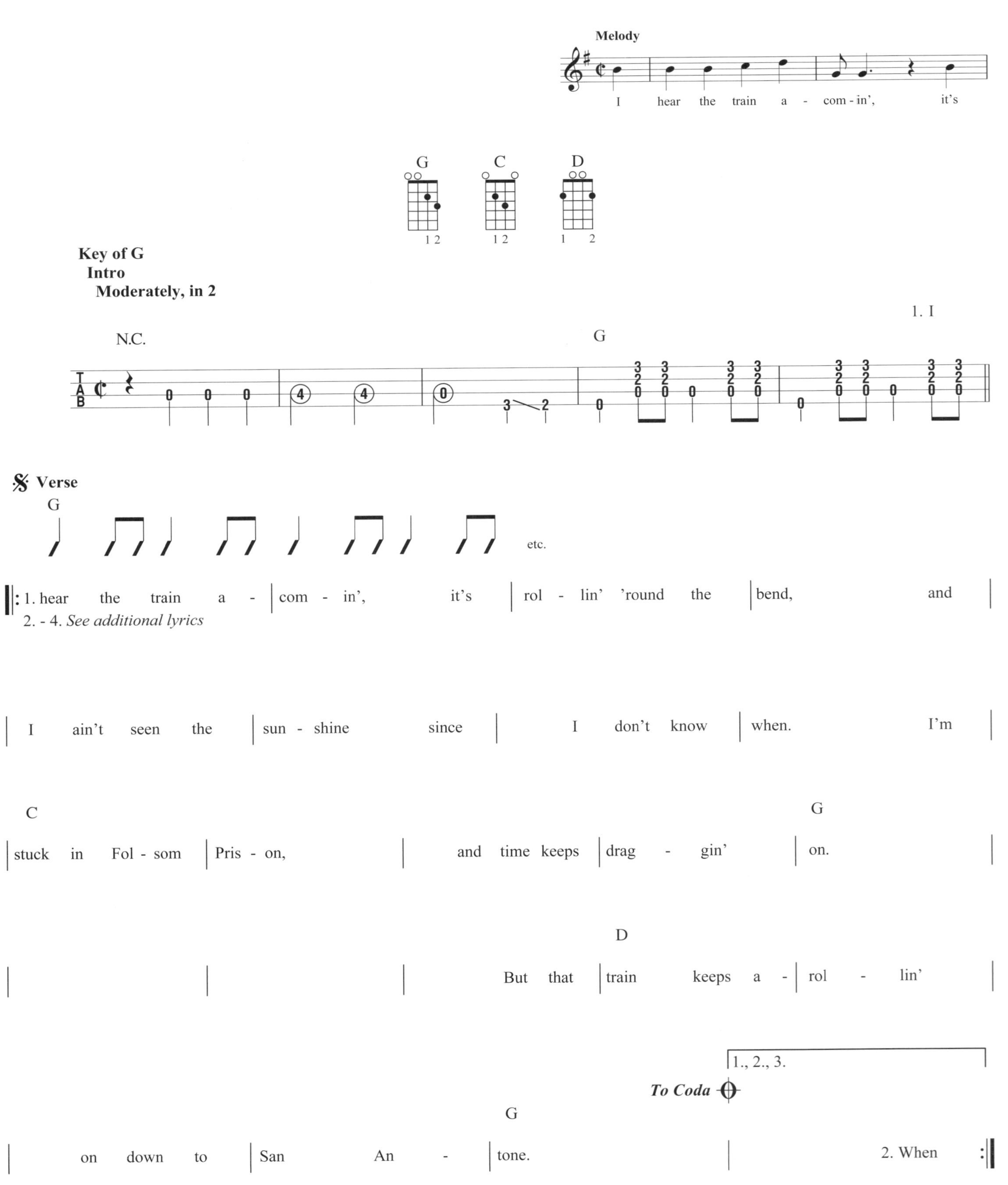

Melody
I hear the train a - com - in', it's
G
C
D
Key of G
Intro
Moderately, in 2
N.C.
G
1. I
Verse
G
etc.
1. hear the train a - com - in', it's rol - lin' 'round the bend, and
2. - 4. See additional lyrics
I ain't seen the sun - shine since I don't know when. I'm
C
G
stuck in Fol - som Pris - on, and time keeps drag - gin' on.
D
But that train keeps a - rol - lin'
1., 2., 3.
To Coda
G
on down to San An - tone. 2. When

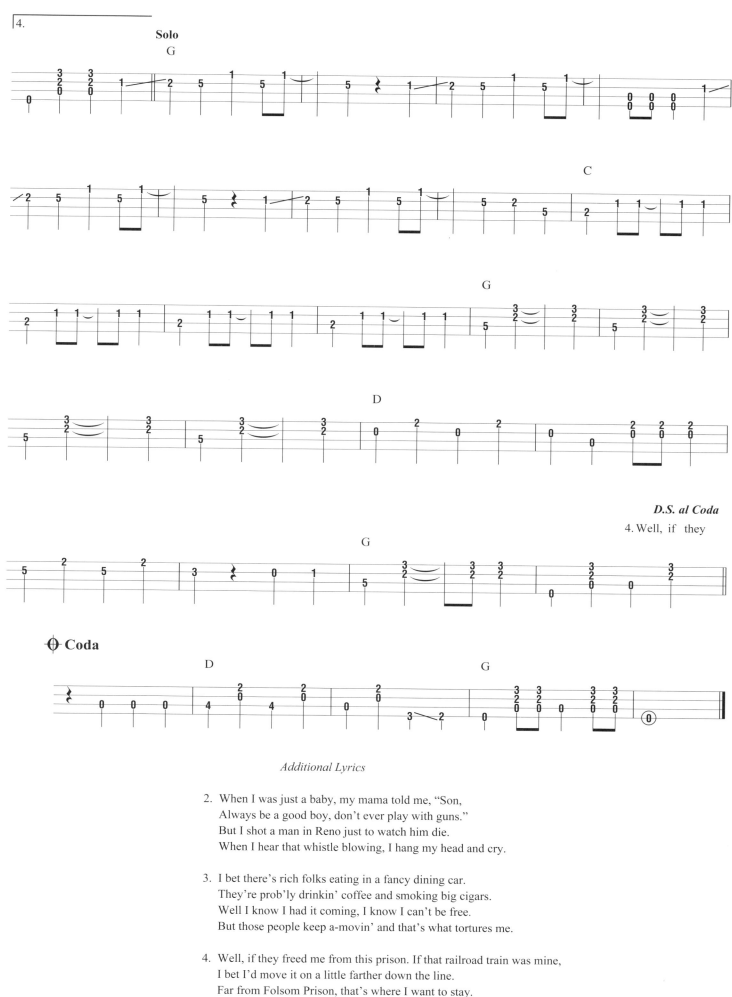

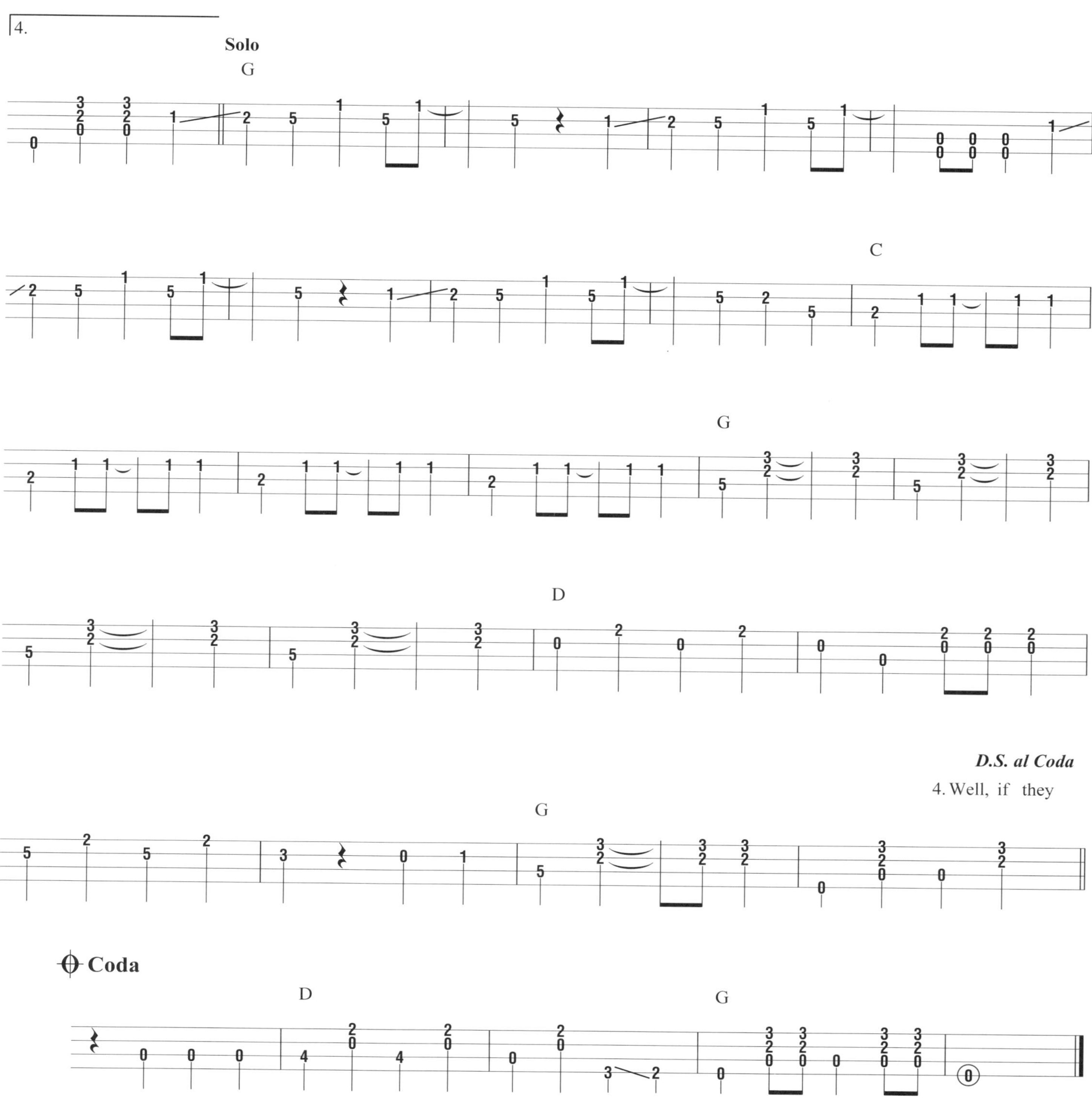
4.
Solo
G
C
G
D
D.S. al Coda
4. Well, if they
G
Coda
D
G

Additional Lyrics

2. When I was just a baby, my mama told me, "Son,
   Always be a good boy, don't ever play with guns."
   But I shot a man in Reno just to watch him die.
   When I hear that whistle blowing, I hang my head and cry.

3. I bet there's rich folks eating in a fancy dining car.
   They're prob'ly drinkin' coffee and smoking big cigars.
   Well I know I had it coming, I know I can't be free.
   But those people keep a-movin' and that's what tortures me.

4. Well, if they freed me from this prison. If that railroad train was mine,
   I bet I'd move it on a little farther down the line.
   Far from Folsom Prison, that's where I want to stay.
   And I'd let that lonesome whistle blow my blues away.

Friend of the Devil

Words by Robert Hunter
Music by Jerry Garcia and John Dawson

Melody:
I lit out from Re - no, I was
G
C
D
Am
Key of G
Intro
Moderately fast, in 2
Play 4 times
Verse
etc.
1. I lit out from Re-no, I was trailed by twen - ty hounds.
2., 3., 4. See additional lyrics
Did-n't get to sleep last night 'til the morn - ing came a - round.
Chorus
Set out run-ning but I take my time, a friend of the dev-il is a friend of mine. If
I get home be - fore day - light, I just might get some sleep to -
1., 2.
3.
To Coda
night.

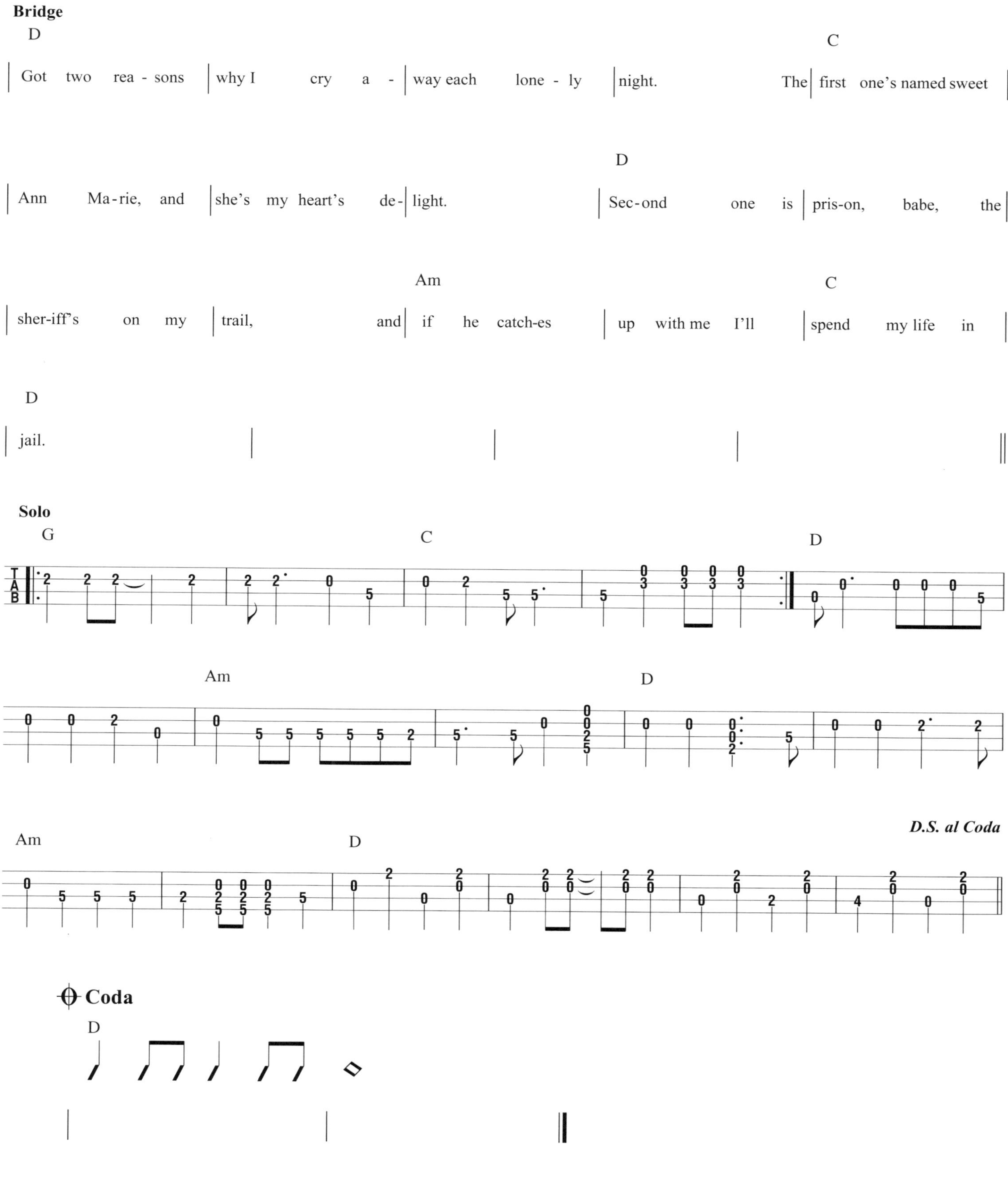
Bridge
D
Got two rea - sons why I cry a - way each lone - ly night.
C
The first one's named sweet
Ann Ma-rie, and she's my heart's de- light.
D
Sec-ond one is pris-on, babe, the
sher-iff's on my trail,
Am
and if he catch-es up with me I'll
C
spend my life in
D
jail.
Solo
G
C
D
Am
D
Am
D
D.S. al Coda
Coda
D

Additional Lyrics

2. Ran into the devil, babe, he loaned me twenty bills.
   Spent the night in Utah in a cave up in the hills.

3. I ran down to the levee but the devil caught me there.
   He took my twenty-dollar bill and he vanished in the air.

4. Got a wife in Chino, babe, and one in Cherokee.
   First one says she's got my child, but it don't look like me.

Going to California

Words and Music by Jimmy Page and Robert Plant

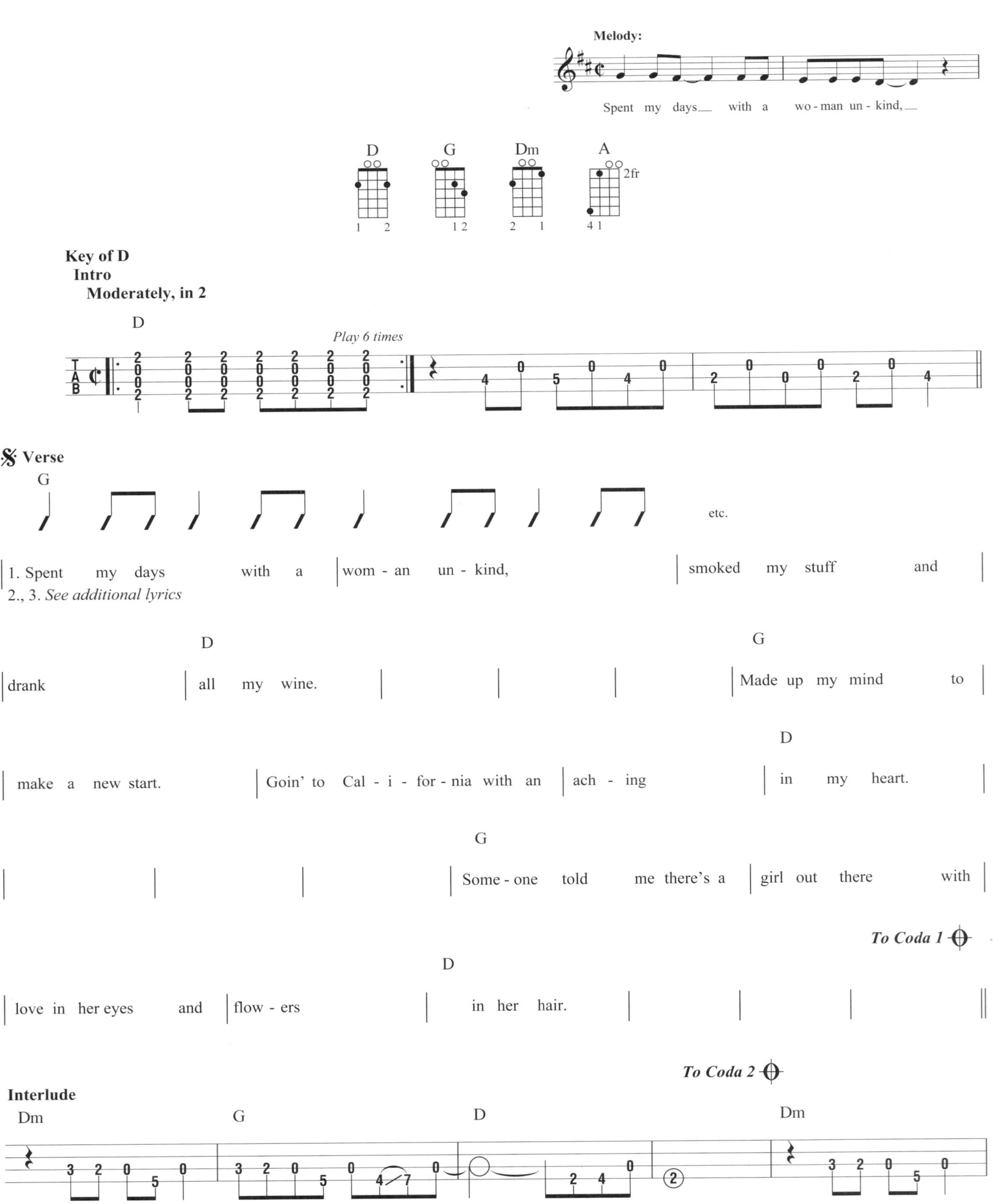
Melody:
Spent my days__ with a wo - man un - kind,__
D
G
Dm
A
2fr
Key of D
Intro
Moderately, in 2
Play 6 times
Verse
etc.
1. Spent my days with a wom - an un - kind, smoked my stuff and
2., 3. See additional lyrics
drank all my wine.
Made up my mind to
make a new start. Goin' to Cal - i - for - nia with an ach - ing in my heart.
Some - one told me there's a girl out there with
To Coda 1
love in her eyes and flow - ers in her hair.
To Coda 2
Interlude

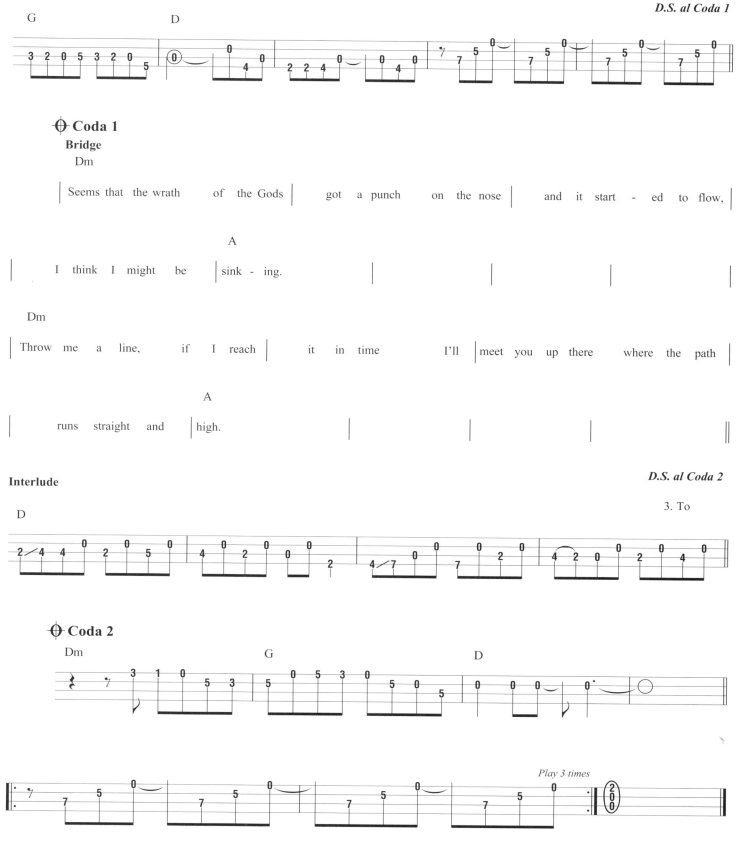

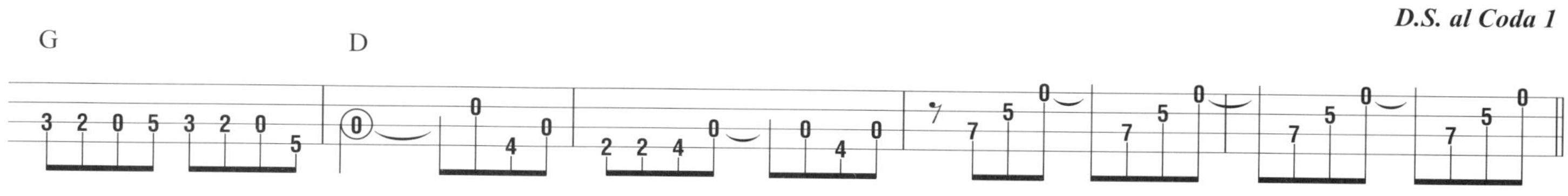

D.S. al Coda 1

G D

Coda 1

Bridge

Dm

Seems that the wrath of the Gods got a punch on the nose and it start - ed to flow,

A

I think I might be sink - ing.

Dm

Throw me a line, if I reach it in time I'll meet you up there where the path

A

runs straight and high.

Interlude

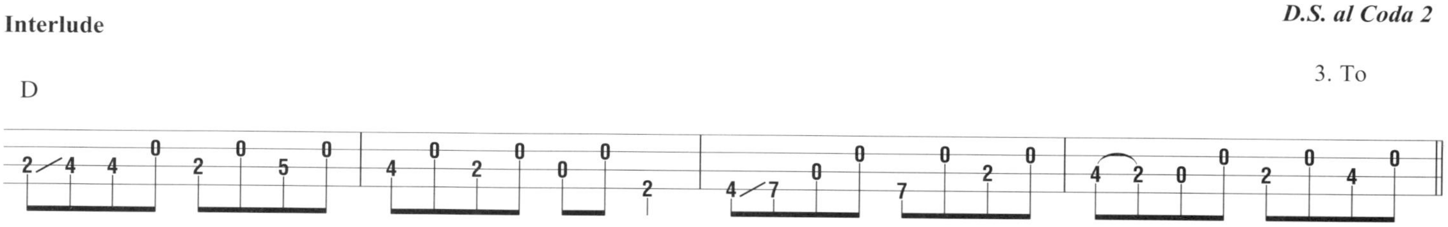

D.S. al Coda 2

D

3. To

Coda 2

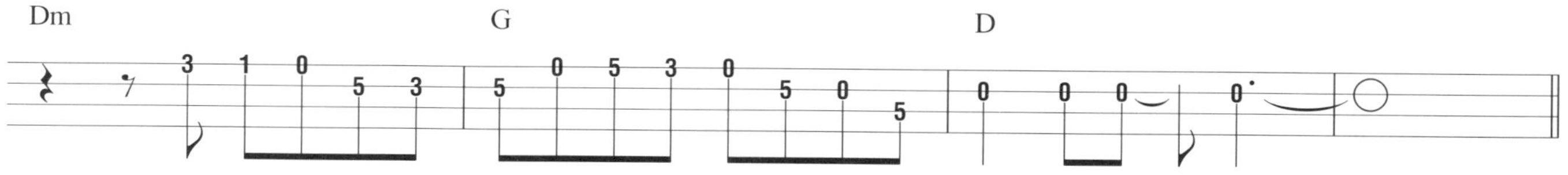

Dm G D

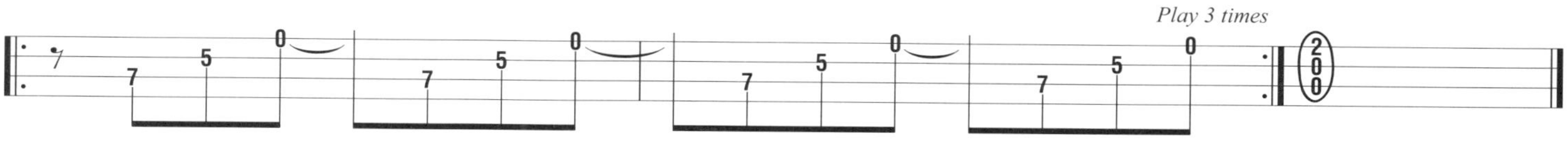

Play 3 times

Additional Lyrics

2. Took my chances on a big jet plane, never let them tell you that they're all the same.
Oh, the sea was red and the sky was grey; wondered how tomorrow could ever follow today.
The mountains and the canyons start to tremble and shake, children of the sun begin to awake.

3. To find a queen without a king, they say she plays guitar and cries and sings... la, la, la, la.
Ride a white mare in the footsteps of dawn, tryin' to find a woman who's never, never, never been born.
Standing on a hill in a mountain of dreams, telling myself it's not as hard, hard, hard as it seems.

Hallelujah

Words and Music by Leonard Cohen

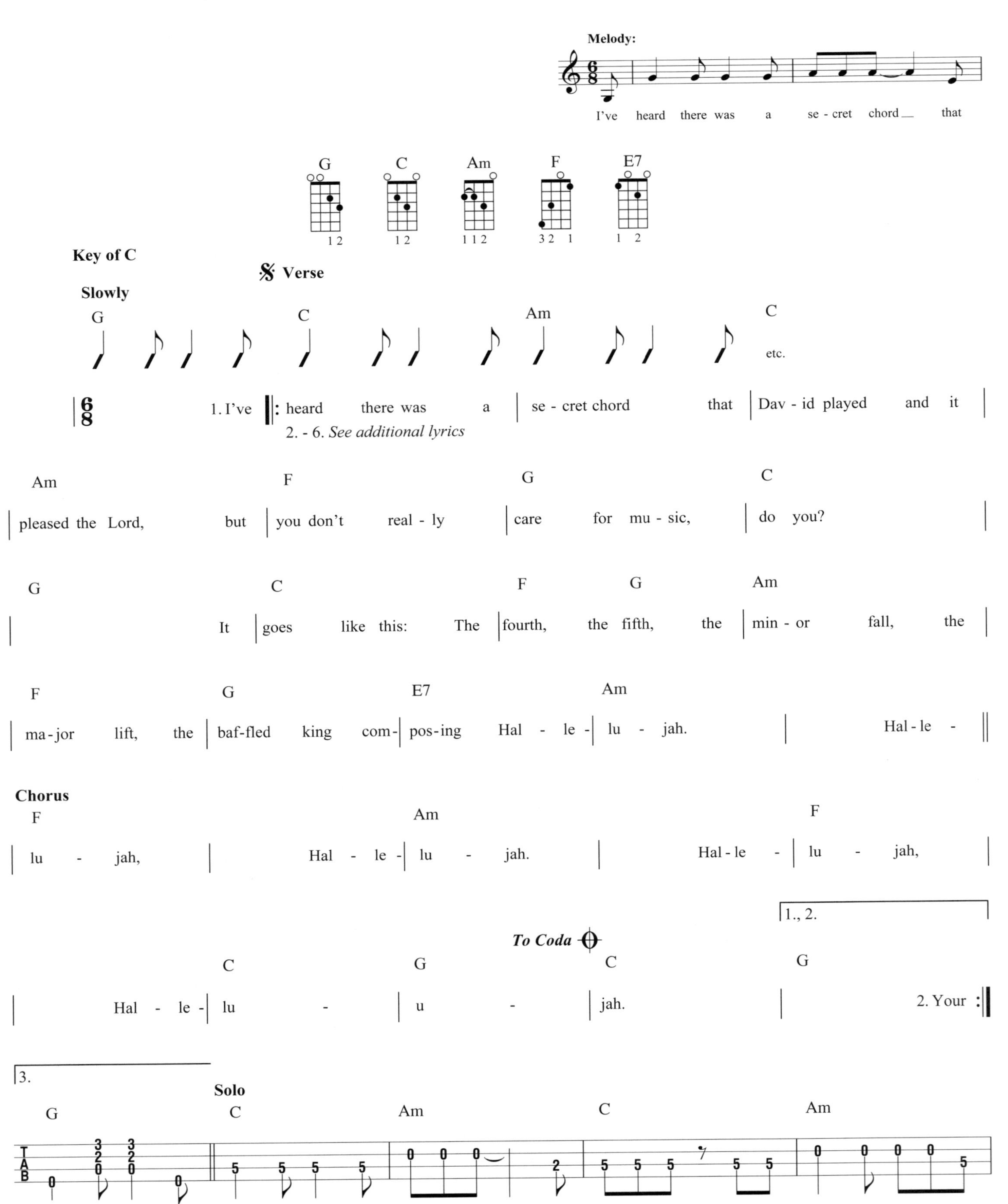
Melody:
I've heard there was a se - cret chord that
G C Am F E7
Key of C
Verse
Slowly
G C Am C
etc.
1. I've heard there was a se - cret chord that Dav - id played and it
2. - 6. See additional lyrics
Am F G C
pleased the Lord, but you don't real - ly care for mu - sic, do you?
G C F G Am
It goes like this: The fourth, the fifth, the min - or fall, the
F G E7 Am
ma - jor lift, the baf - fled king com - pos - ing Hal - le - lu - jah. Hal - le -
Chorus
F Am F
lu - jah, Hal - le - lu - jah. Hal - le - lu - jah,
1., 2.
To Coda
C G C G
Hal - le - lu - u - jah. 2. Your
3.
Solo
G C Am C Am

F G C G C
F G Am F G E7
Am F Am
D.S. al Coda
F C G C G
Coda
C
jah.

Additional Lyrics

2. Your faith was strong but you needed proof.
   You saw her bathing on the roof.
   Her beauty and the moonlight overthrew ya.
   She tied you to her kitchen chair.
   She broke your throne and she cut your hair,
   And from your lips she drew the Hallelujah.

3. Baby, I've been here before.
   I know this room and I've walked this floor.
   I used to live alone before I knew ya.
   And I've seen your flag on the marble arch,
   And love is not a victory march.
   It's a cold and it's a broken Hallelujah.

4. (Solo)

5. There was a time when you let me know
   What's really going on below,
   But now you never show that to me, do ya?
   But remember when I moved in you,
   And the holy dove was moving too,
   And every breath we drew was Hallelujah.

6. Maybe there's a God above,
   But all I've ever learned from love was
   How to shoot somebody who out-drew ya.
   And it's not a cry that you hear at night,
   It's not somebody who's seen the light,
   It's a cold and it's a broken Hallelujah.

Ho Hey

Words and Music by Jeremy Fraites and Wesley Schultz

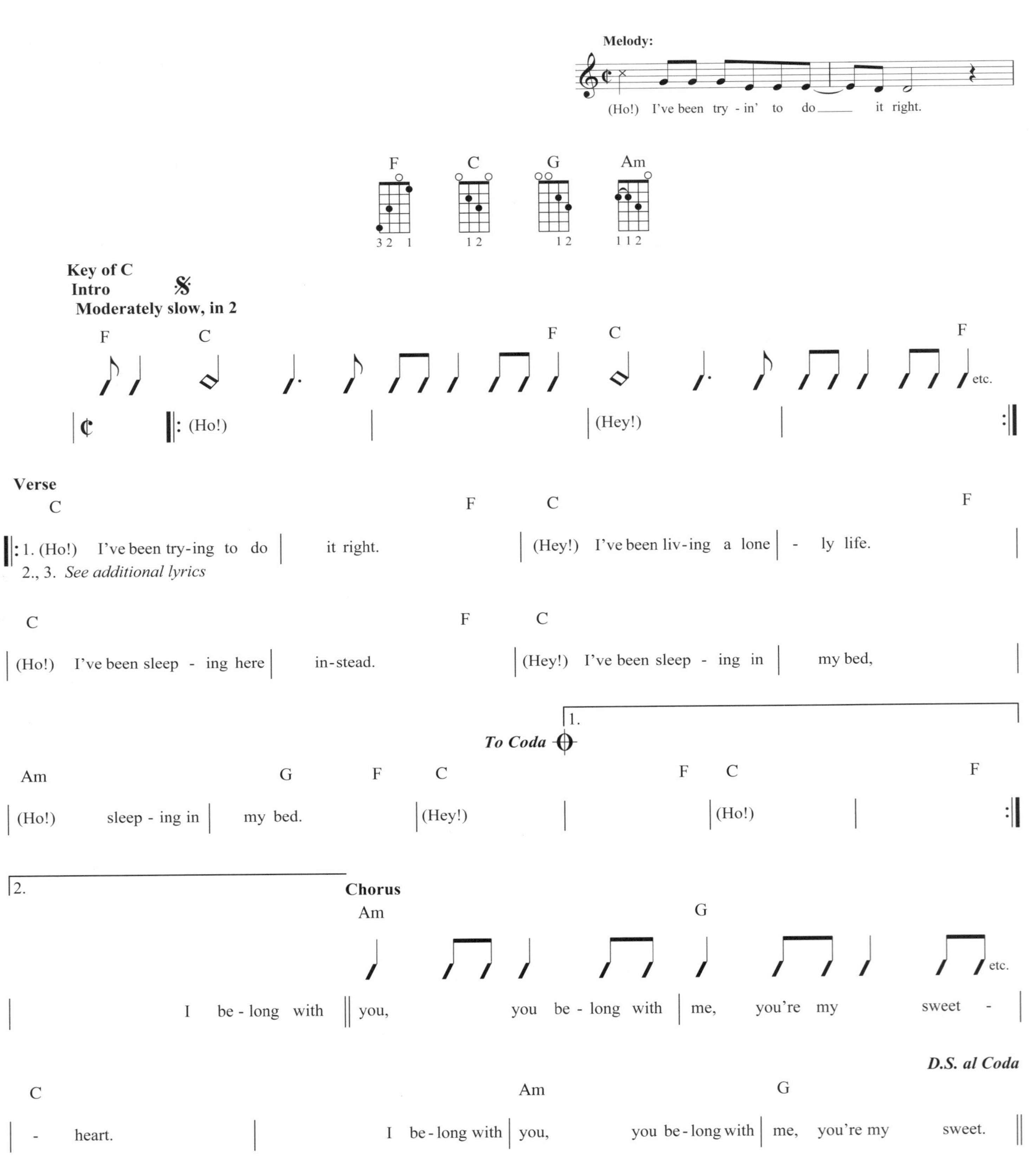

Melody:
(Ho!) I've been try - in' to do it right.
F
C
G
Am
3 2 1
1 2
1 2
1 1 2
Key of C
Intro
Moderately slow, in 2
F
C
F
C
F
etc.
(Ho!)
(Hey!)
Verse
C
F
C
F
1. (Ho!) I've been try-ing to do it right.
(Hey!) I've been liv-ing a lone - ly life.
2., 3. See additional lyrics
C
F
C
(Ho!) I've been sleep - ing here in-stead.
(Hey!) I've been sleep - ing in my bed,
1.
To Coda
Am
G
F
C
F
C
F
(Ho!) sleep - ing in my bed.
(Hey!)
(Ho!)
2.
Chorus
Am
G
etc.
I be - long with you, you be - long with me, you're my sweet -
D.S. al Coda
C
Am
G
- heart. I be - long with you, you be - long with me, you're my sweet.

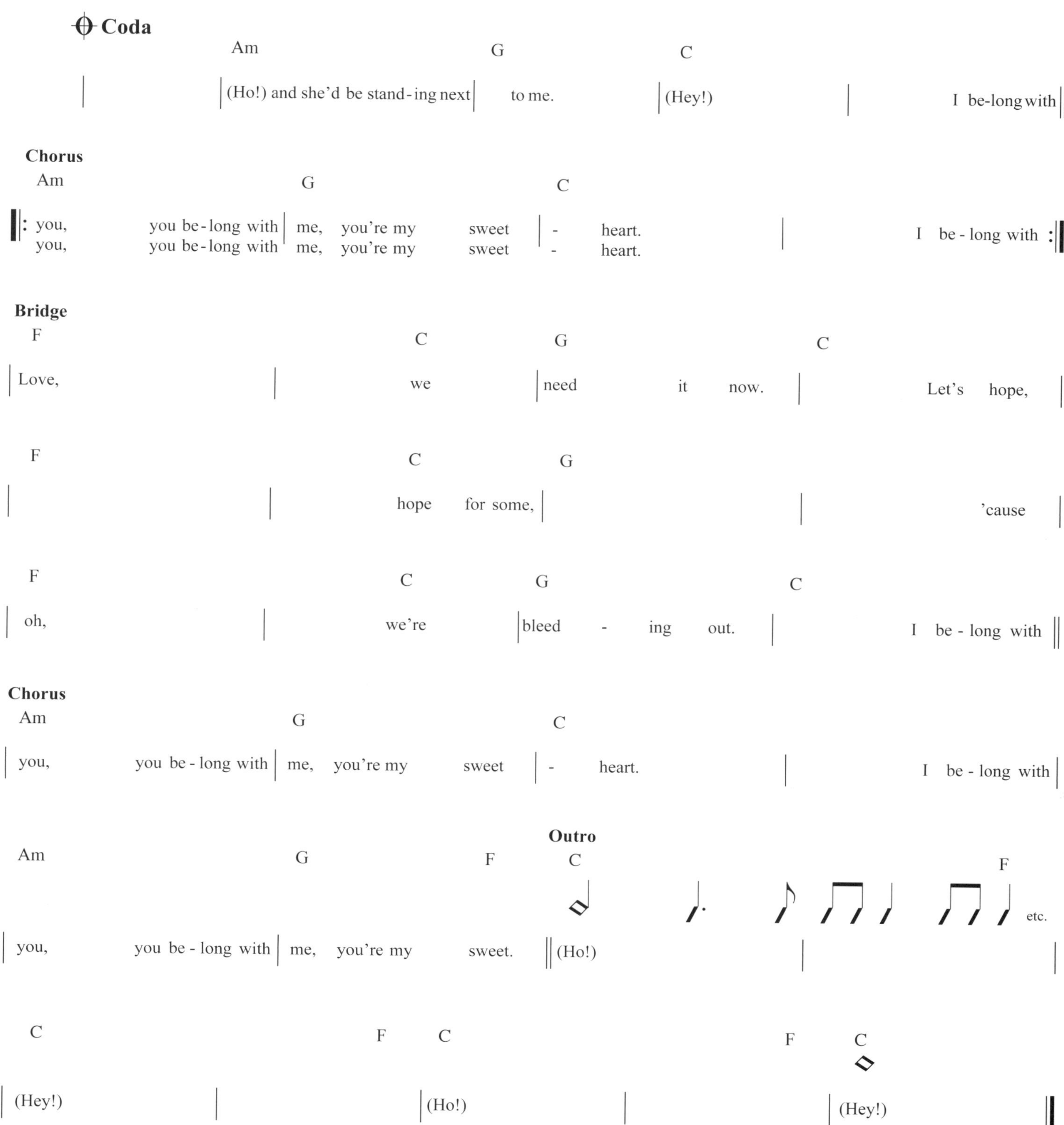
Coda
Am G C
(Ho!) and she'd be stand-ing next to me. (Hey!) I be-long with
Chorus
Am G C
you, you be-long with me, you're my sweet - heart. I be-long with
you, you be-long with me, you're my sweet - heart.
Bridge
F C G C
Love, we need it now. Let's hope,
F C G
hope for some, 'cause
F C G C
oh, we're bleed - ing out. I be-long with
Chorus
Am G C
you, you be-long with me, you're my sweet - heart. I be-long with
Am G F
Outro
C F
etc.
you, you be-long with me, you're my sweet. (Ho!)
C F C F C
(Hey!) (Ho!) (Hey!)

Additional Lyrics

2. (Ho!) So show me family,
   (Hey!) All the blood that I will bleed.
   (Ho!) I don't know where I belong,
   (Hey!) I don't know where I went wrong,
   (Ho!) But I can write a song.
   (Hey!)

3. (Ho!) I don't think you're right for him.
   (Hey!) Look at what it might have been if you
   (Ho!) Took a bus to China Town,
   (Hey!) I'd be standing on Canal
   (Ho!) And Bowery.
   (Hey!)

I Am a Man of Constant Sorrow

Words and Music by Carter Stanley

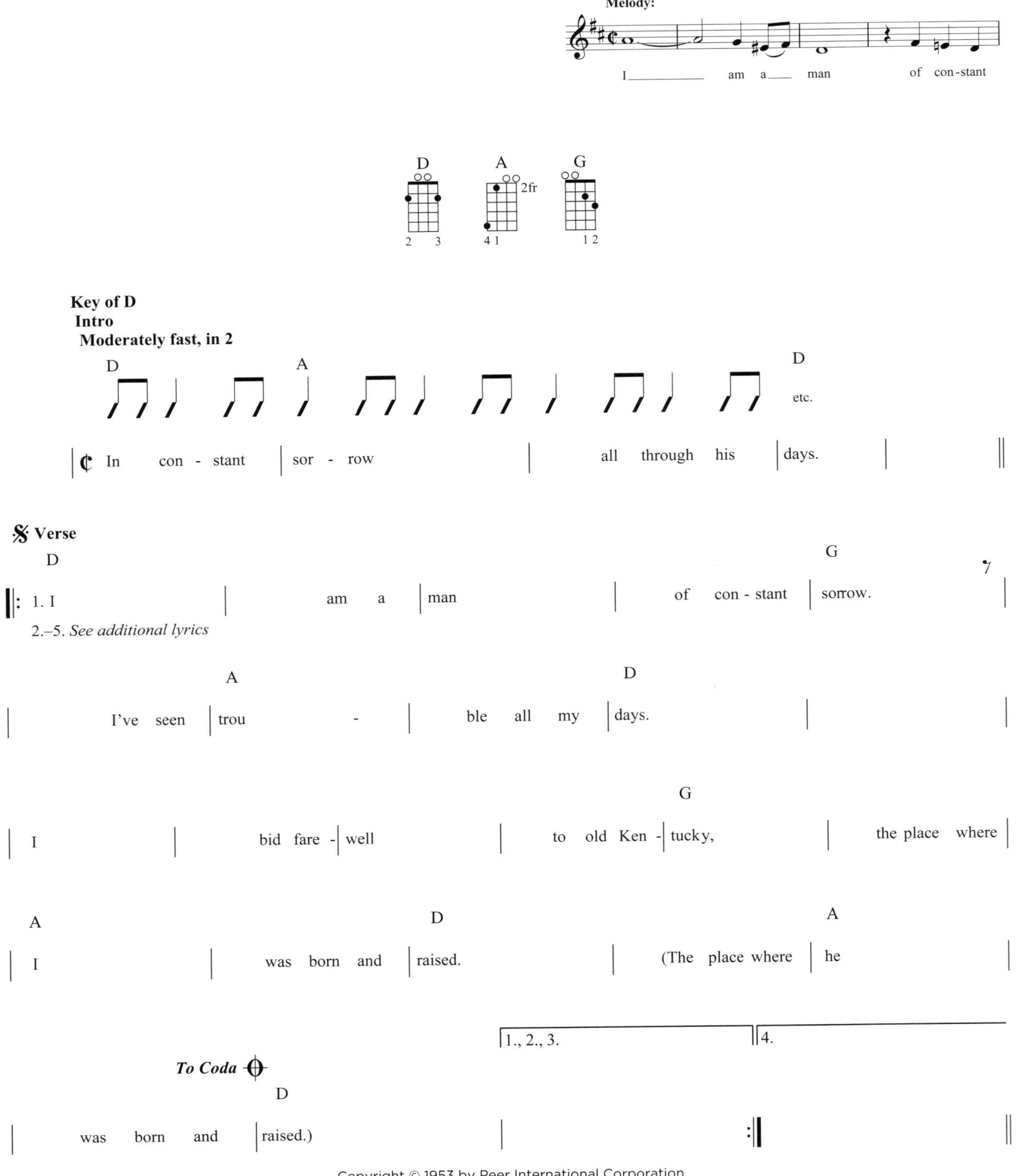

Melody:
I am a man of con-stant
D
A
2fr
G
2 3
4 1
1 2
Key of D
Intro
Moderately fast, in 2
D
A
D
etc.
In con - stant sor - row all through his days.
Verse
D
G
1. I am a man of con - stant sorrow.
2.–5. See additional lyrics
A
D
I've seen trou - ble all my days.
G
I bid fare - well to old Ken - tucky, the place where
A
D
A
I was born and raised. (The place where he
1., 2., 3.
4.
To Coda
D
was born and raised.)

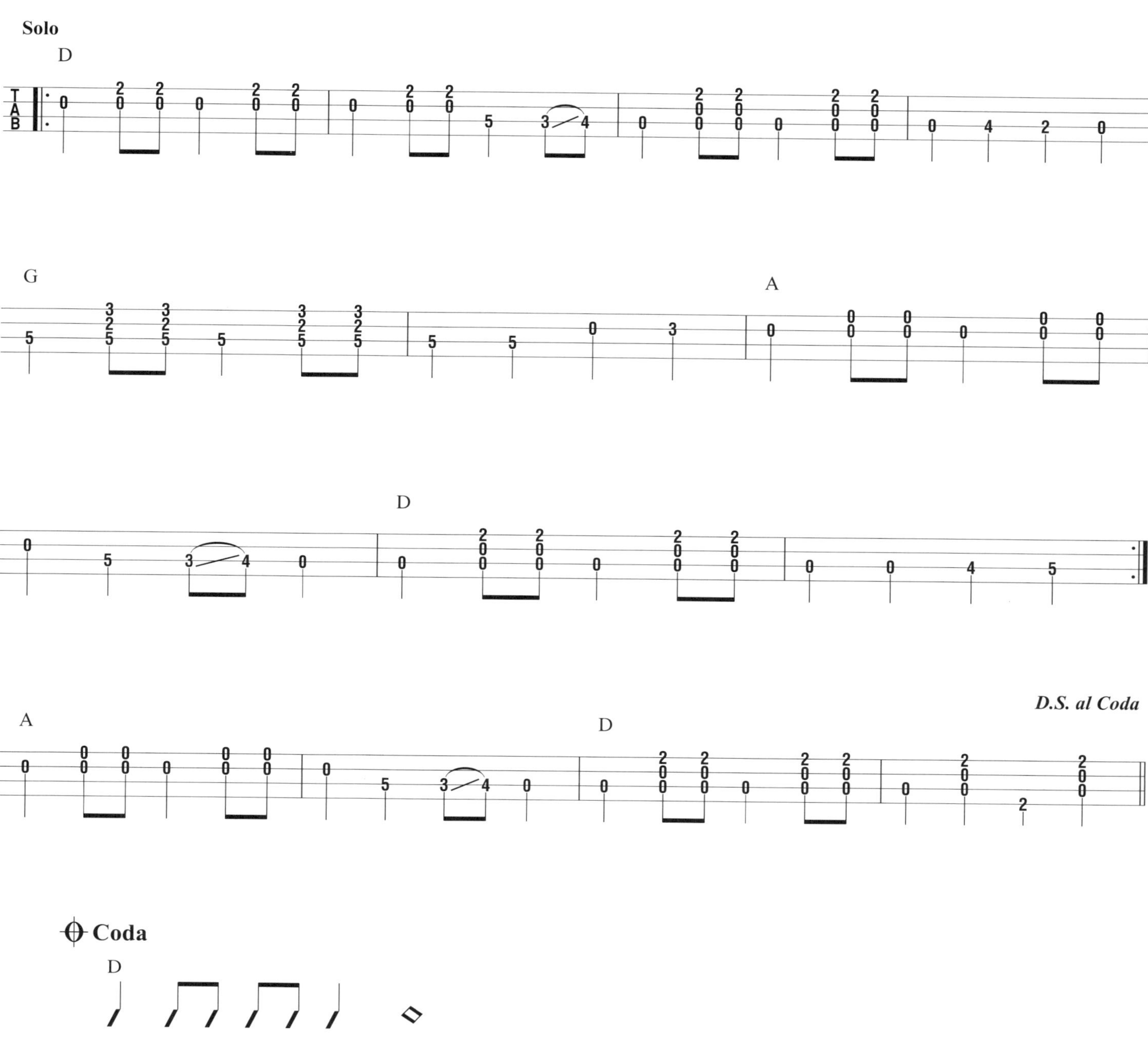
Solo
D
G
A
D
A
D.S. al Coda
D
Coda
D
shore.

Additional Lyrics

2. For six long years I've been in trouble; no pleasure here on Earth I found.
For in this world I'm bound to ramble; I have no friends to help me now.
(He has no friends to help him now.)

3. It's fare-thee-well my old true lover, I never expect to see you again.
For I'm bound to ride that northern railroad, perhaps I'll die upon this train.
(Perhaps he'll die upon this train.)

4. You can bury me in some deep valley, for many years where I may lay.
And you may learn to love another while I am sleeping in my grave.
(While he is sleeping in his grave.)

5. Maybe your friends think I'm just a stranger, my face you never will see no more.
But there is one promise that is given: I'll meet you on God's golden shore.
(He'll meet you on God's golden shore.)

I Walk the Line

Words and Music by John R. Cash

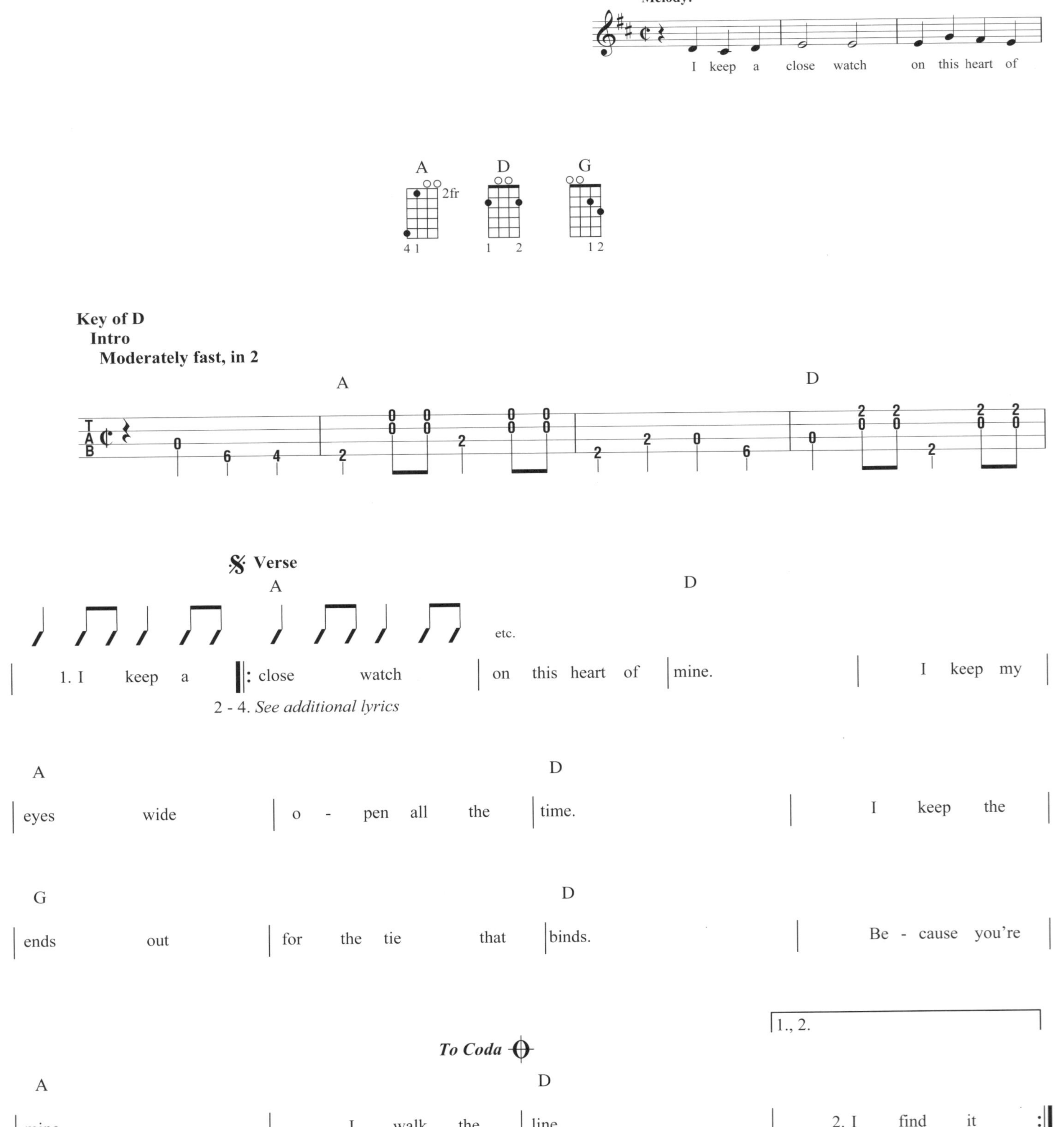

Melody:
I keep a close watch on this heart of
A
2fr
D
G
Key of D
Intro
Moderately fast, in 2
Verse
1. I keep a close watch on this heart of mine. I keep my
2 - 4. *See additional lyrics*
eyes wide o - pen all the time. I keep the
ends out for the tie that binds. Be - cause you're
To Coda
1., 2.
mine, I walk the line. 2. I find it

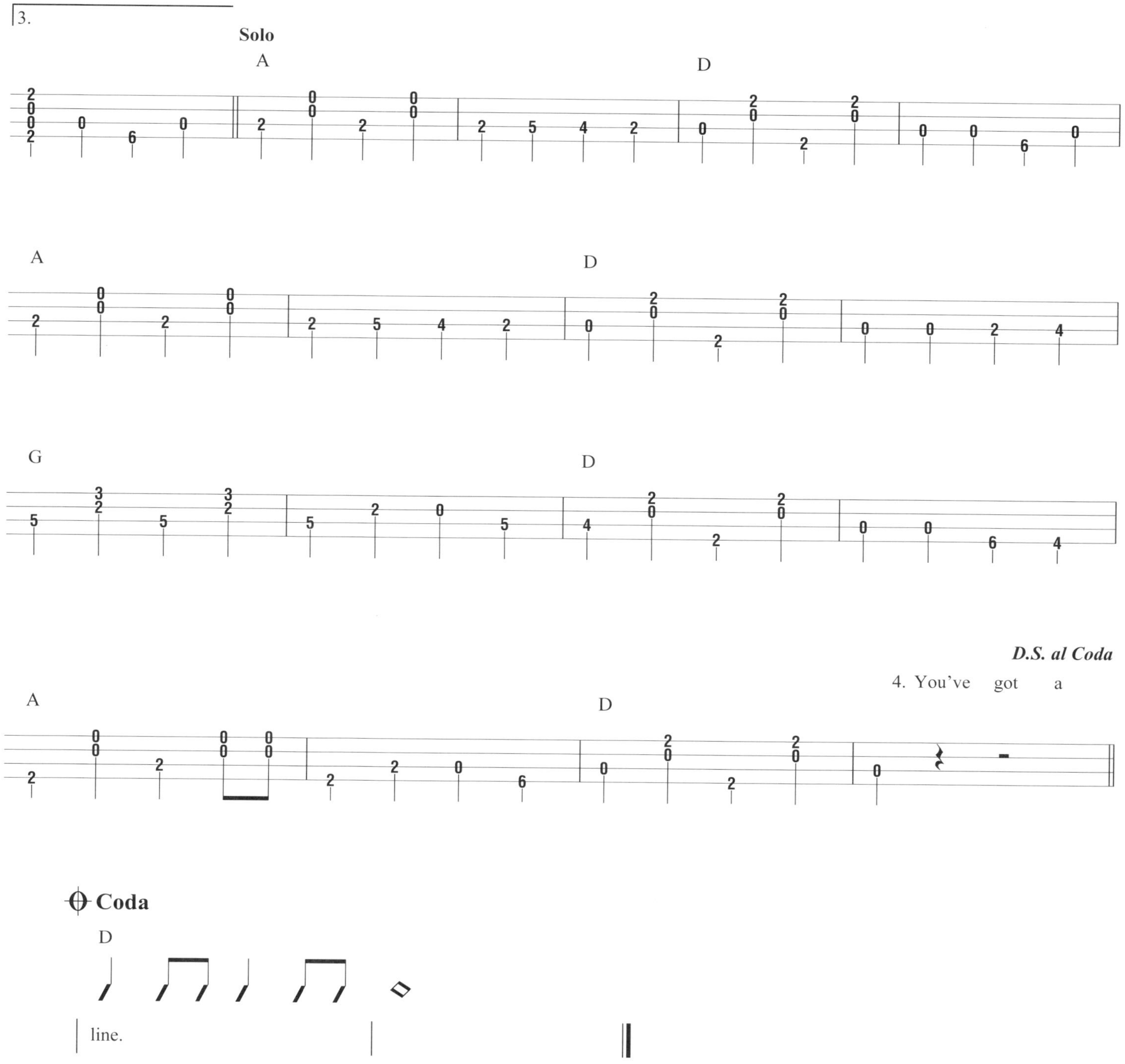

3.

Solo

A D

A D

G D

A D

D.S. al Coda

4. You've got a

Coda

D
line.

Additional Lyrics

2. I find it very, very easy to be true.
   I find myself alone when each day's through.
   Yes, I'll admit that I'm a fool for you.
   Because you're mine, I walk the line.

3. As sure as night is dark and day is light.
   I keep you on my mind both day and night.
   And happiness I've known prove that it's right.
   Because you're mine, I walk the line.

4. You've got a way to keep me on your side.
   You give me cause for love that I can't hide.
   For you I know I'd even try to turn the tide.
   Because you're mine, I walk the line.

I Will Wait

Words and Music by Mumford & Sons

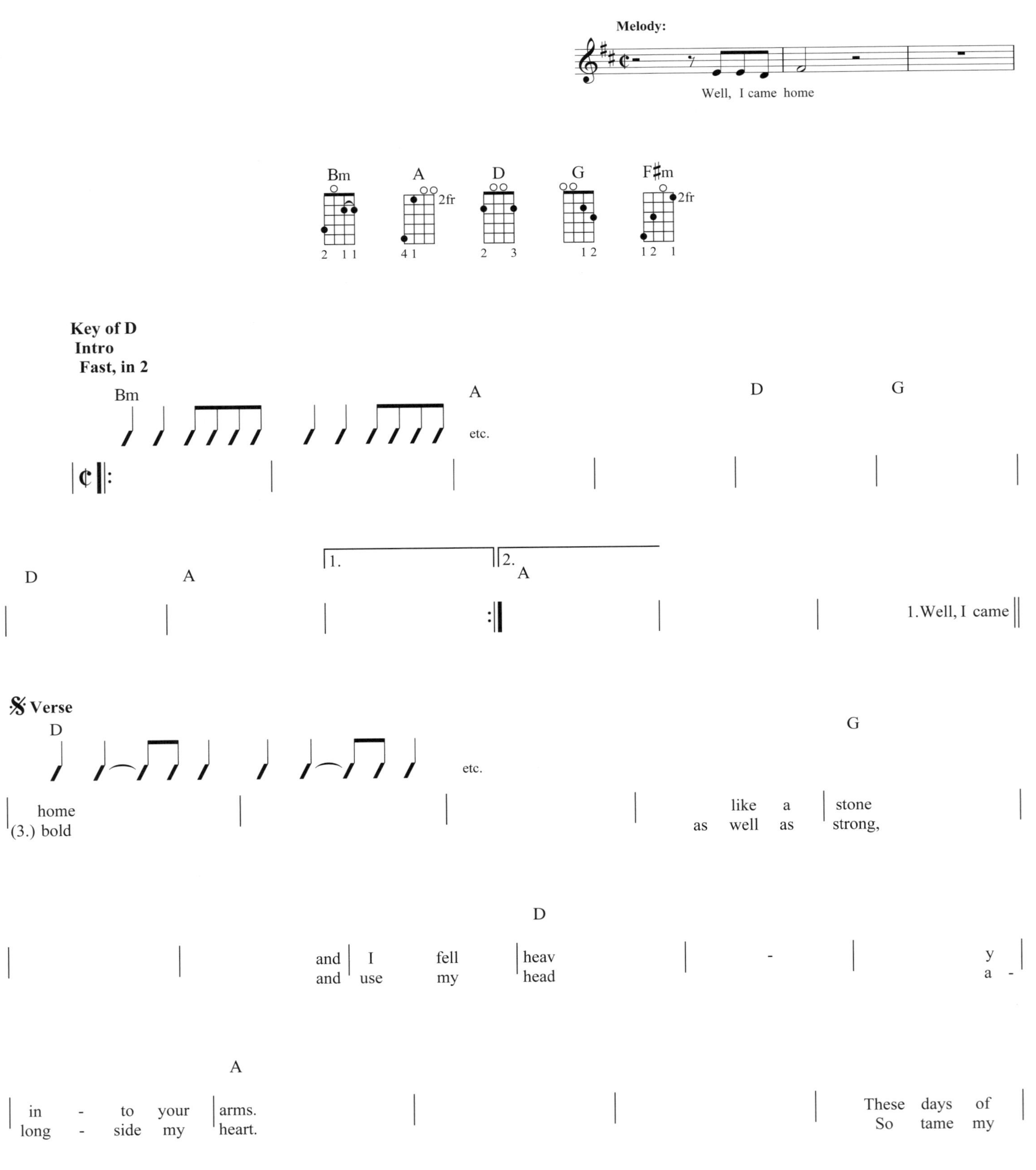
Melody:
Well, I came home
Bm
A
D
G
F♯m
2fr
2 1 1
4 1
2 3
1 2
1 2 1
Key of D
Intro
Fast, in 2
etc.
1.
2.
1.Well, I came
Verse
home
(3.) bold
like a stone
as well as strong,
and I fell heav - y
and use my head a -
in - to your arms.
long - side my heart.
These days of
So tame my

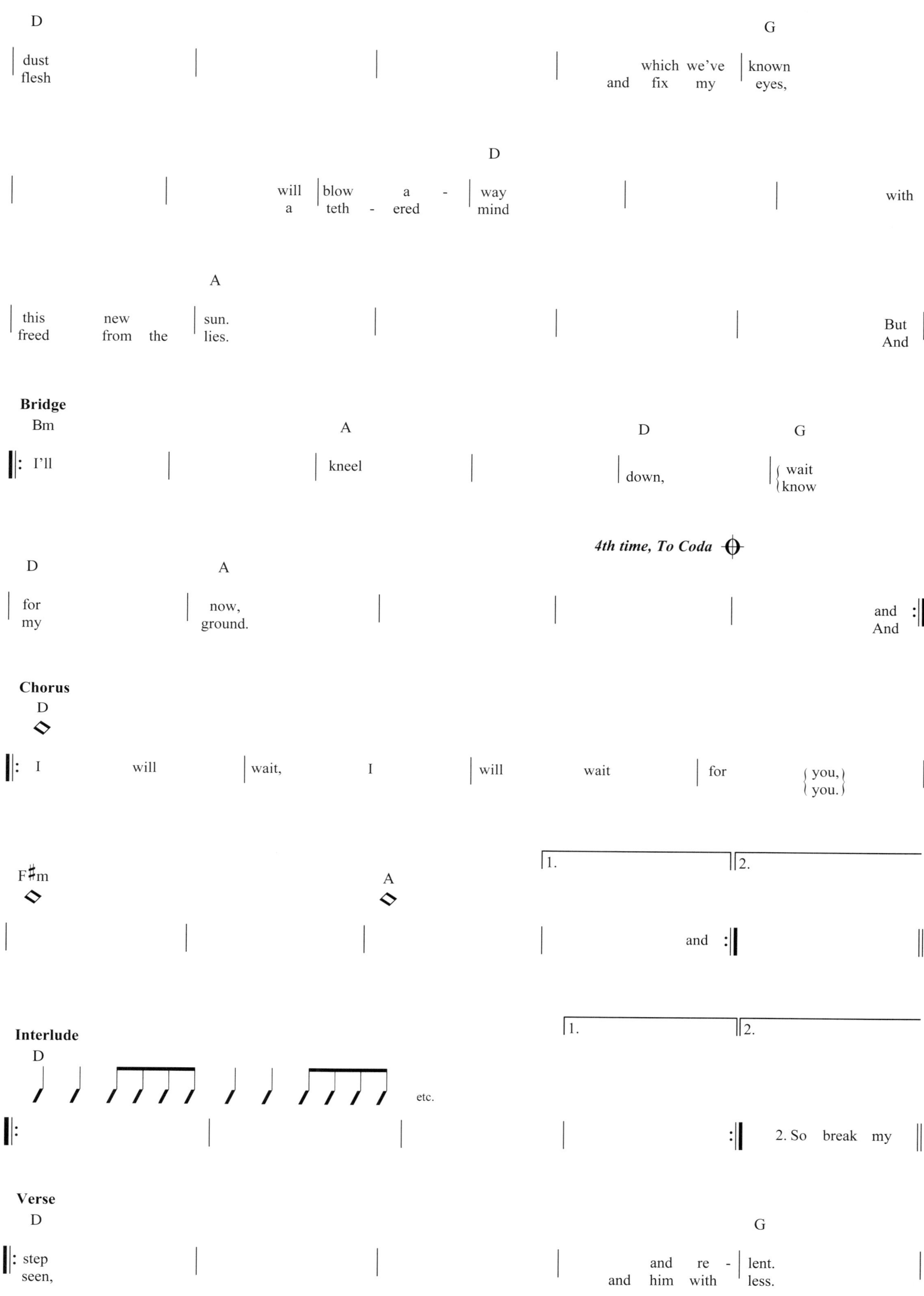
D
dust
flesh
G
which we've known
and fix my eyes,
D
will blow a - way
a teth - ered mind
with
A
this new sun.
freed from the lies.
But
And
Bridge
Bm
I'll
A
kneel
D
down,
G
wait
know
D
A
for now,
my ground.
4th time, To Coda
and
And
Chorus
D
I will wait, I will wait for you,
you.
F♯m
A
1.
2.
and
Interlude
D
etc.
1.
2.
2. So break my
Verse
D
step
seen,
G
and re - lent.
and him with less.

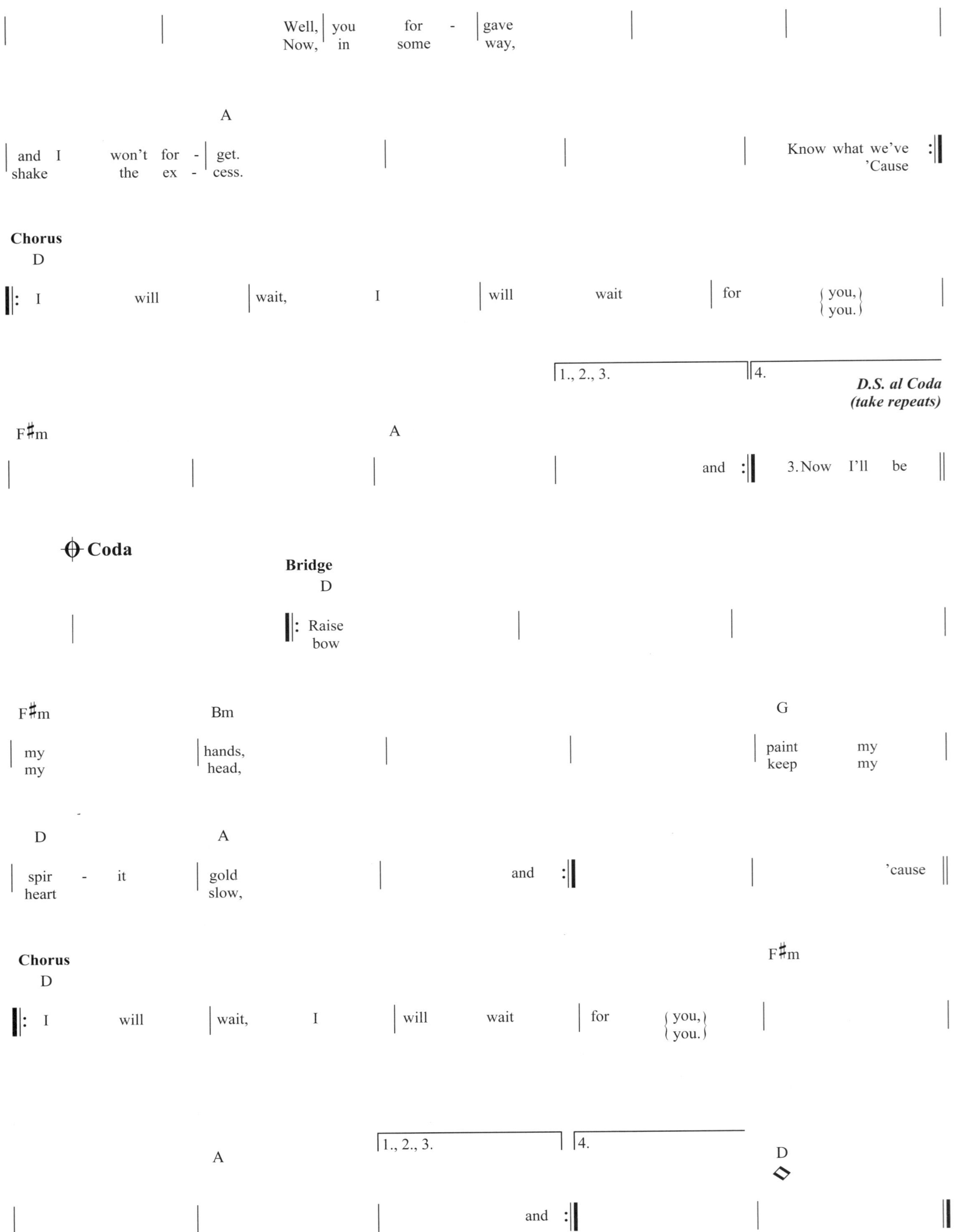
D
Well, you for - gave
Now, in some way,
A
and I won't for - get.
shake the ex - cess.
Know what we've
'Cause
Chorus
D
I will wait, I will wait for you, you.
1., 2., 3.
4.
D.S. al Coda
(take repeats)
F♯m
A
and
3. Now I'll be
Coda
Bridge
D
Raise
bow
F♯m
Bm
G
my hands,
my head,
paint my
keep my
D
A
spir - it gold
heart slow,
and
'cause
Chorus
D
F♯m
I will wait, I will wait for you, you.
A
1., 2., 3.
4.
D
and

In the Jailhouse Now

Words and Music by Jimmie Rodgers

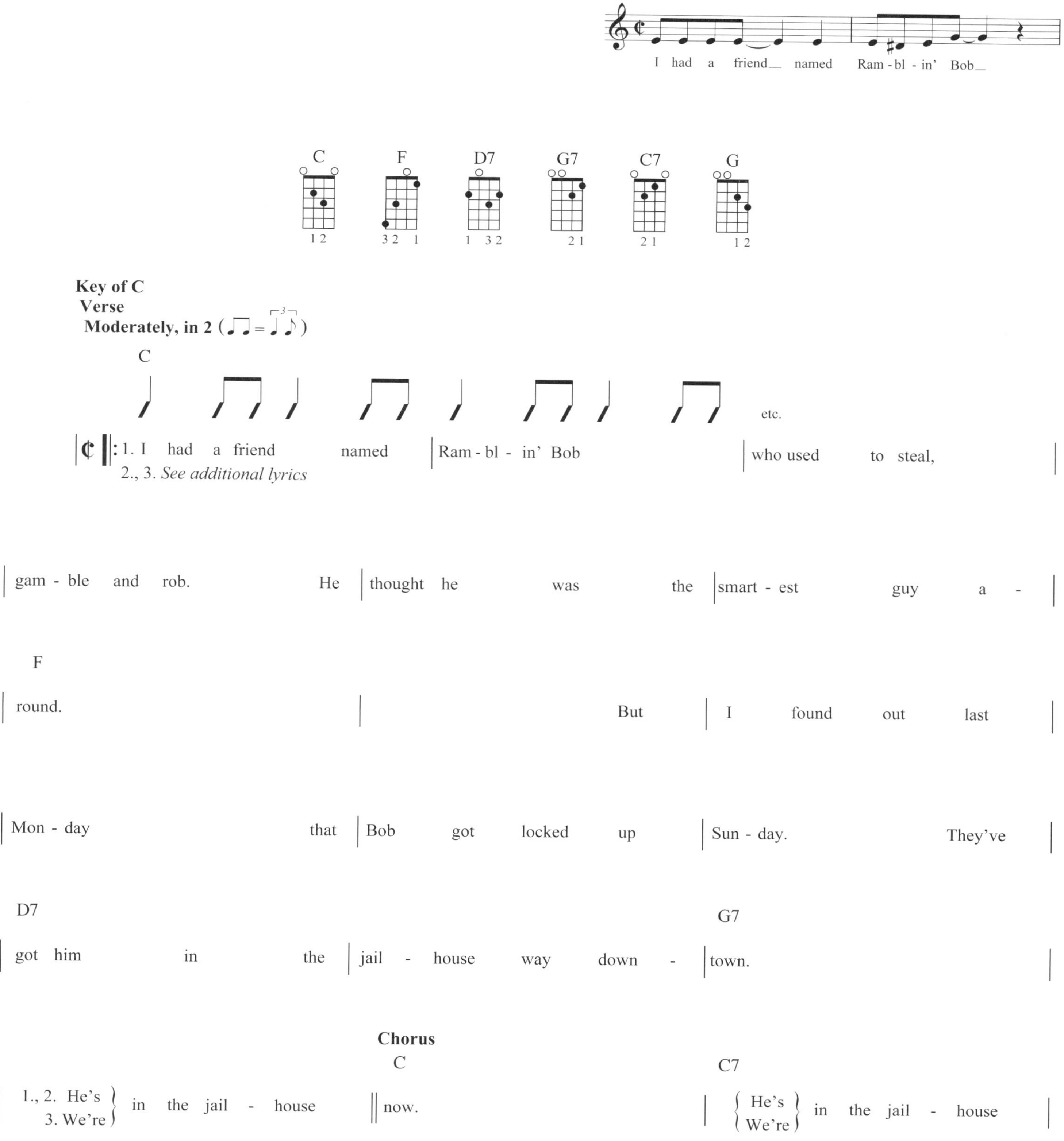

Melody:
I had a friend named Ram-bl-in' Bob
C
F
D7
G7
C7
G
Key of C
Verse
Moderately, in 2
C
etc.
1. I had a friend named Ram-bl-in' Bob who used to steal,
2., 3. See additional lyrics
gam-ble and rob. He thought he was the smart-est guy a-
F
round. But I found out last
Mon-day that Bob got locked up Sun-day. They've
D7
got him in the jail-house way down-
G7
town.
Chorus
C
1., 2. He's
3. We're
in the jail-house now.
C7
He's
We're
in the jail-house

F

now. | | Well, I | told him once or / told that judge right

G7

twice to stop / to his face | play - in' cards and / I don't like to | shoot - in' dice. / see this place.

He's / We're in the jail - house | now.

C

| | A - lee - o ||

Interlude

F

lay - ee - hee - o - | hee. | |

C

| A - lee - o | lay - ee - o - dee - o - | hoo, |

G7

| yo - de - | lay - ee - hee, yo - de - | lay - ee - hee, yo - de - |

1., 2. | 3.

To Coda ⊕

C

lay - hee. | :|| ||

Solo

C

F

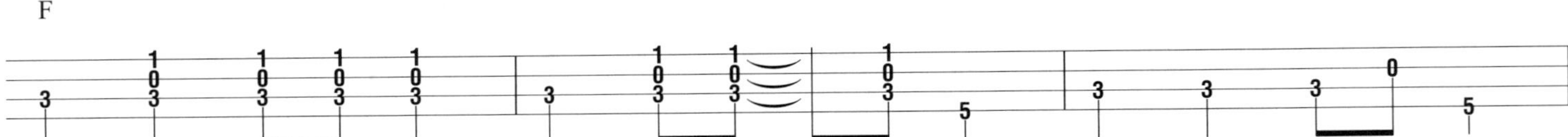

D7
G
G7
C
C7
F
G7
C
D.C. al Coda
Coda
C

Additional Lyrics

2. Bob liked to play his poker, pinochle, whist and euchre,
   But shootin' dice was his favorite game.
   Well, he got throwed in jail, with nobody to go his bail.
   The judge done said that he refused a fine.

3. I went out last Tuesday, I met a girl named Susie.
   I said I was the swellest guy around.
   Well, we started to spendin' my money and she started to callin' me Honey.
   We took in every cabaret in town.

I'll Fly Away

Words and Music by Albert E. Brumley

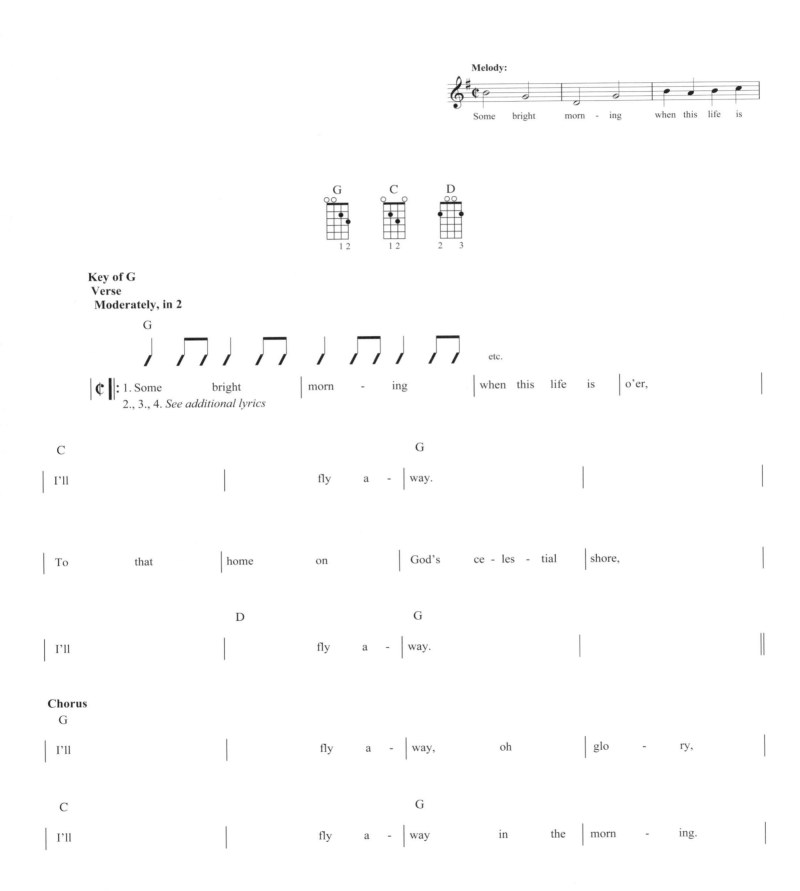

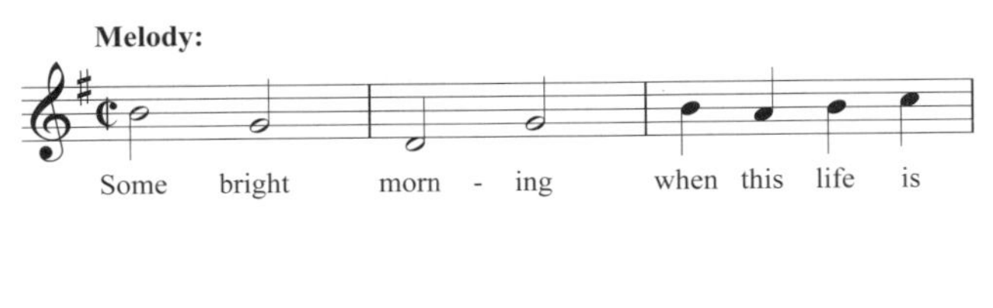
Melody:
Some bright morn - ing when this life is

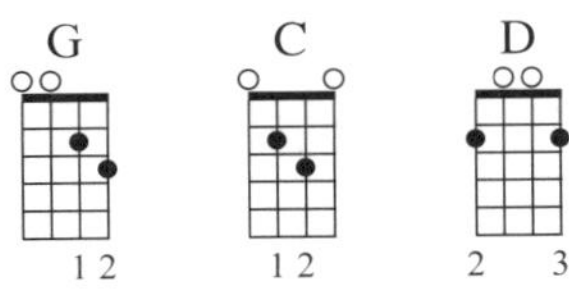
G
C
D
1 2
1 2
2 3

Key of G
Verse
Moderately, in 2

G

etc.

| 1. Some bright | morn - ing | when this life is | o'er, |
2., 3., 4. *See additional lyrics*

C | G
| I'll | fly a - | way. | |

| To that | home on | God's ce - les - tial | shore, |

D | G
| I'll | fly a - | way. | ||

Chorus

G
| I'll | fly a - | way, oh | glo - ry, |

C | G
| I'll | fly a - | way in the | morn - ing. |

When I die, hal - le - lu - jah by and by,
To Coda
1., 2.
3.
D
G
I'll fly a - way.
Solo
G
C
G
D
G
D.C. al Coda
Coda
G
way.

Additional Lyrics

2. When the shadows of this life have grown, I'll fly away.
   Like a bird from these prison walls has flown, I'll fly away.

3. Oh, how glad and happy when we meet, I'll fly away.
   No more cold iron shackles on my feet, I'll fly away.

4. Just a few more weary days and then, I'll fly away,
   To a land where joys will never end, I'll fly away.

Jambalaya
(On the Bayou)

Words and Music by Hank Williams

Melody:
Good-bye Joe, me got - ta go, me, oh, my, oh.

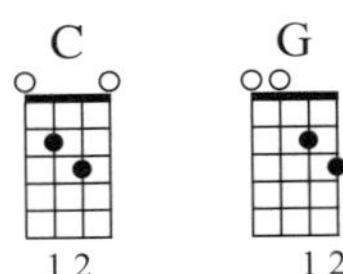
C
G
1 2
1 2

Key of C

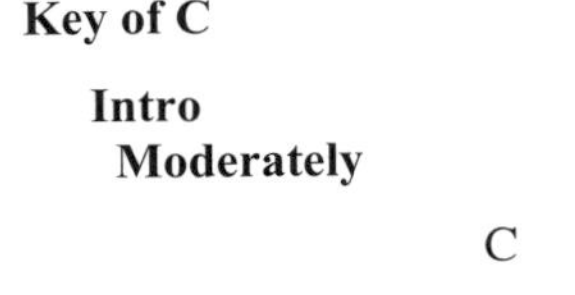
Intro
Moderately

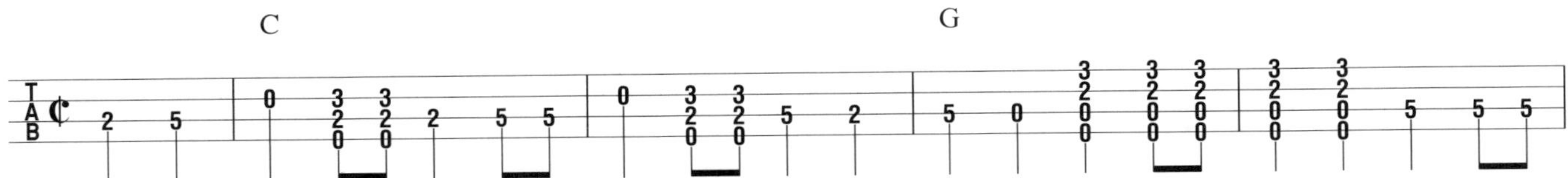
C
G

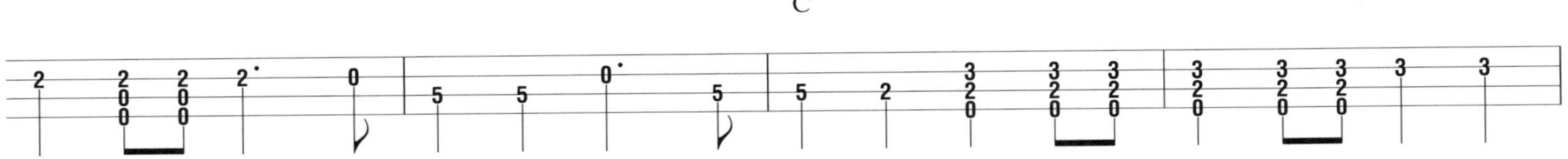
C

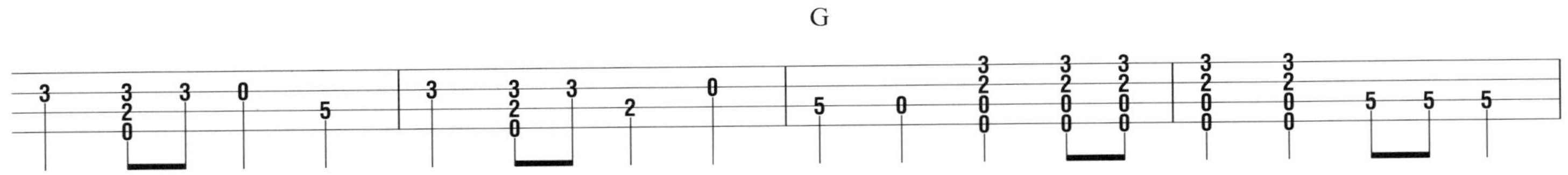
G

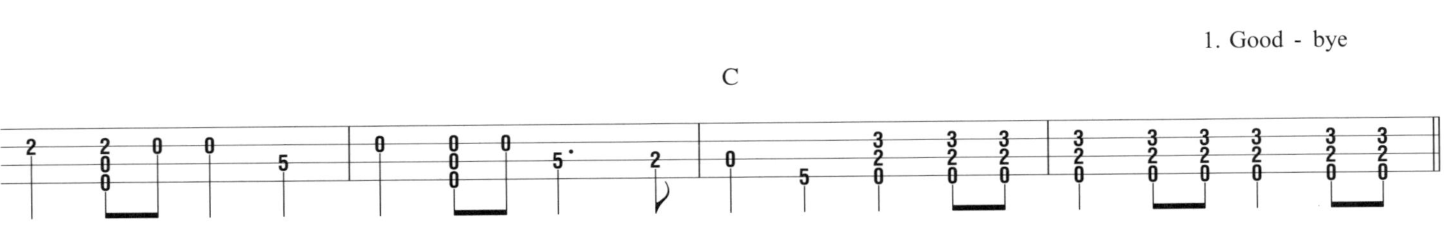
1. Good - bye
C

Verse
C
G
etc.
Joe, me got-ta go, me, oh my, oh, me got-ta go pole the
2., 3. See additional lyrics
pi - rogue down the
C
bay - ou. My Y - vonne, the sweet - est one, me, oh
G
my, oh. Son of a gun, we'll have big fun on the
C
bay - ou. Jam - ba -
Chorus
C
la - ya and a craw - fish pie and fil - let
G
gum - bo, 'cause to - night I'm gon - na
see my ma cher a -
C
mi - o, pick gui - tar, fill fruit jar and be
G
gay, oh. Son of a gun, we'll have big fun on the
C
bay - ou.
1., 2.
2.Thi - bo -
3.
Son of a
G
gun, we'll have big fun on the
C
bay - ou.
Son of a
G
gun we'll have big fun on the
C
bay - ou.

Additional Lyrics

2. Thibodaux, Fontaineaux, the place is buzzin'.
   Kinfolk come to see Yvonne by the dozen.
   Dress in style and go hog-wild, me, oh my, oh.
   Son of a gun, we'll have big fun on the bayou.

3. Settle down far from town, get me a pirogue
   And I'll catch all the fish in the bayou.
   Swap my mon' to buy Yvonne what she need, oh.
   Son of a gun, we'll have big fun on the bayou.

Losing My Religion

Words and Music by William Berry, Peter Buck, Michael Mills and Michael Stipe

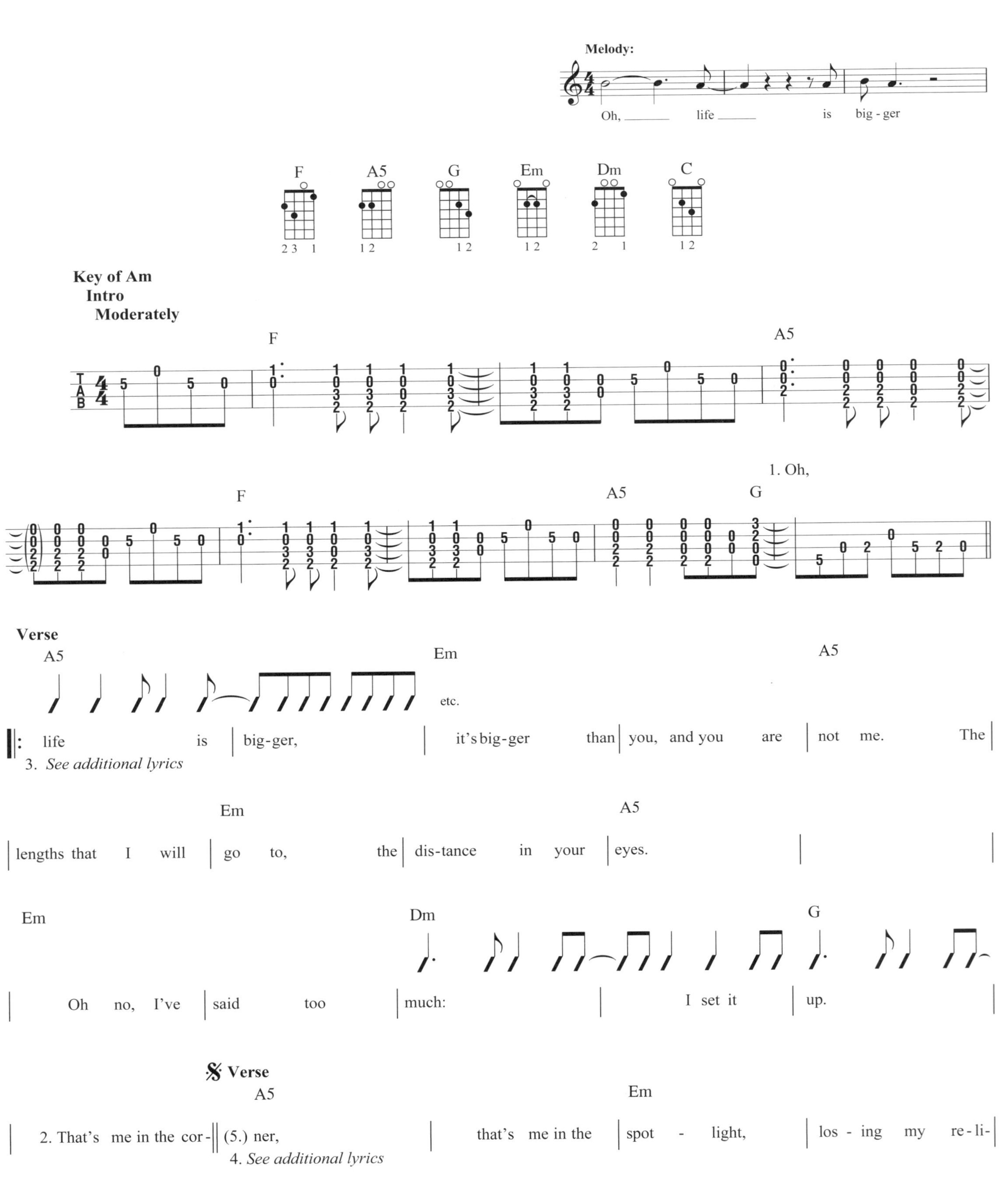

Melody:
Oh, life is big - ger
F
A5
G
Em
Dm
C
Key of Am
Intro
Moderately
1. Oh,
Verse
etc.
life is big-ger, it's big-ger than you, and you are not me. The
3. See additional lyrics
lengths that I will go to, the dis-tance in your eyes.
Oh no, I've said too much: I set it up.
Verse
2. That's me in the cor- (5.) ner, that's me in the spot - light, los - ing my re-li-
4. See additional lyrics

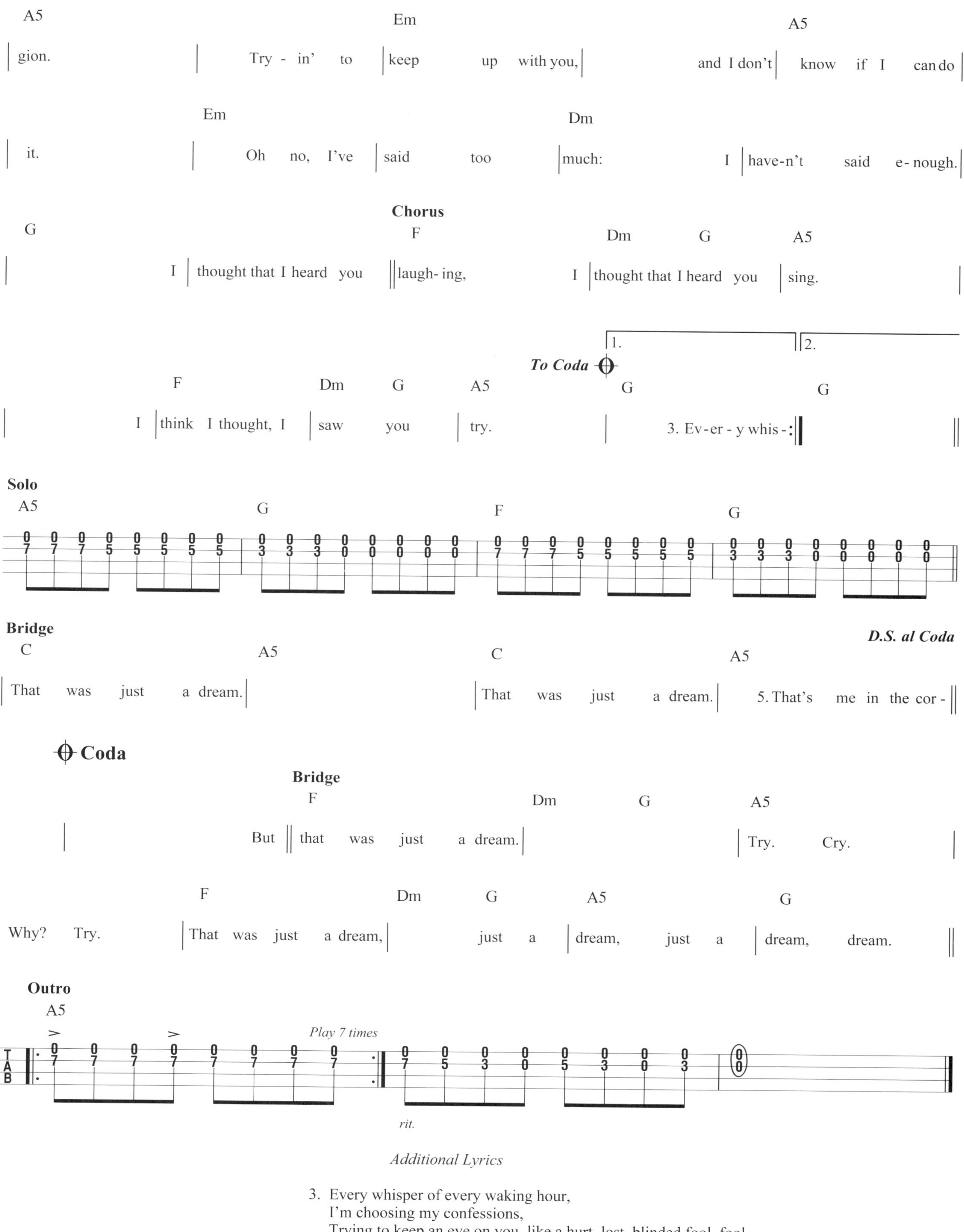
A5 Em A5
gion. Try - in' to keep up with you, and I don't know if I can do
Em Dm
it. Oh no, I've said too much: I have-n't said e - nough.
Chorus
G F Dm G A5
I thought that I heard you laugh- ing, I thought that I heard you sing.
To Coda
1. 2.
F Dm G A5 G G
I think I thought, I saw you try. 3. Ev - er - y whis -
Solo
A5 G F G
Bridge
C A5 C A5
D.S. al Coda
That was just a dream. That was just a dream. 5. That's me in the cor -
Coda
Bridge
F Dm G A5
But that was just a dream. Try. Cry.
F Dm G A5 G
Why? Try. That was just a dream, just a dream, just a dream, dream.
Outro
A5
Play 7 times
T
A
B
rit.

Additional Lyrics

3. Every whisper of every waking hour,
I'm choosing my confessions,
Trying to keep an eye on you, like a hurt, lost, blinded fool, fool.
Oh no, I've said too much. I set it up.

4. Consider this, consider this hint of the century.
Consider this: the slip that brought me to my knees failed.
What if all these fantasies come flailing around?
Now I've said too much.

Maggie May

Words and Music by Rod Stewart and Martin Quittenton

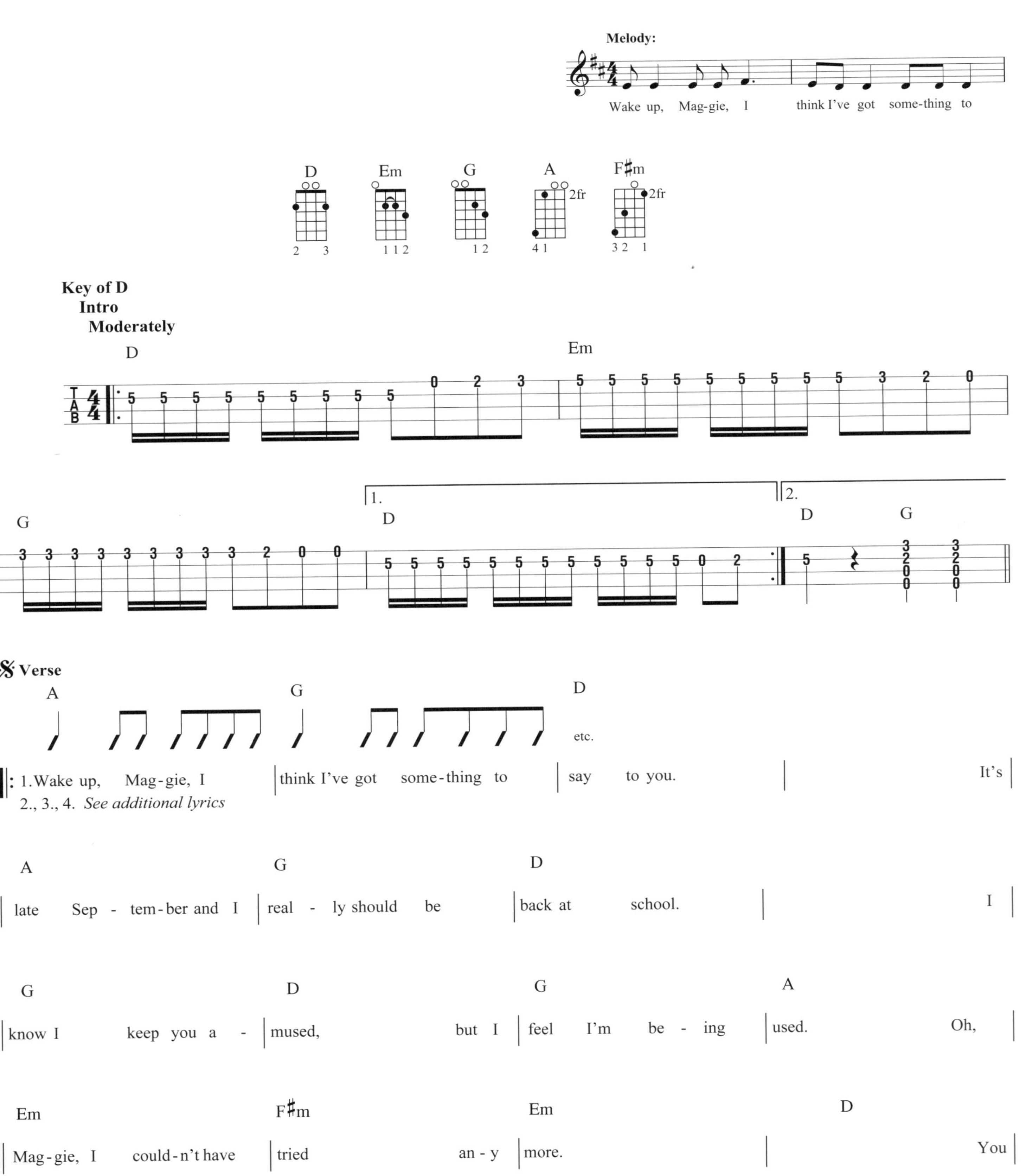

Melody:
Wake up, Mag-gie, I think I've got some-thing to
D
Em
G
A
F♯m
2fr
2fr
Key of D
Intro
Moderately
1.
2.
𝄋 Verse
etc.
1.Wake up, Mag-gie, I think I've got some-thing to say to you. It's
2., 3., 4. See additional lyrics
late Sep - tem-ber and I real - ly should be back at school. I
know I keep you a - mused, but I feel I'm be - ing used. Oh,
Mag-gie, I could-n't have tried an - y more. You

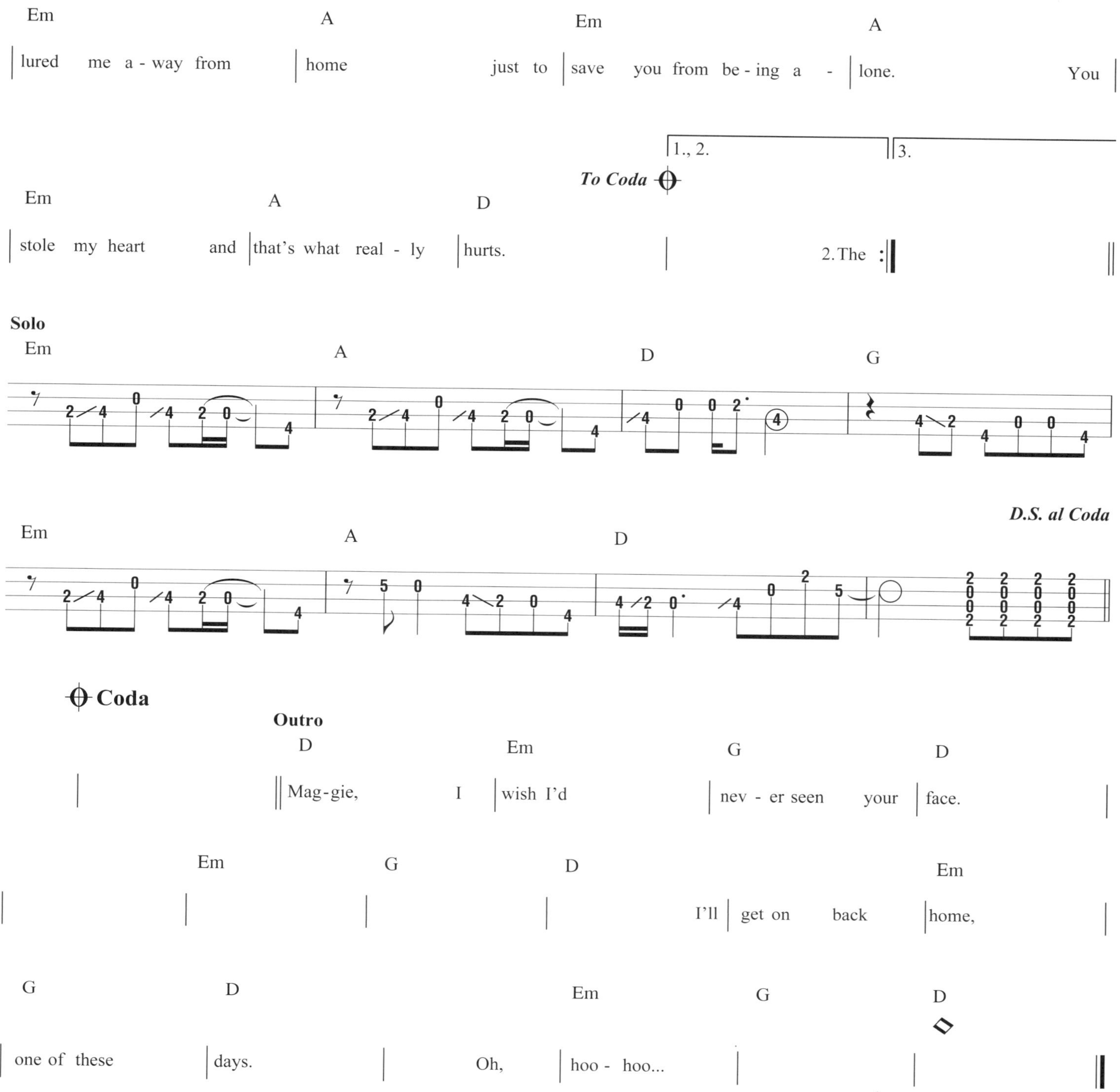
Em
A
Em
A
lured me a - way from
home
just to
save you from be - ing a - lone.
You
1., 2.
3.
To Coda
Em
A
D
stole my heart and
that's what real - ly
hurts.
2. The
Solo
Em
A
D
G
Em
A
D
D.S. al Coda
Coda
Outro
D
Em
G
D
Mag-gie, I
wish I'd
nev - er seen your
face.
Em
G
D
Em
I'll
get on back
home,
G
D
Em
G
D
one of these
days.
Oh,
hoo - hoo...

Additional Lyrics

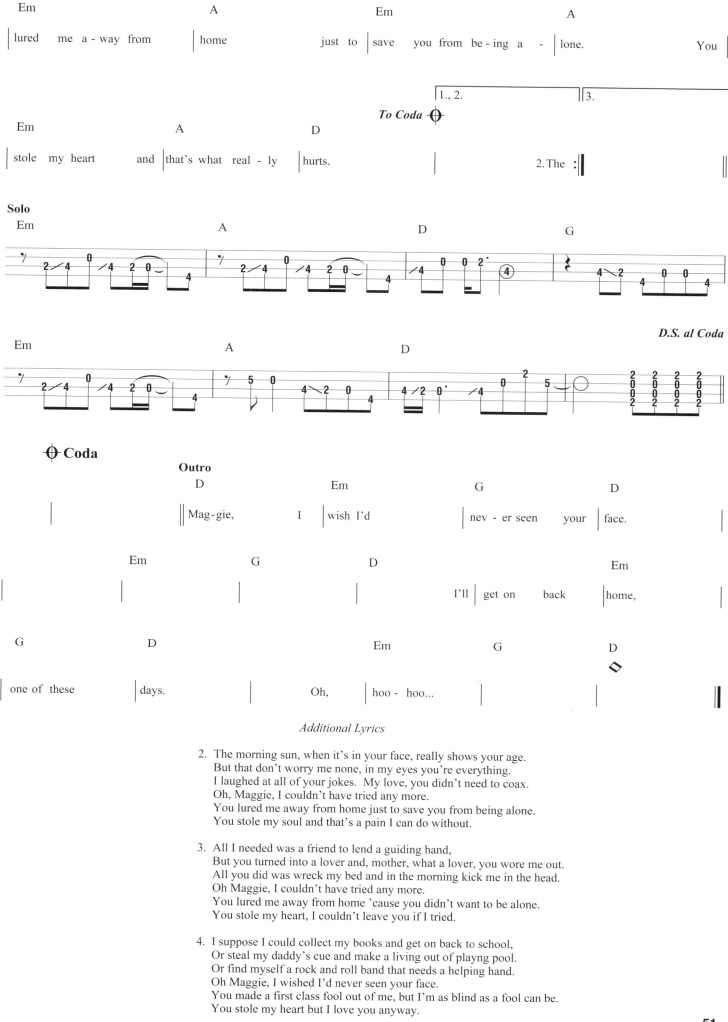

2. The morning sun, when it's in your face, really shows your age.
   But that don't worry me none, in my eyes you're everything.
   I laughed at all of your jokes. My love, you didn't need to coax.
   Oh, Maggie, I couldn't have tried any more.
   You lured me away from home just to save you from being alone.
   You stole my soul and that's a pain I can do without.

3. All I needed was a friend to lend a guiding hand,
   But you turned into a lover and, mother, what a lover, you wore me out.
   All you did was wreck my bed and in the morning kick me in the head.
   Oh Maggie, I couldn't have tried any more.
   You lured me away from home 'cause you didn't want to be alone.
   You stole my heart, I couldn't leave you if I tried.

4. I suppose I could collect my books and get on back to school,
   Or steal my daddy's cue and make a living out of playng pool.
   Or find myself a rock and roll band that needs a helping hand.
   Oh Maggie, I wished I'd never seen your face.
   You made a first class fool out of me, but I'm as blind as a fool can be.
   You stole my heart but I love you anyway.

Mandolin Wind

Words and Music by Rod Stewart

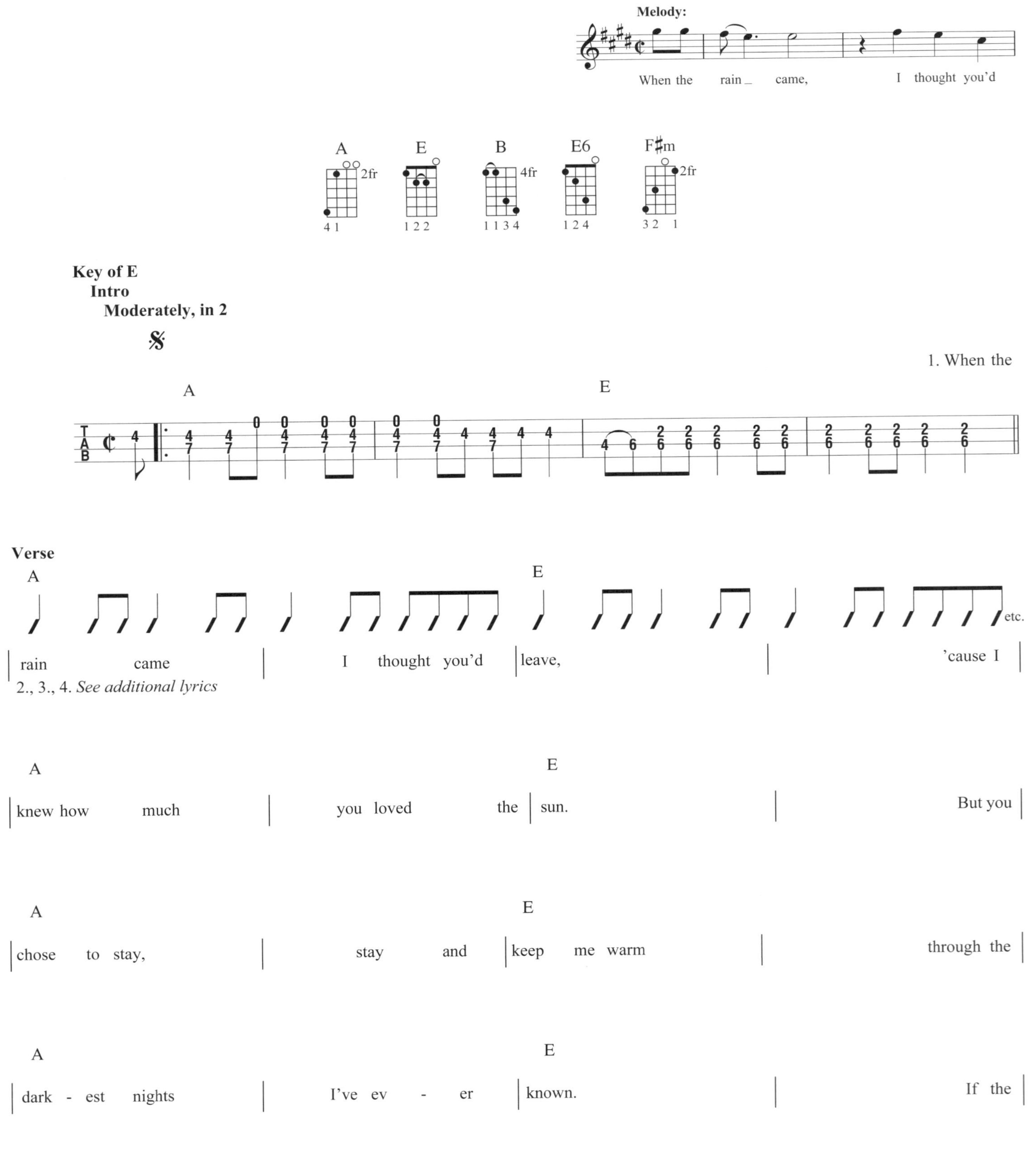

Melody:
When the rain came, I thought you'd
A
E
B
E6
F♯m
2fr
4fr
Key of E
Intro
Moderately, in 2
1. When the
Verse
rain came I thought you'd leave, 'cause I
2., 3., 4. See additional lyrics
knew how much you loved the sun. But you
chose to stay, stay and keep me warm through the
dark - est nights I've ev - er known. If the

To Coda 

B
man - do - lin wind

A
could - n't change a thing, then I know I

E6
rit.
love

E
ya.

Free time

1., 2.

3.

E

Solo

A

E

A

E

A

E

A

E

B

A

F♯m

B

2nd time, D.S. al Coda

Coda
F♯m
B
could-n't change a thing,
no, no.
A
La da da da,
la da,
la da da da,
F♯m
B
la da da da,
la da da da da.
Outro
B
A
The cold - est win-ter
in al - most
four - teen years
F♯m
B
could nev - er,
nev - er change your
mind, yeah.
A
F♯m
B
And I love ya,
yes in-deed and I
love ya,
A
and I love ya,
Lord - y I
love ya.
F♯m
B

Additional Lyrics

2. Oh, the snow fell without a break. Buffalo died in the frozen fields, you know.
   Through the coldest winter in almost fourteen years, I couldn't believe you kept a smile.
   Now I can rest assured knowing that we've seen the worst and I know I love ya.

3. Oh, I never was good with romantic words, so the next few lines come really hard.
   Don't have much but what I've got is yours, except, of course, my steel guitar.
   'Cause I know you don't play, but I'll teach you one day, because I love ya.

4. I recall the night we knelt and prayed, noticing your face was thin and pale.
   I found it hard to hide my tears. I felt ashamed, I felt I'd let you down.
   No mandolin wind couldn't change a thing, couldn't change a thing, no, no.

Mr. Bojangles

Words and Music by Jerry Jeff Walker

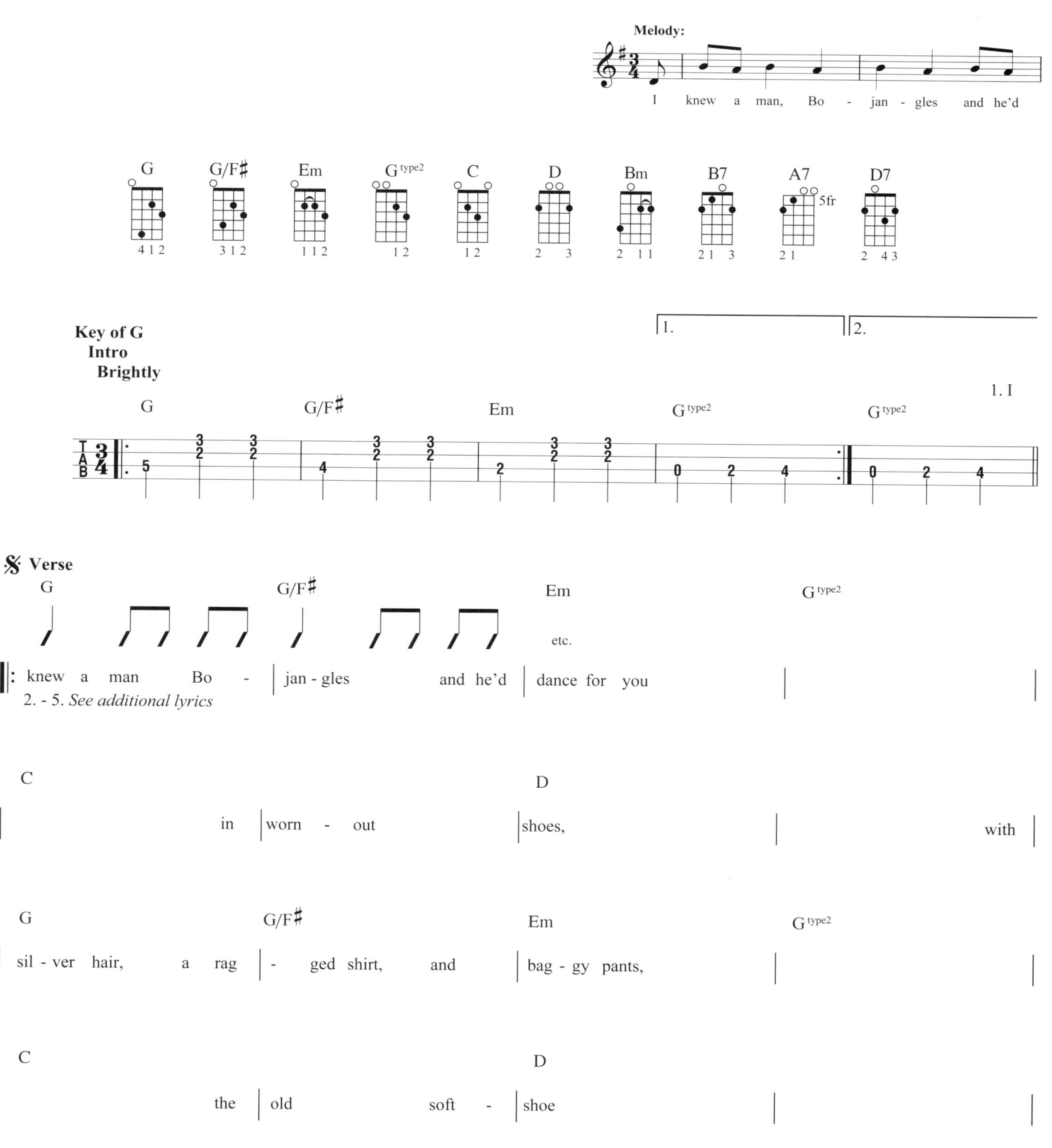
Melody:
I knew a man, Bo - jan - gles and he'd
G
G/F♯
Em
G type2
C
D
Bm
B7
A7
5fr
D7
Key of G
Intro
Brightly
1.
2.
1. I
Verse
knew a man Bo - jan - gles and he'd dance for you
2. - 5. See additional lyrics
etc.
in worn - out shoes, with
sil - ver hair, a rag - ged shirt, and bag - gy pants,
the old soft - shoe

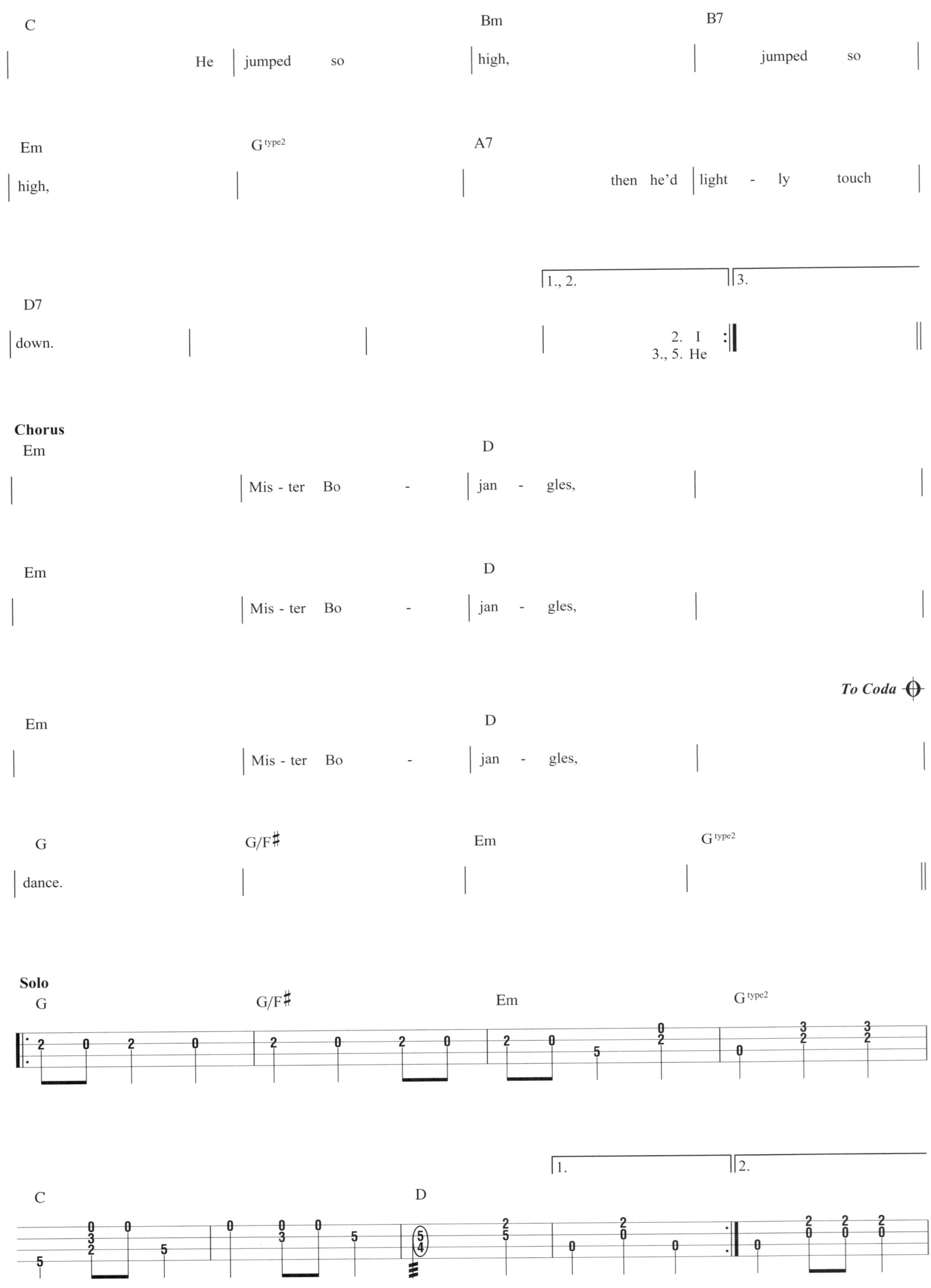
C Bm B7
He jumped so high, jumped so
Em G type2 A7
high, then he'd light - ly touch
D7
1., 2. 3.
down. 2. I 3., 5. He
Chorus
Em D
Mis - ter Bo - jan - gles,
Em D
Mis - ter Bo - jan - gles,
To Coda
Em D
Mis - ter Bo - jan - gles,
G G/F♯ Em G type2
dance.
Solo
G G/F♯ Em G type2
C D
1. 2.

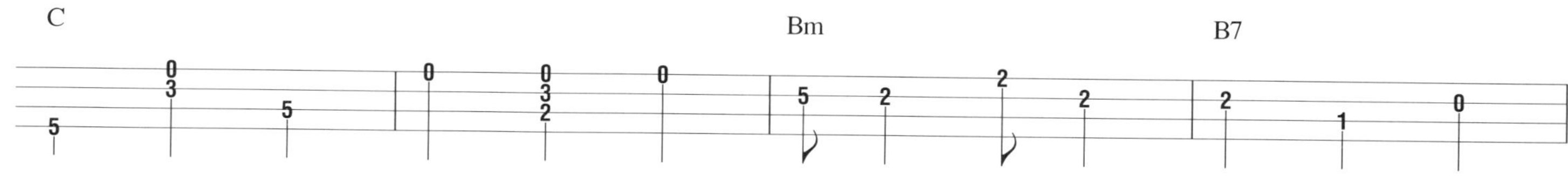
C
Bm
B7

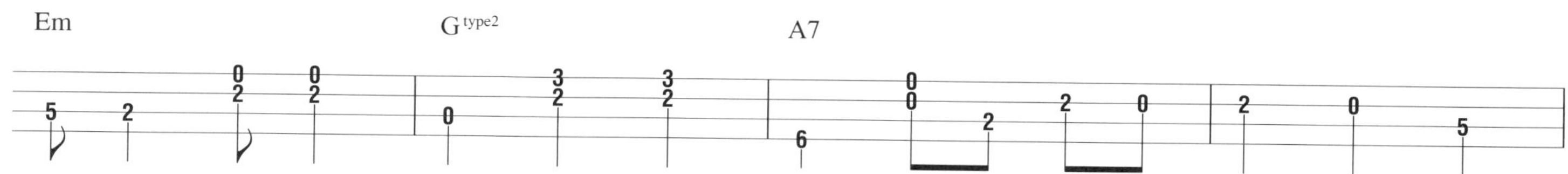
Em
G type2
A7

D.S. al Coda
(take 1st & 2nd endings)

4. He

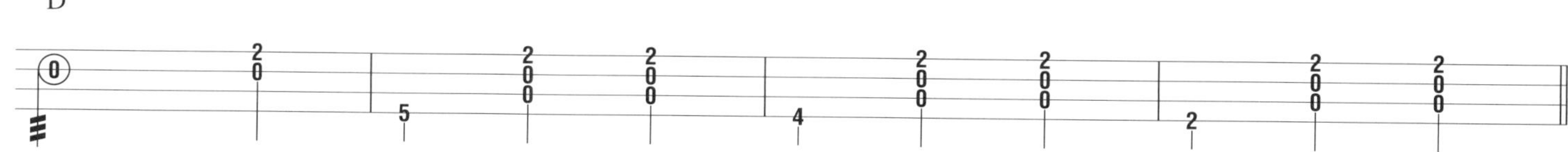
D

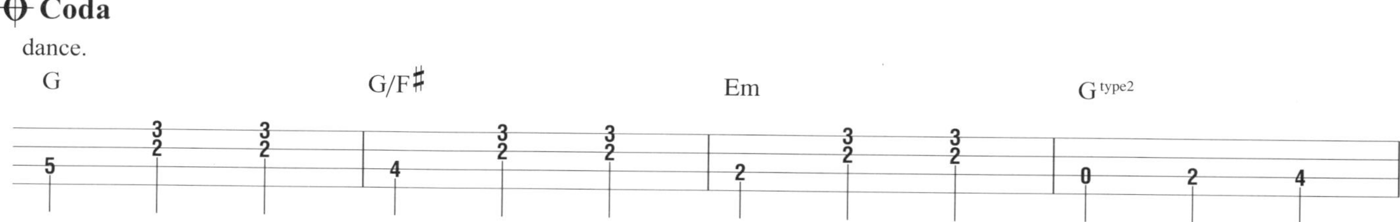
Coda
dance.
G
G/F♯
Em
G type2

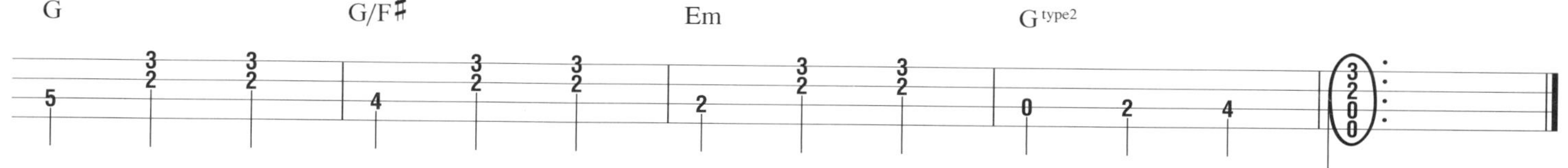
G
G/F♯
Em
G type2

Additional Lyrics

2. I met him in a cell in New Orleans, I was down and out.
   He looked to me to be the eyes of age, as he spoke right out.
   He talked of life, talked of life, he laughed, clicked his heels and stepped.

3. He said his name "Bojangles" and he danced a lick across the cell.
   He grabbed his pants and spread his stance, oh, he jumped so high and then he clicked his heels.
   He let go a laugh, let go a laugh and shook back his clothes all around.

4. He danced for those at minstrel shows and county fairs throughtout the south.
   He spoke through tears of fifteen years how his dog and him traveled about.
   The dog up and died, he up and died, and after twenty years he still grieves.

5. He said, "I dance now at every chance in honky tonks, for drinks and tips.
   But most the time I spend behind these county bars, 'cause I drinks a bit."
   He shook his head, and as he shook his head, I heard someone ask him, please...

'O Sole Mio

Words by Giovanni Capurro
Music by Eduardo di Capua

Melody:
G
Am
D7
Gmaj7
Cm
5fr
A
Key of G
Intro
Slowly

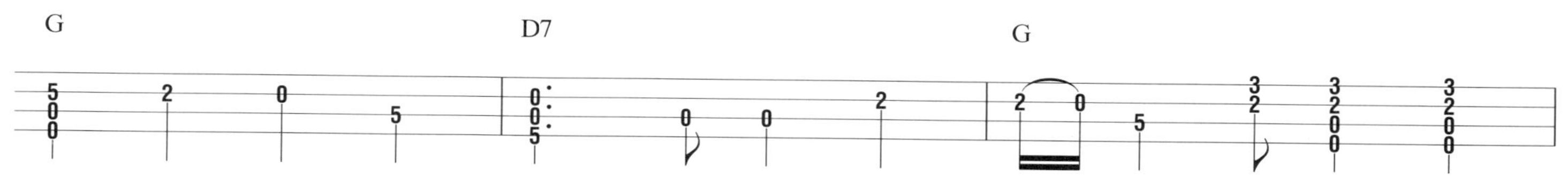
G
D7
G

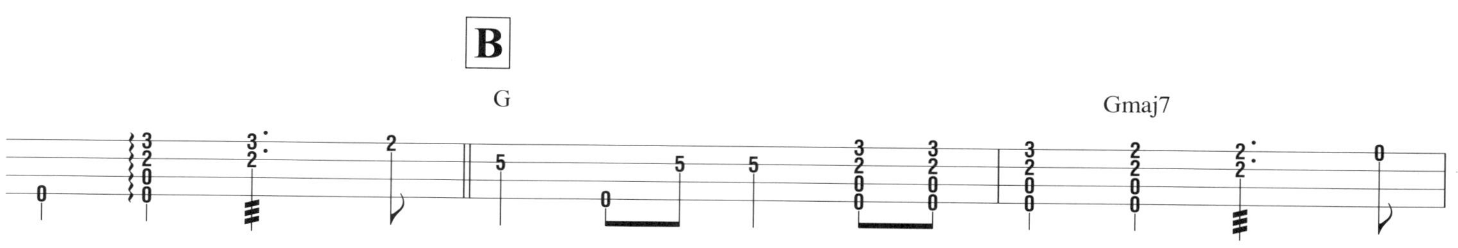
B
G
Gmaj7

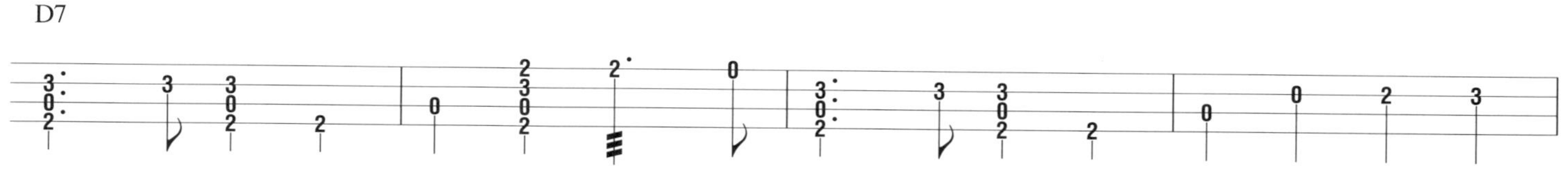
D7

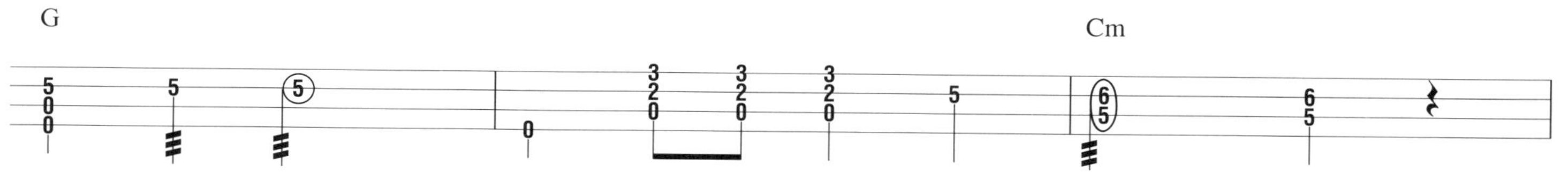
G
Cm

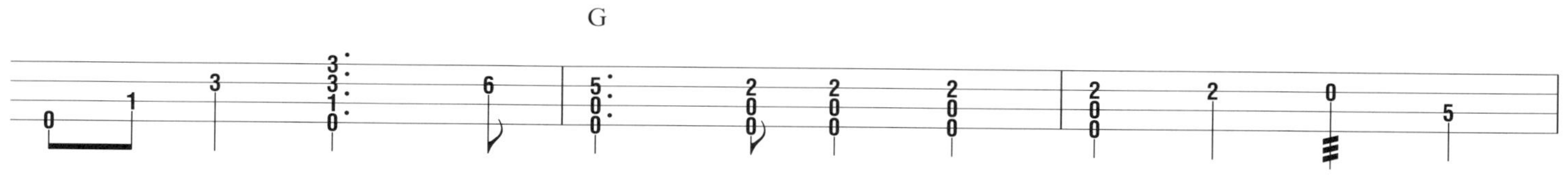
G

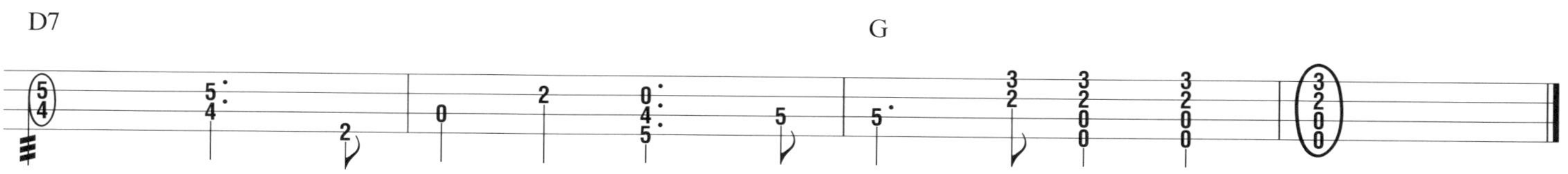
D7
G

Old Joe Clark

Tennessee Folksong

Melody:
A
E
G
2fr
4 1
2 1 1 3
1 2
A
Key of A
Intro
Fast, in 2
B

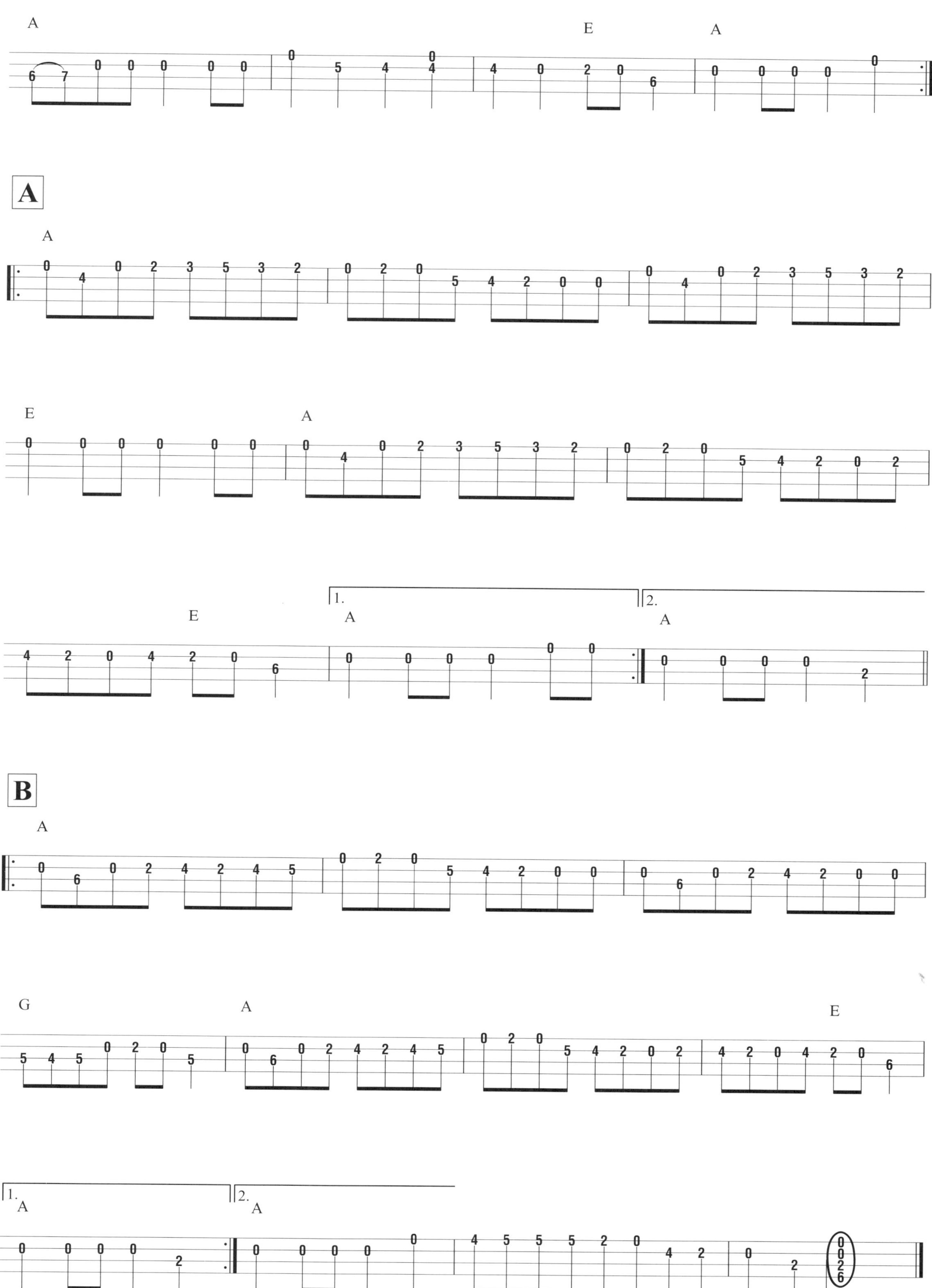
A
E
A
A
A
E
A
1.
2.
E
A
A
B
A
G
A
E
1.
A
2.
A

Poor Wayfaring Stranger

Traditional Folksong

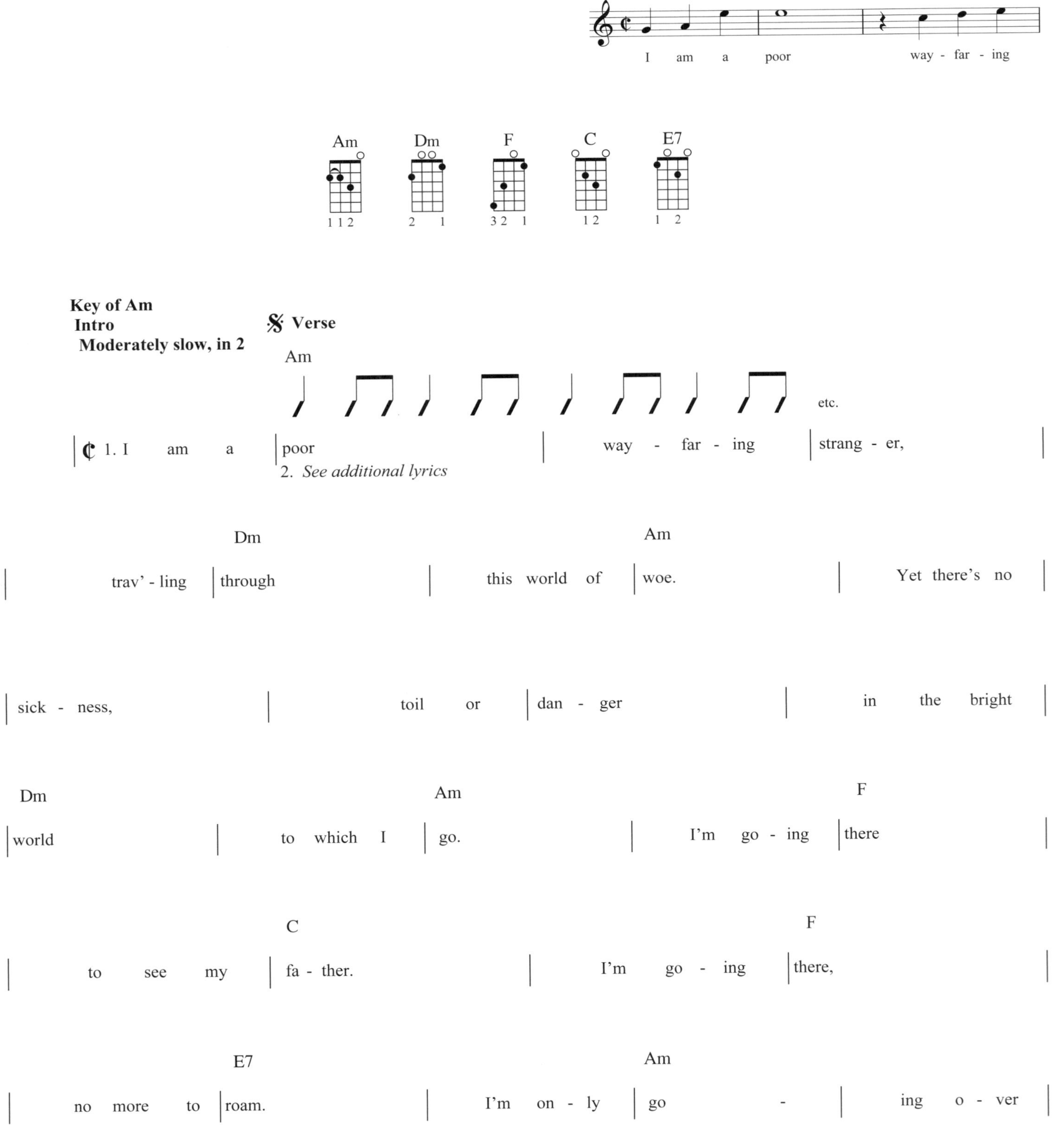
Melody:
I am a poor way - far - ing
Am
Dm
F
C
E7
1 1 2
2 1
3 2 1
1 2
1 2
Key of Am
Intro
Moderately slow, in 2
Verse
Am
etc.
1. I am a poor way - far - ing strang - er,
2. See additional lyrics
Dm
Am
trav' - ling through this world of woe. Yet there's no
sick - ness, toil or dan - ger in the bright
Dm
Am
F
world to which I go. I'm go - ing there
C
F
to see my fa - ther. I'm go - ing there,
E7
Am
no more to roam. I'm on - ly go - ing o - ver

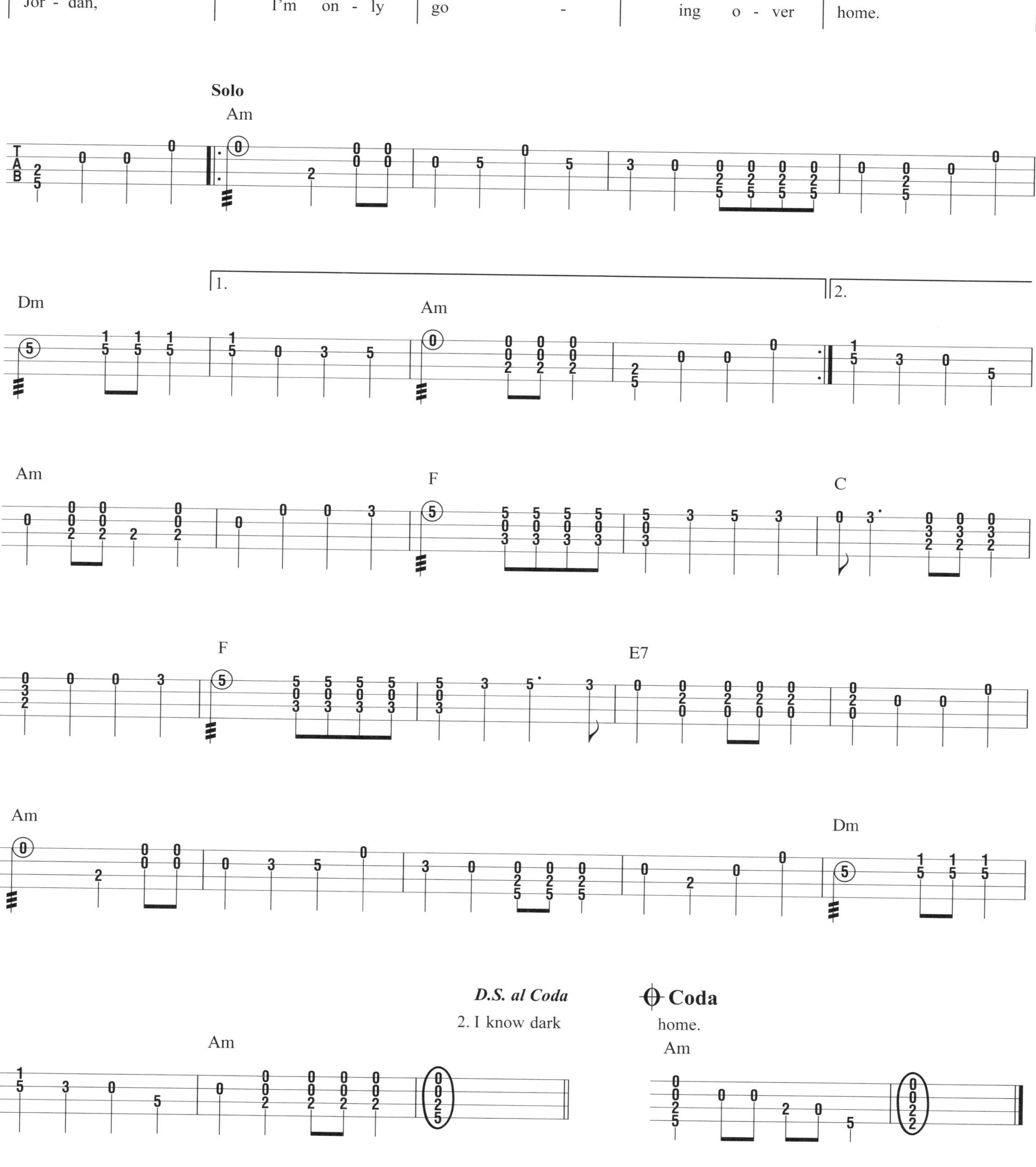
To Coda
Dm
Am
Jor - dan,
I'm on - ly
go -
ing o - ver
home.
Solo
Am
Dm
1.
Am
2.
Am
F
C
F
E7
Am
Dm
D.S. al Coda
2. I know dark
Am
Coda
home.
Am

Additional Lyrics

2. I know dark clouds will gather 'round me. I know my way is rough and steep.
Yet beautiful fields lie just before me, where God's redeemed their vigils keep.
I'm going there to see my mother. She said she'd meet me when I come.
I'm only going over Jordan, I'm only going over home.

Redemption Song

Words and Music by Bob Marley

Melody:
Old pi - rates, yes they rob I, sold I
G C D Em Am
Key of G
Intro
Moderately
G C G D G
C G D G
1. Old
Verse
G Em C G
etc.
pi - rates, yes, they rob I, sold I to the merch - ant
2. See additional lyrics
Am G Em
ships. Min - utes af - ter they took I

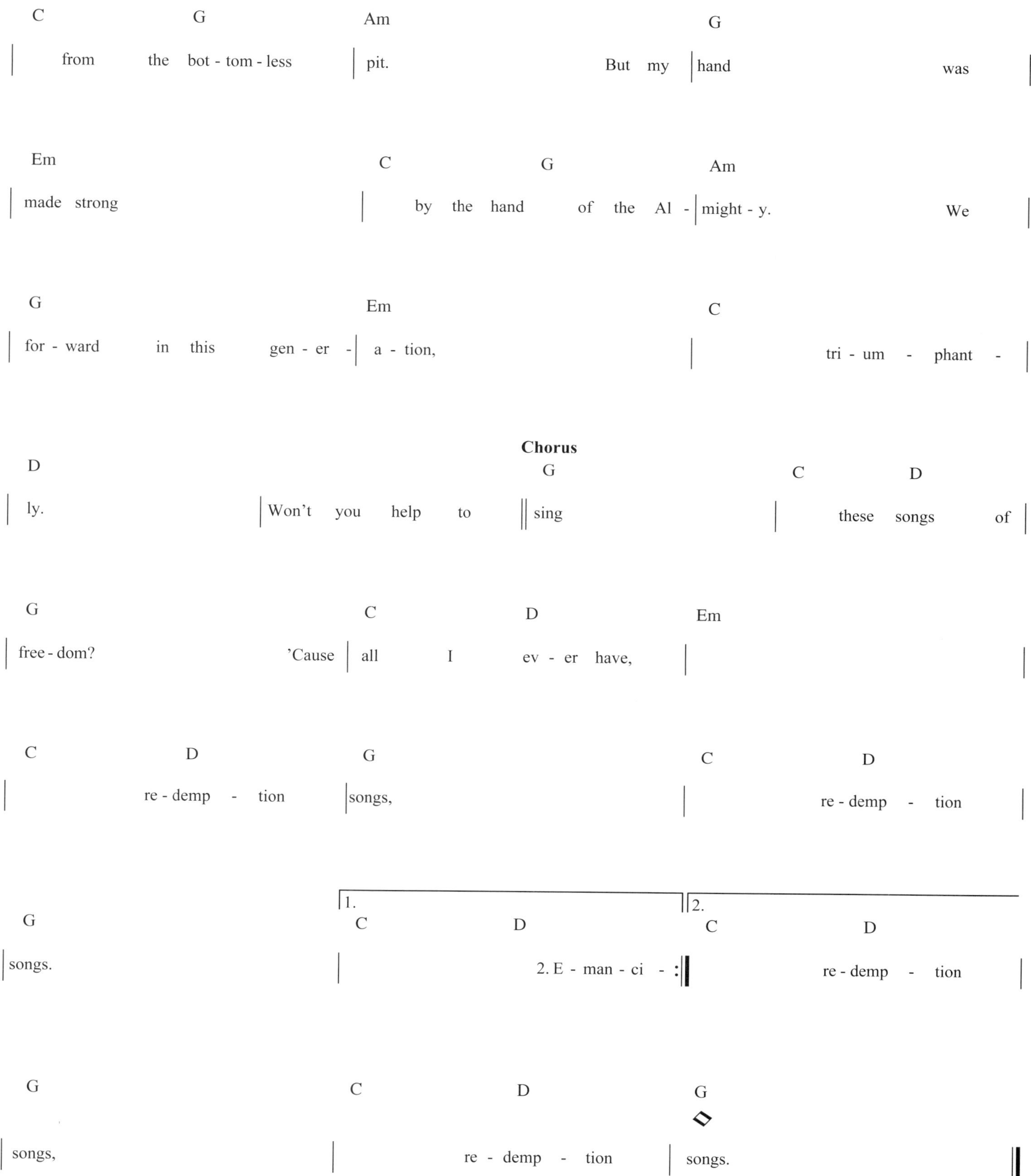
C G Am G
from the bot - tom - less pit. But my hand was
Em C G Am
made strong by the hand of the Al - might - y. We
G Em C
for - ward in this gen - er - a - tion, tri - um - phant -
D
ly. Won't you help to
Chorus
G C D
sing these songs of
G C D Em
free - dom? 'Cause all I ev - er have,
C D G C D
re - demp - tion songs, re - demp - tion
G
songs.
1.
C D
2. E - man - ci -
2.
C D
re - demp - tion
G C D G
songs, re - demp - tion songs.

Additional Lyrics

2. Emancipate yourselves from mental slavery, none but ourselves can free our minds.
Have no fear for atomic energy, 'cause none of them can stop the time.
How long shall they kill our prophets while we stand aside and look?
Some say it's just a part of it, we've got to fulfill the book.

Return to Me

Words and Music by Danny Di Minno and Carmen Lombardo

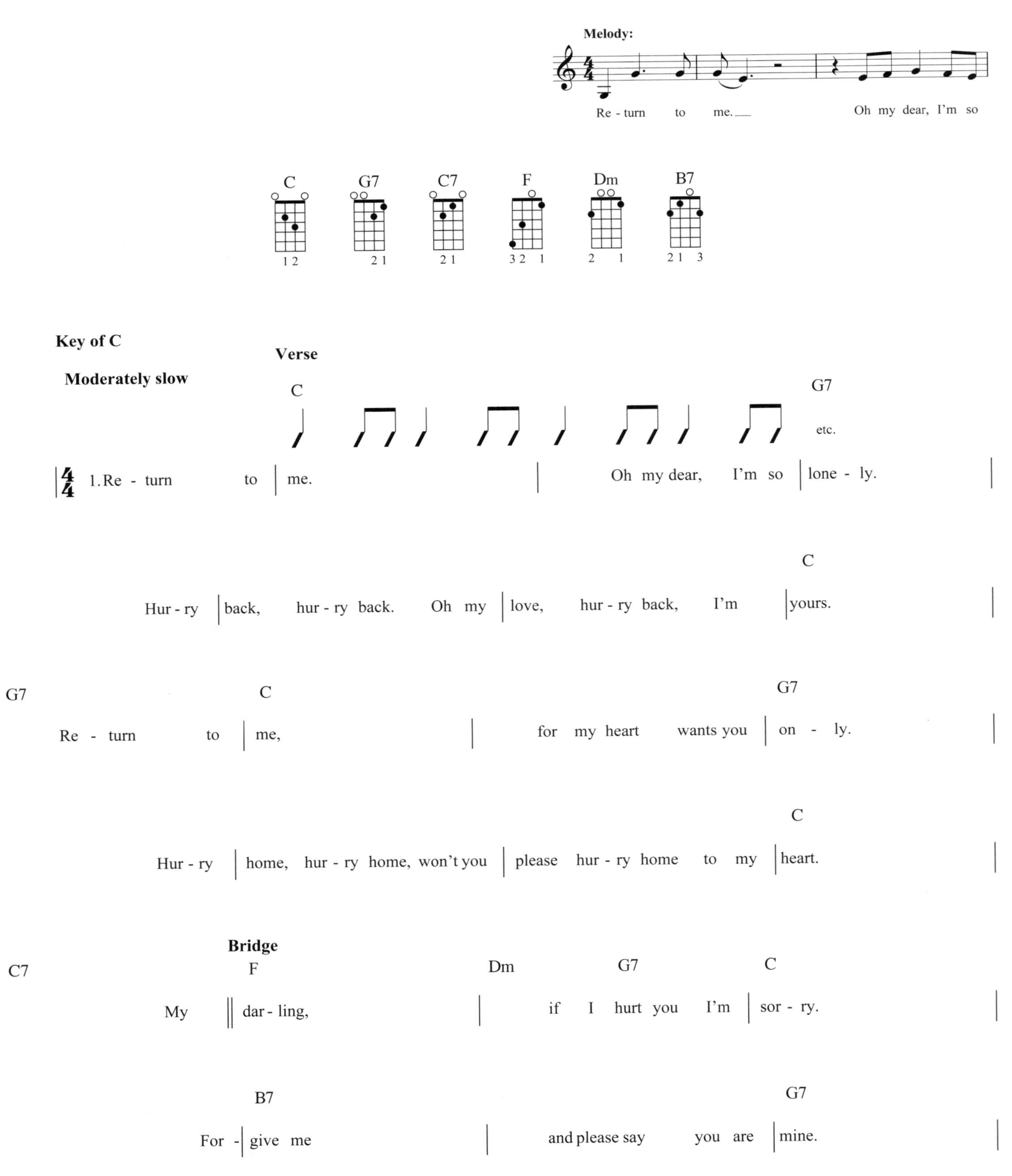

Melody:
Re - turn to me. Oh my dear, I'm so
C G7 C7 F Dm B7
Key of C
Moderately slow
Verse
C G7
etc.
1. Re - turn to me. Oh my dear, I'm so lone - ly.
C
Hur - ry back, hur - ry back. Oh my love, hur - ry back, I'm yours.
G7 C G7
Re - turn to me, for my heart wants you on - ly.
C
Hur - ry home, hur - ry home, won't you please hur - ry home to my heart.
Bridge
C7 F Dm G7 C
My dar - ling, if I hurt you I'm sor - ry.
B7 G7
For - give me and please say you are mine.

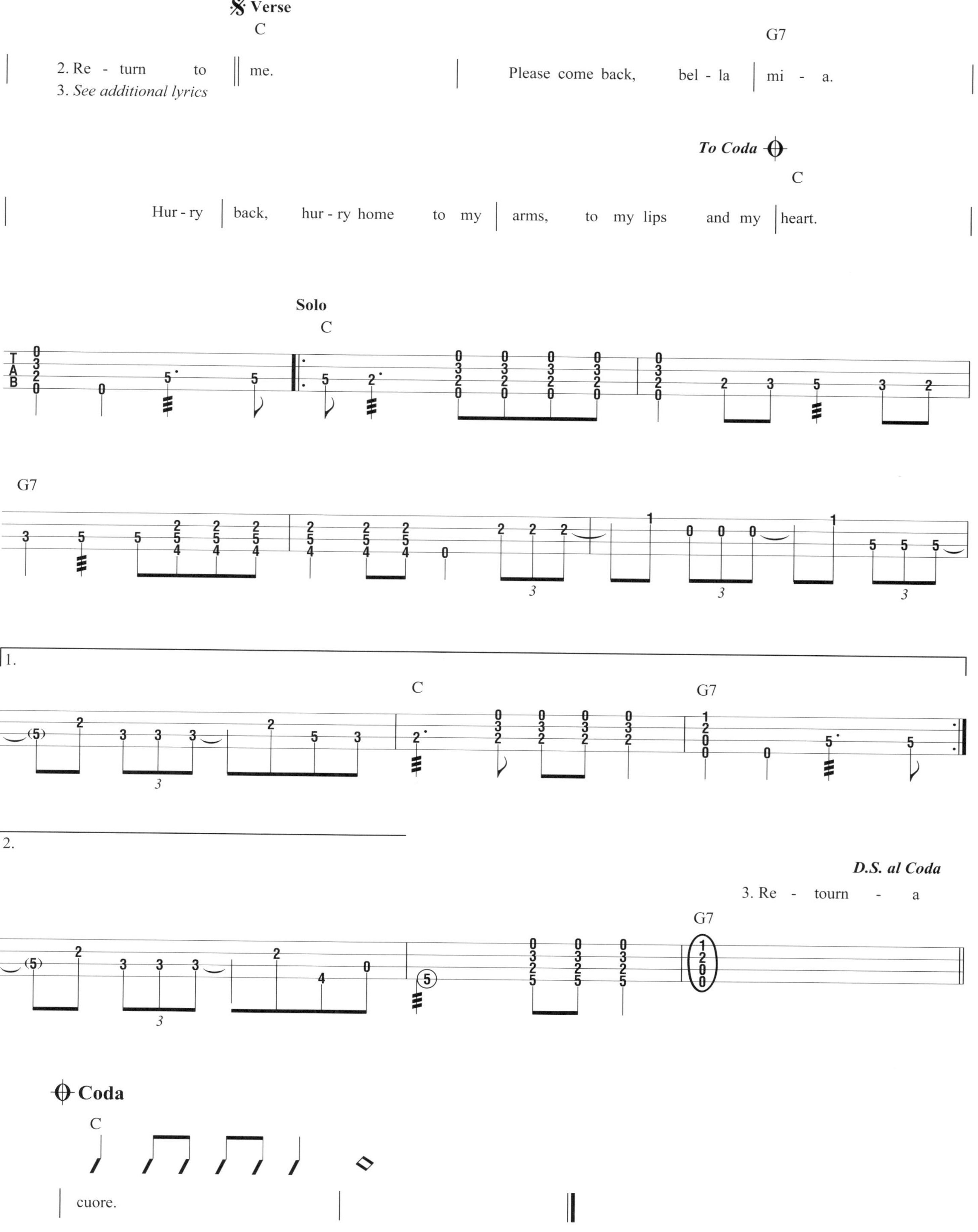

Verse
C
G7
2. Re - turn to me.
3. See additional lyrics
Please come back, bel - la mi - a.
To Coda
C
Hur - ry back, hur - ry home to my arms, to my lips and my heart.
Solo
C
T
A
B
G7
1.
C
G7
2.
D.S. al Coda
3. Re - tourn - a
G7
Coda
C
cuore.

Additional Lyrics

3. Retorna me. Cara mia, ti amo.
 Solo tu, solo tu, solo tu, solo tu, mio cuore.

Ripple

Words by Robert Hunter
Music by Jerry Garcia

Melody:
If my words did glow ___ with the gold ___ of

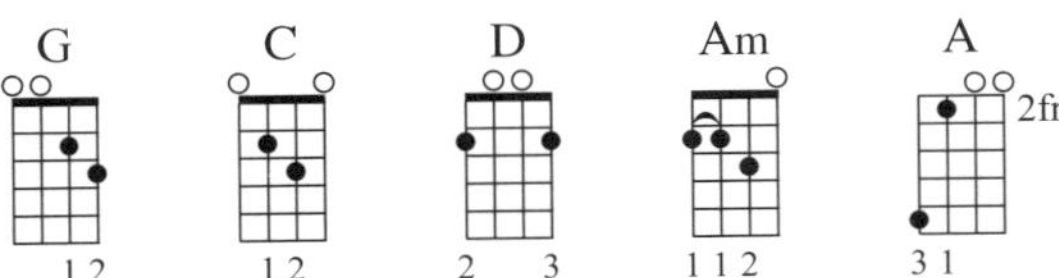
G
C
D
Am
A
2fr
1 2
1 2
2 3
1 1 2
3 1

Key of G
Intro
Moderately, in 2

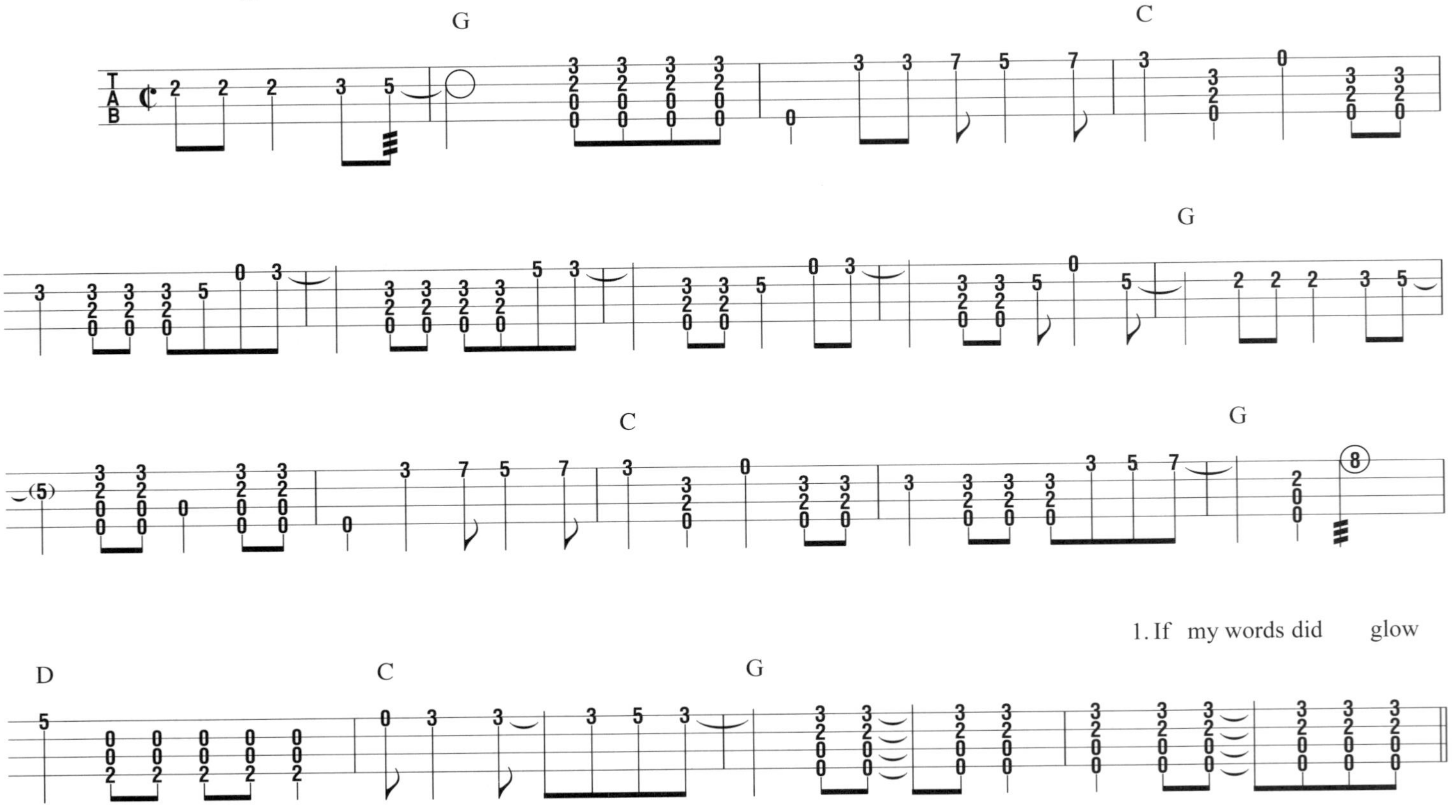

G C

G

C G

D C G

1. If my words did glow

Verse

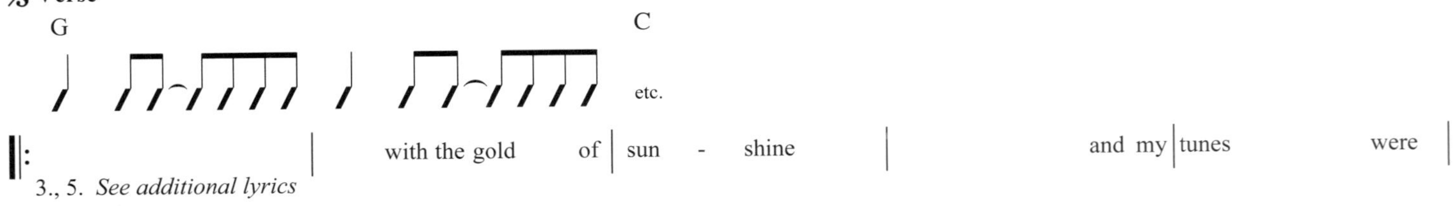

G C

etc.

with the gold of sun - shine and my tunes were

3., 5. *See additional lyrics*

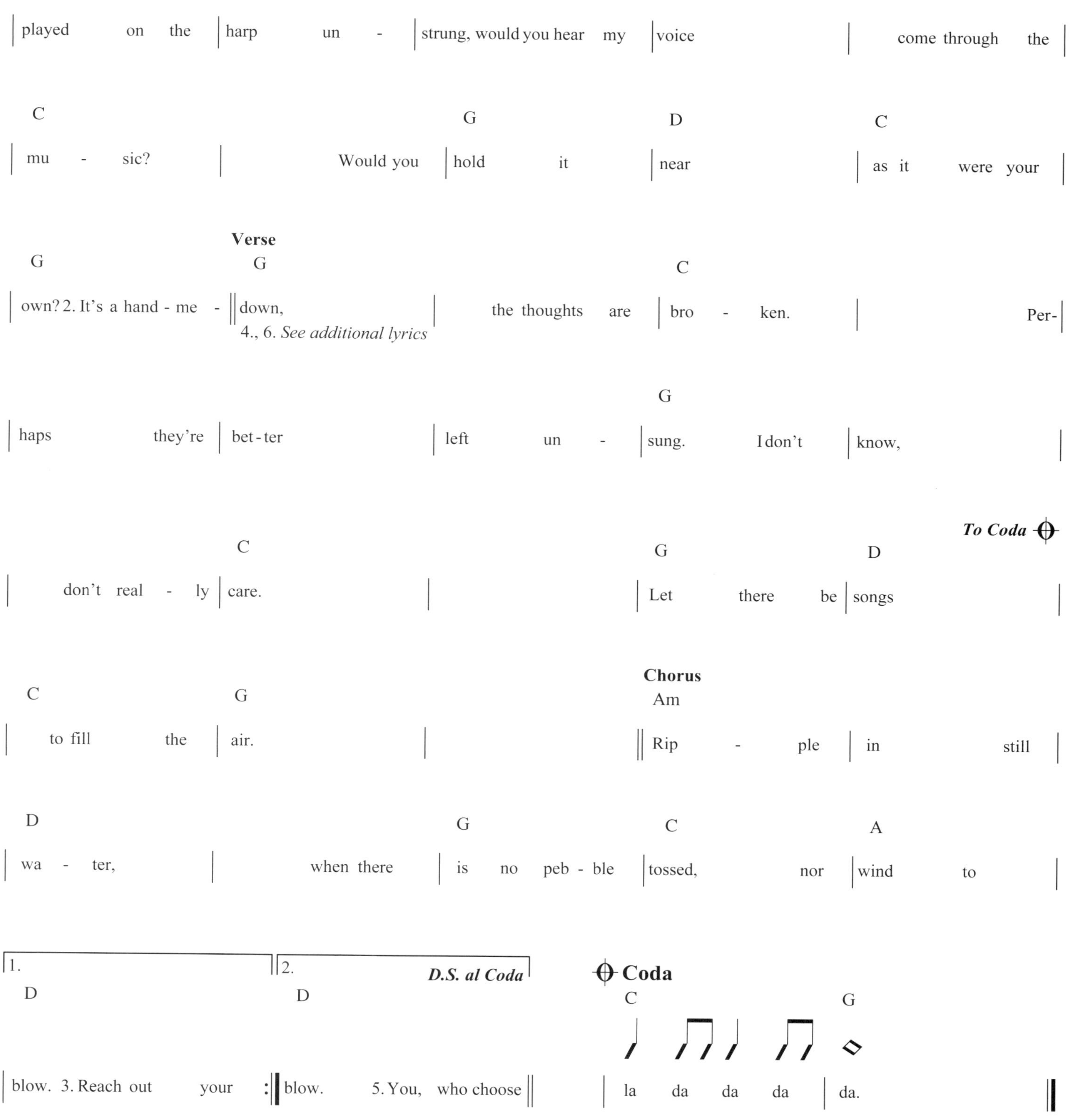

G
played on the harp un - strung, would you hear my voice come through the
C G D C
mu - sic? Would you hold it near as it were your
Verse
G G C
own? 2. It's a hand - me - down, the thoughts are bro - ken. Per-
4., 6. See additional lyrics
G
haps they're bet - ter left un - sung. I don't know,
To Coda
C G D
don't real - ly care. Let there be songs
Chorus
C G Am
to fill the air. Rip - ple in still
D G C A
wa - ter, when there is no peb - ble tossed, nor wind to
1. 2. D.S. al Coda
D D
blow. 3. Reach out your blow. 5. You, who choose
Coda
C G
la da da da da.

Additional Lyrics

3. Reach out your hand if your cup be empty. If your cup is full, may it be again.
Let it be known there is a fountain that was not made by the hands of men.

4. There is a road, no simple highway, between the dawn and the dark of night.
And if you go, no one may follow. That path is for your steps alone.

5. You who choose to lead, must follow, but if you fall you fall alone.
If you should stand then who's to guide you? If I knew the way, I would take you home.

6. La dee da da da, la da da da da, da da da, da da, da da da da da.
La da da da da, la da da da da, la da da da, la da da da da.

Rocky Top

Words and Music by Boudleaux Bryant and Felice Bryant

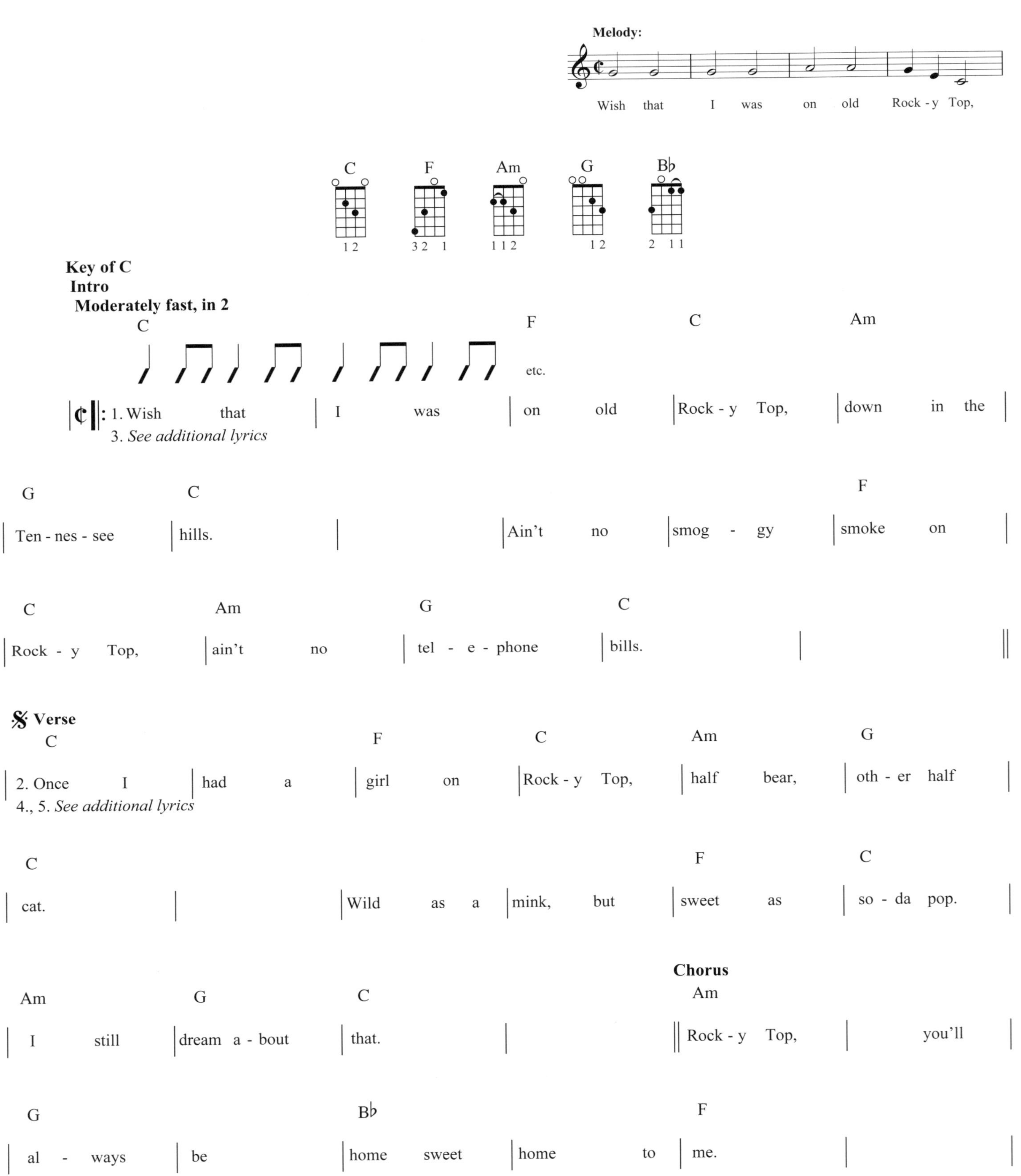
Melody:
Wish that I was on old Rock - y Top,
C F Am G B♭
1 2
3 2 1
1 1 2
1 2
2 1 1
Key of C
Intro
Moderately fast, in 2
C F C Am
etc.
1. Wish that I was on old Rock - y Top, down in the
3. See additional lyrics
G C F
Ten - nes - see hills. Ain't no smog - gy smoke on
C Am G C
Rock - y Top, ain't no tel - e - phone bills.
Verse
C F C Am G
2. Once I had a girl on Rock - y Top, half bear, oth - er half
4., 5. See additional lyrics
C F C
cat. Wild as a mink, but sweet as so - da pop.
Chorus
Am G C Am
I still dream a - bout that. Rock - y Top, you'll
G B♭ F
al - ways be home sweet home to me.

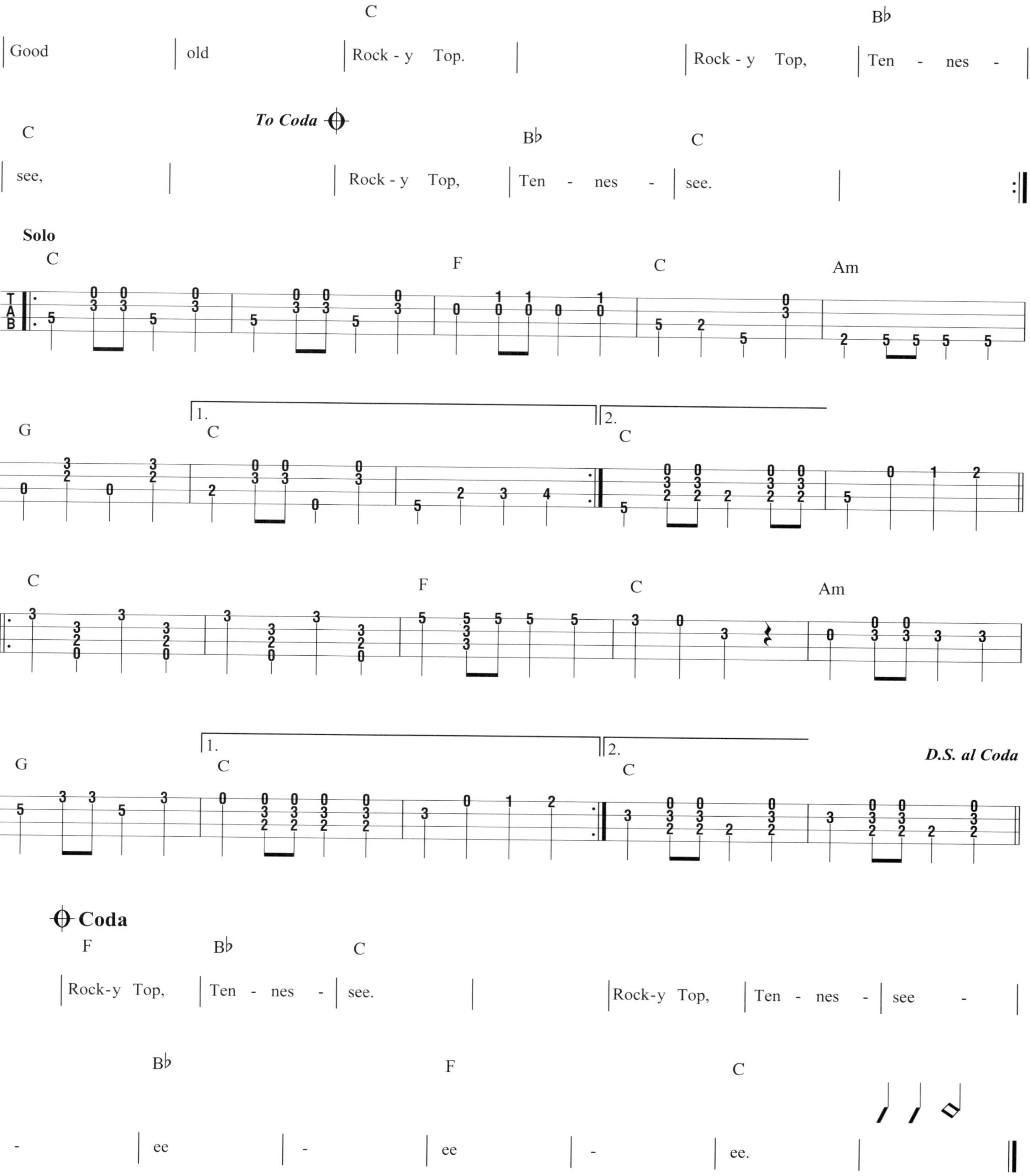
C
Bb
Good old Rock - y Top. Rock - y Top, Ten - nes -
C
To Coda
Bb
C
see, Rock - y Top, Ten - nes - see.
Solo
C
F
C
Am
G
1.
C
2.
C
C
F
C
Am
G
1.
C
2.
C
D.S. al Coda
Coda
F
Bb
C
Rock-y Top, Ten - nes - see. Rock-y Top, Ten - nes - see -
Bb
F
C
- ee - ee - ee.

Additional Lyrics

3. Once two strangers climbed old Rocky Top, lookin' for a moonshine still.
   Strangers ain't come down from Rocky Top, reckon they never will.

4. Corn won't grow at all on Rocky Top, dirt's too rocky by far.
   That's why all the folks on Rocky Top get their corn from a jar.

5. I've had years of cramped-up city life, trapped like a duck in a pen.
   All I know is, it's a pity life can't be simple again.

Roll in My Sweet Baby's Arms

Traditional

Melody:
Ain't gon - na work on the rail - road,

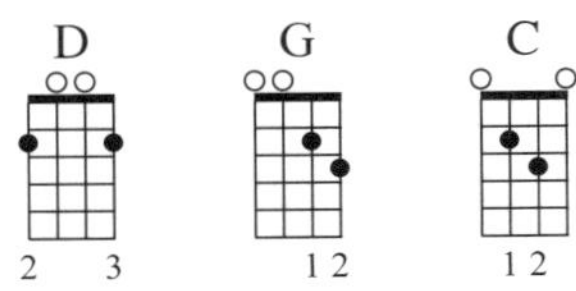
D
G
C
2 3
1 2
1 2

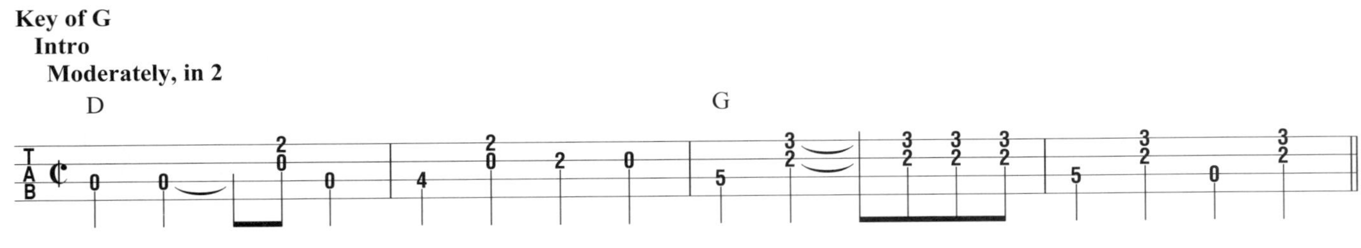
Key of G
Intro
Moderately, in 2
D
G

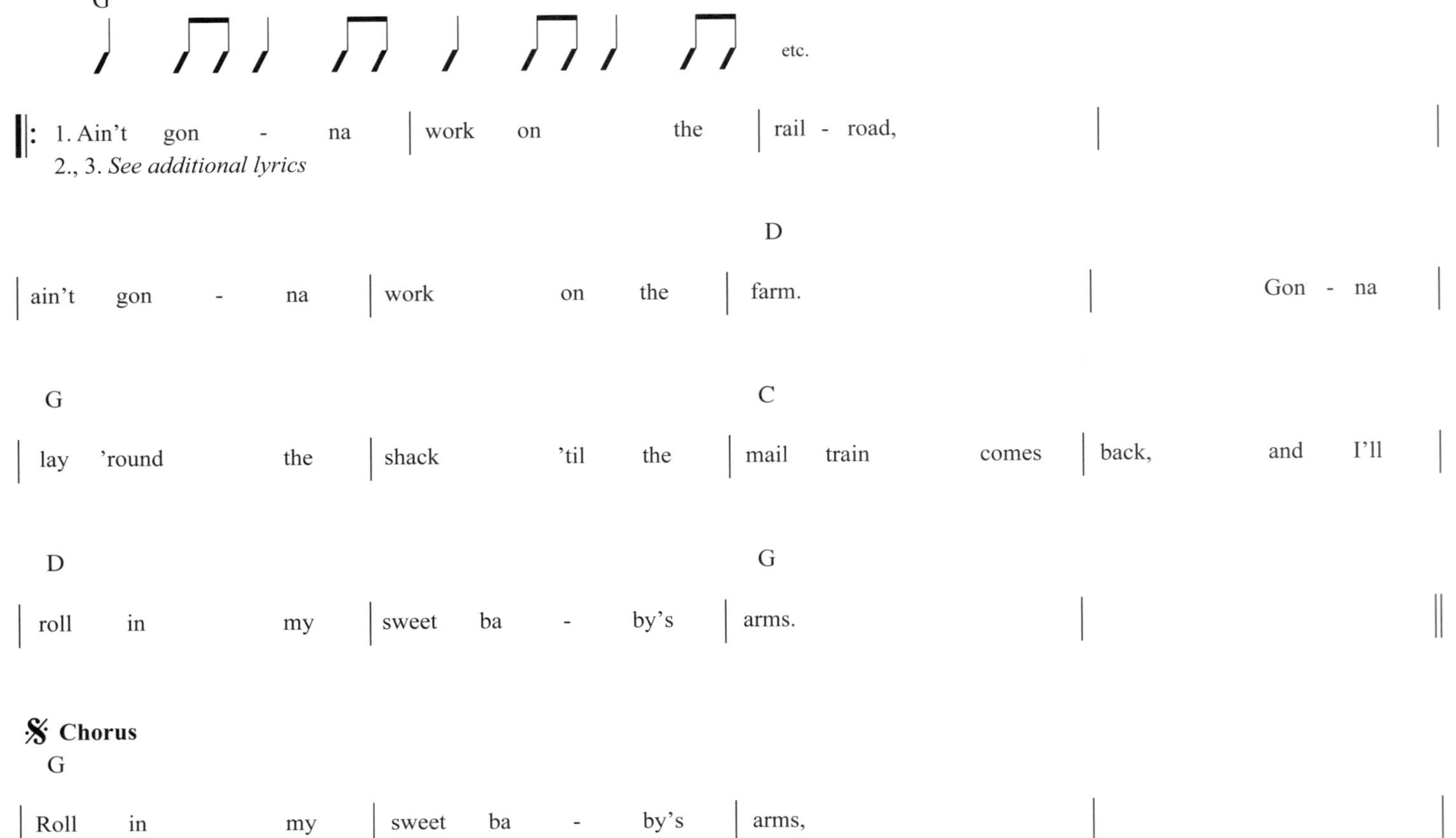
Verse
G
etc.
1. Ain't gon - na work on the rail - road,
2., 3. See additional lyrics
ain't gon - na work on the farm.
D
Gon - na
G
lay 'round the shack 'til the
C
mail train comes back, and I'll
D
roll in my sweet ba - by's
G
arms.
Chorus
G
Roll in my sweet ba - by's arms,

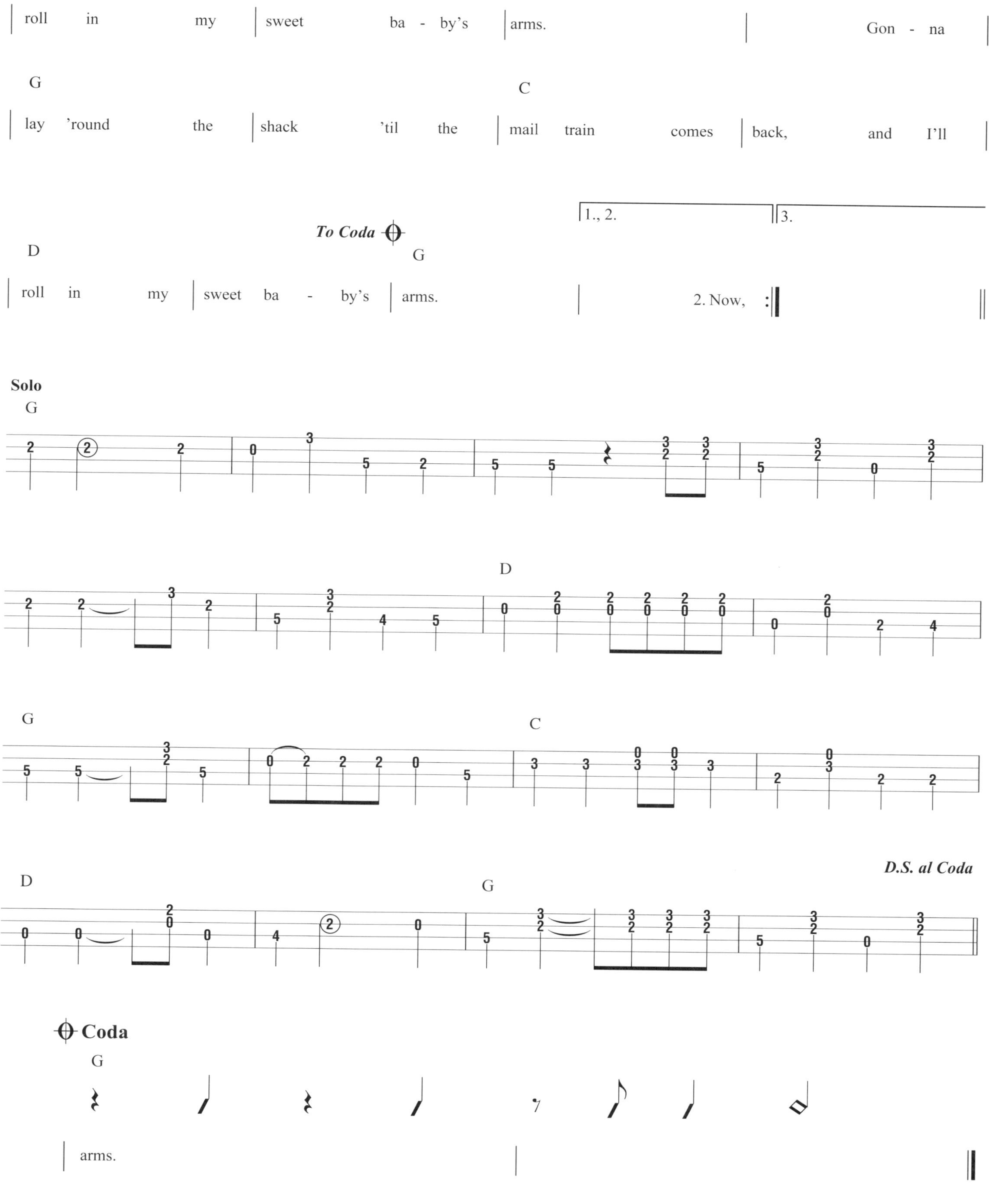
D
roll in my sweet ba - by's arms. Gon - na
G
C
lay 'round the shack 'til the mail train comes back, and I'll
To Coda
1., 2.
3.
D
G
roll in my sweet ba - by's arms. 2. Now,
Solo
G
D
G
C
D
G
D.S. al Coda
Coda
G
arms.

Additional Lyrics

2. Now, where were you last Friday night while I was lying in jail?
   Walking the streets with another man, wouldn't even go my bail.

3. I know your parents don't like me. They drove me away from your door.
   If I had my life to live over, I'd never go there any more.

Rye Whiskey

Words and Music by Paul Kowert, Gabriel Witcher,
Christopher Eldridge, Christopher Thile and Noam Pikelny

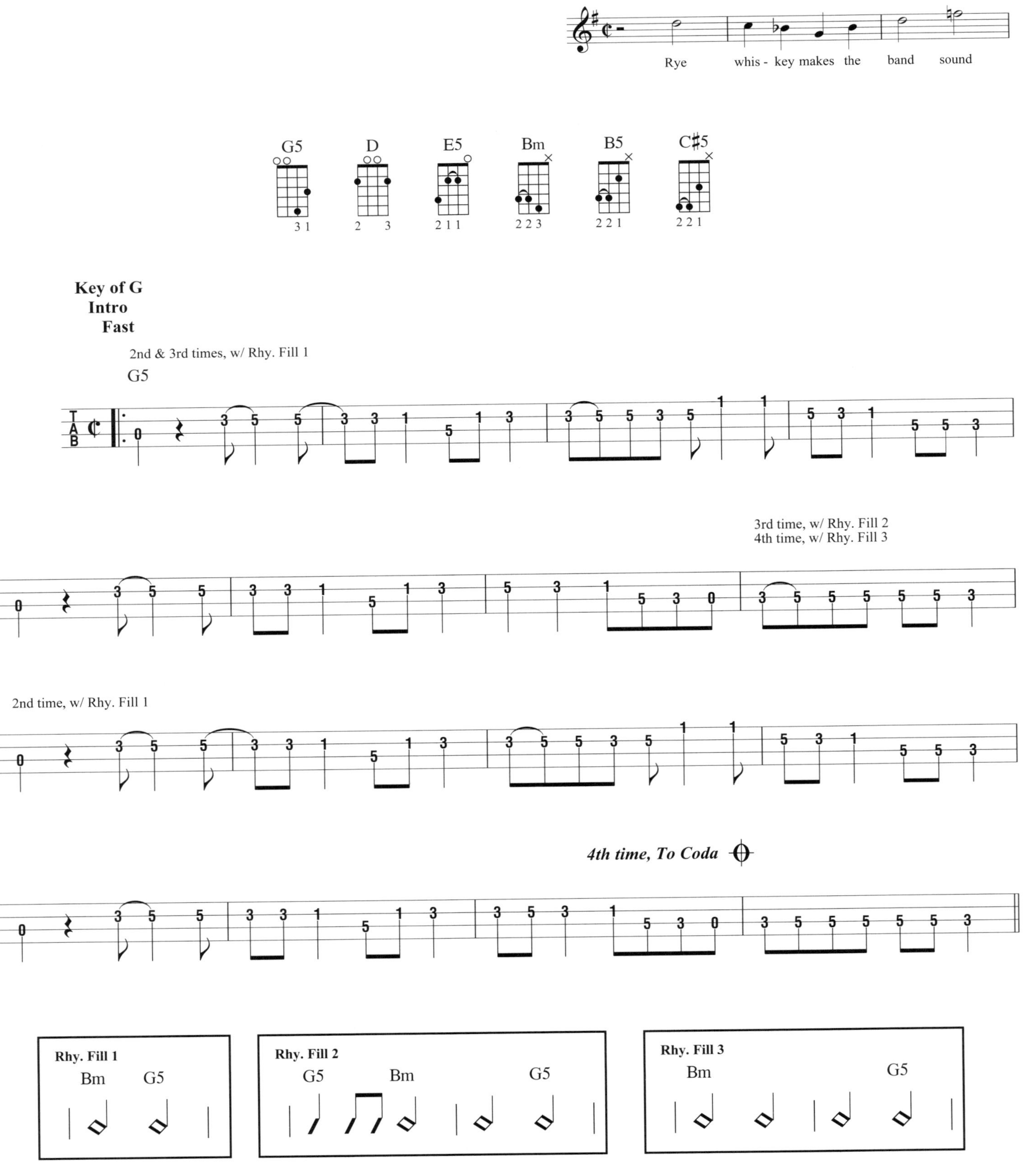

Melody:
Rye whis - key makes the band sound
G5
D
E5
Bm
B5
C♯5
Key of G
Intro
Fast
2nd & 3rd times, w/ Rhy. Fill 1
3rd time, w/ Rhy. Fill 2
4th time, w/ Rhy. Fill 3
2nd time, w/ Rhy. Fill 1
4th time, To Coda
Rhy. Fill 1
Rhy. Fill 2
Rhy. Fill 3

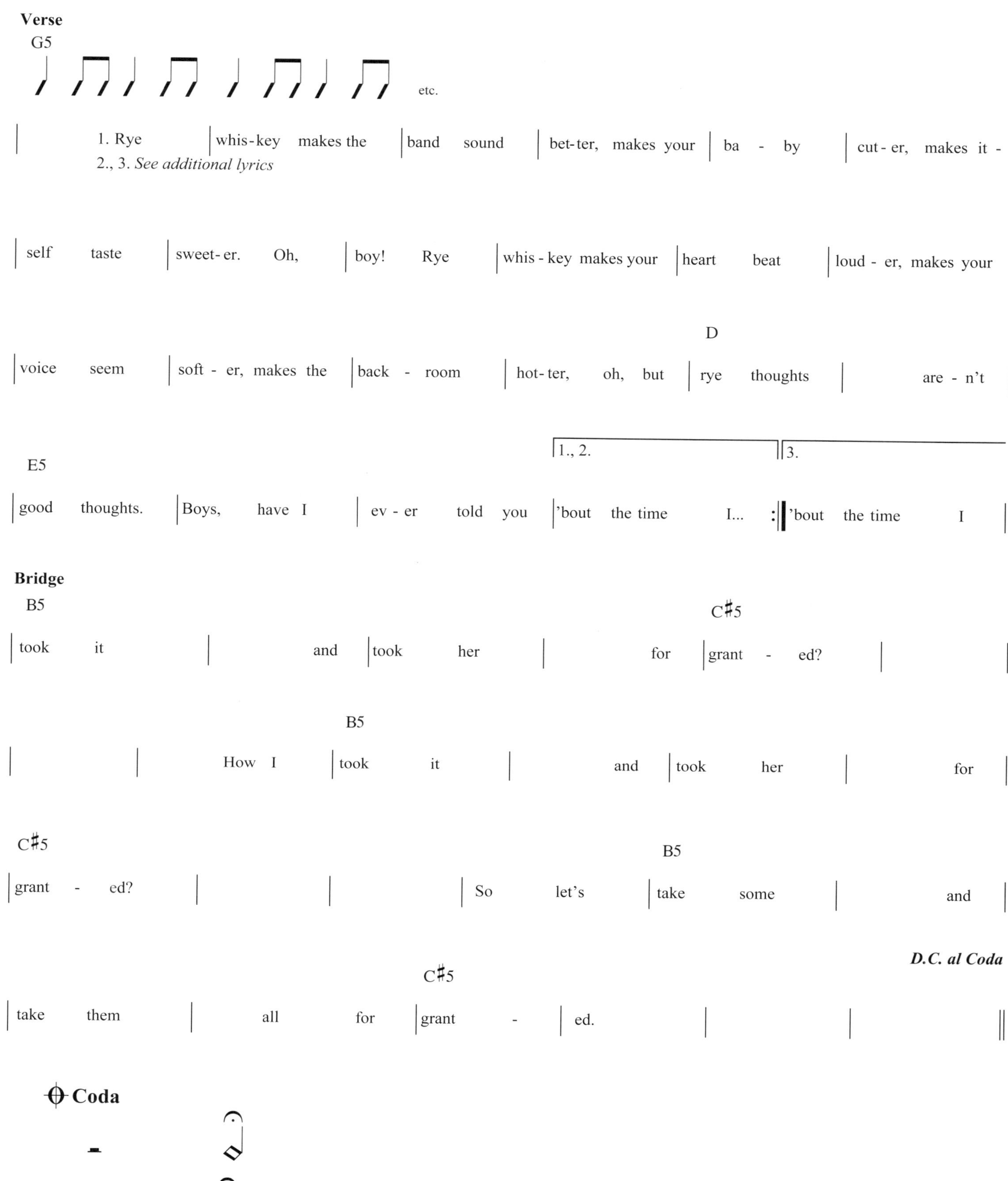
Verse
G5
etc.
1. Rye whis-key makes the band sound bet-ter, makes your ba - by cut-er, makes it -
2., 3. See additional lyrics
self taste sweet-er. Oh, boy! Rye whis-key makes your heart beat loud - er, makes your
D
voice seem soft - er, makes the back - room hot-ter, oh, but rye thoughts are - n't
E5
1., 2.
3.
good thoughts. Boys, have I ev - er told you 'bout the time I... 'bout the time I
Bridge
B5
C♯5
took it and took her for grant - ed?
B5
How I took it and took her for
C♯5
B5
grant - ed? So let's take some and
D.C. al Coda
C♯5
take them all for grant - ed.
Coda
5

Additional Lyrics

2. Rye whiskey wraps your troubles up into a bright blue package, ties a bow around it.
   Oh, boy! Just throw it on the pile in the corner, see you're not alone in not being alone tonight.
   But rye love isn't good love. Boys, have I ever told you 'bout the time I...

3. I used to wake up bright and early, got my work done quickly, held my baby tightly.
   Oh, boy! Rye whiskey makes the sun set faster, makes the spirit more willing, but the body weaker
   Because rye sleep isn't good sleep. Boys, have I ever told you 'bout the time I...

Soldier's Joy

Traditional

Melody:

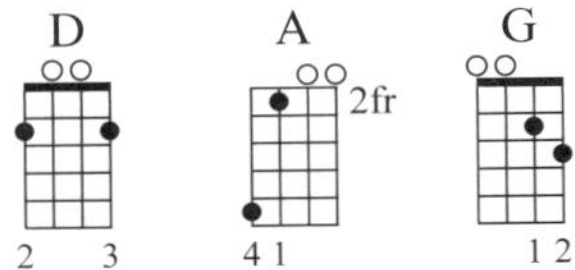

D
A
2fr
G
2 3
4 1
1 2

Key of D
Intro
Moderately, in 2

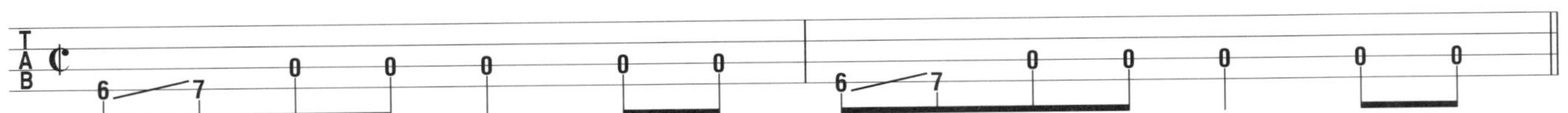

D

A
D
A
D
A
D
B
D
G
D
A
D
G
D
A
D

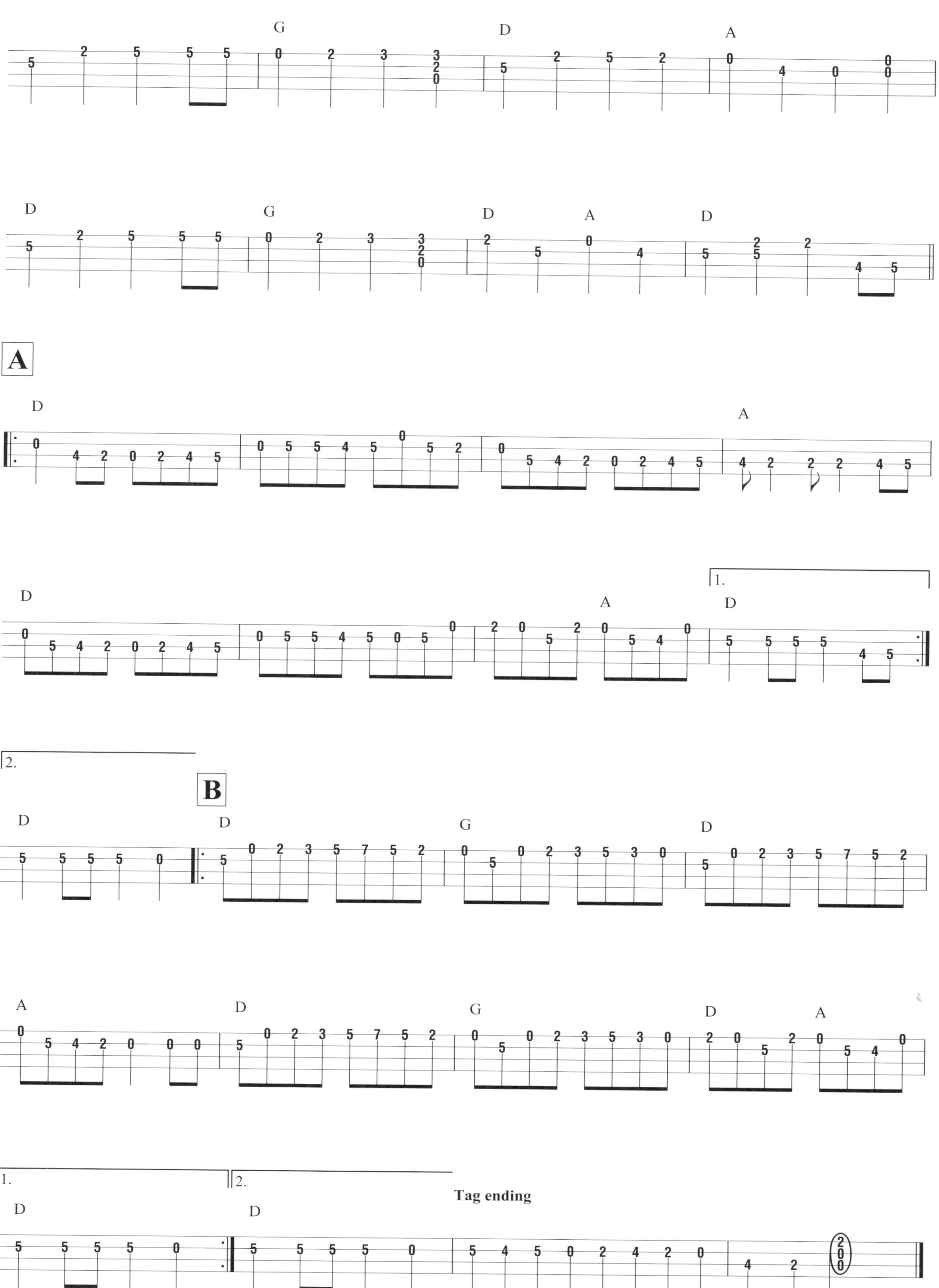
G D A
D G D A D
A
D A
1. A D
2.
B
D D G D
A D G D A
1. 2.
Tag ending
D D

Somewhere, My Love

Lara's Theme from DOCTOR ZHIVAGO

Lyric by Paul Francis Webster
Music by Maurice Jarre

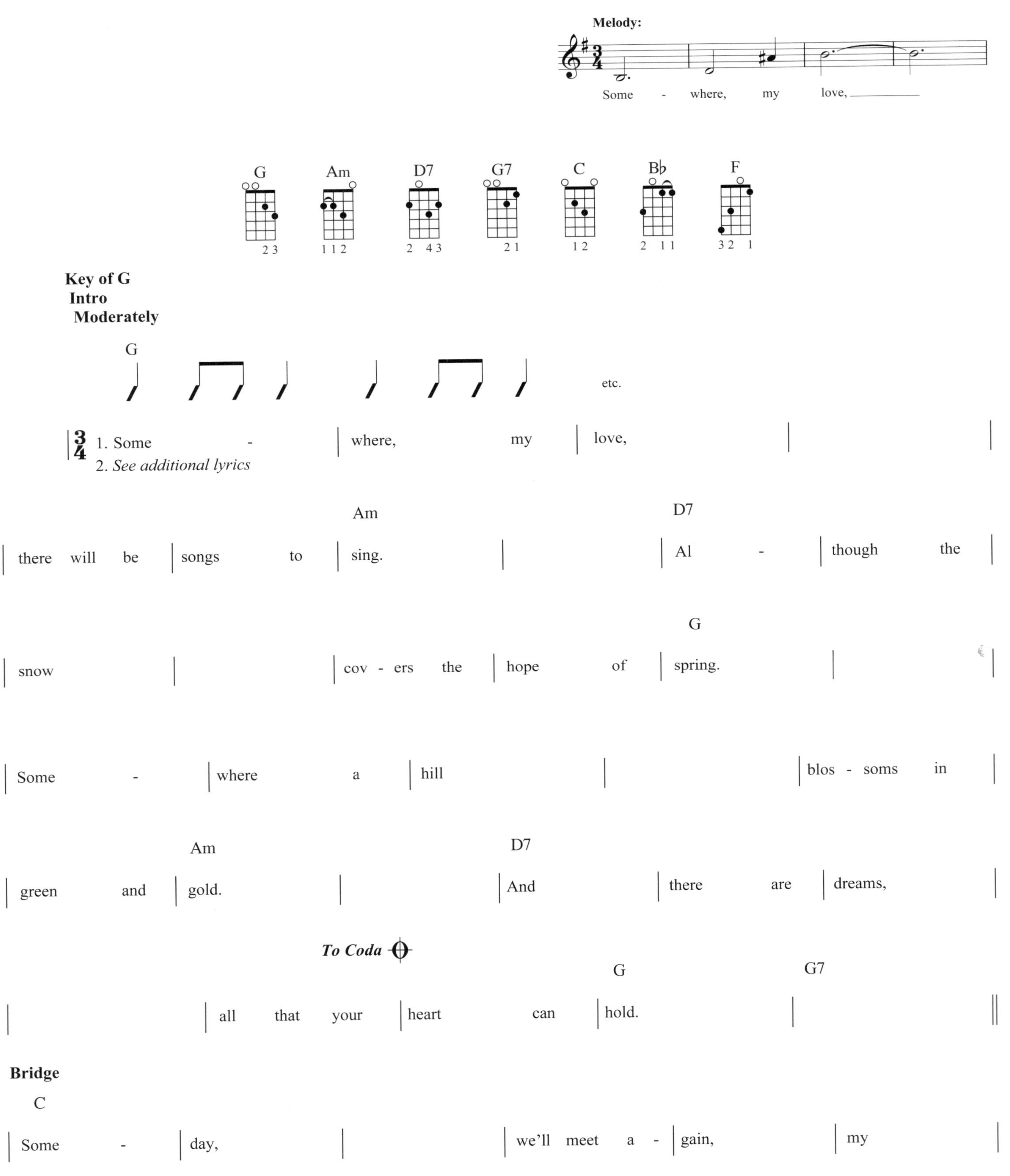
Melody:
Some - where, my love,
G Am D7 G7 C B♭ F
Key of G
Intro
Moderately
G
etc.
1. Some - where, my love,
2. See additional lyrics
Am D7
there will be songs to sing. Al - though the
G
snow cov - ers the hope of spring.
Some - where a hill blos - soms in
Am D7
green and gold. And there are dreams,
To Coda
G G7
all that your heart can hold.
Bridge
C
Some - day, we'll meet a - gain, my

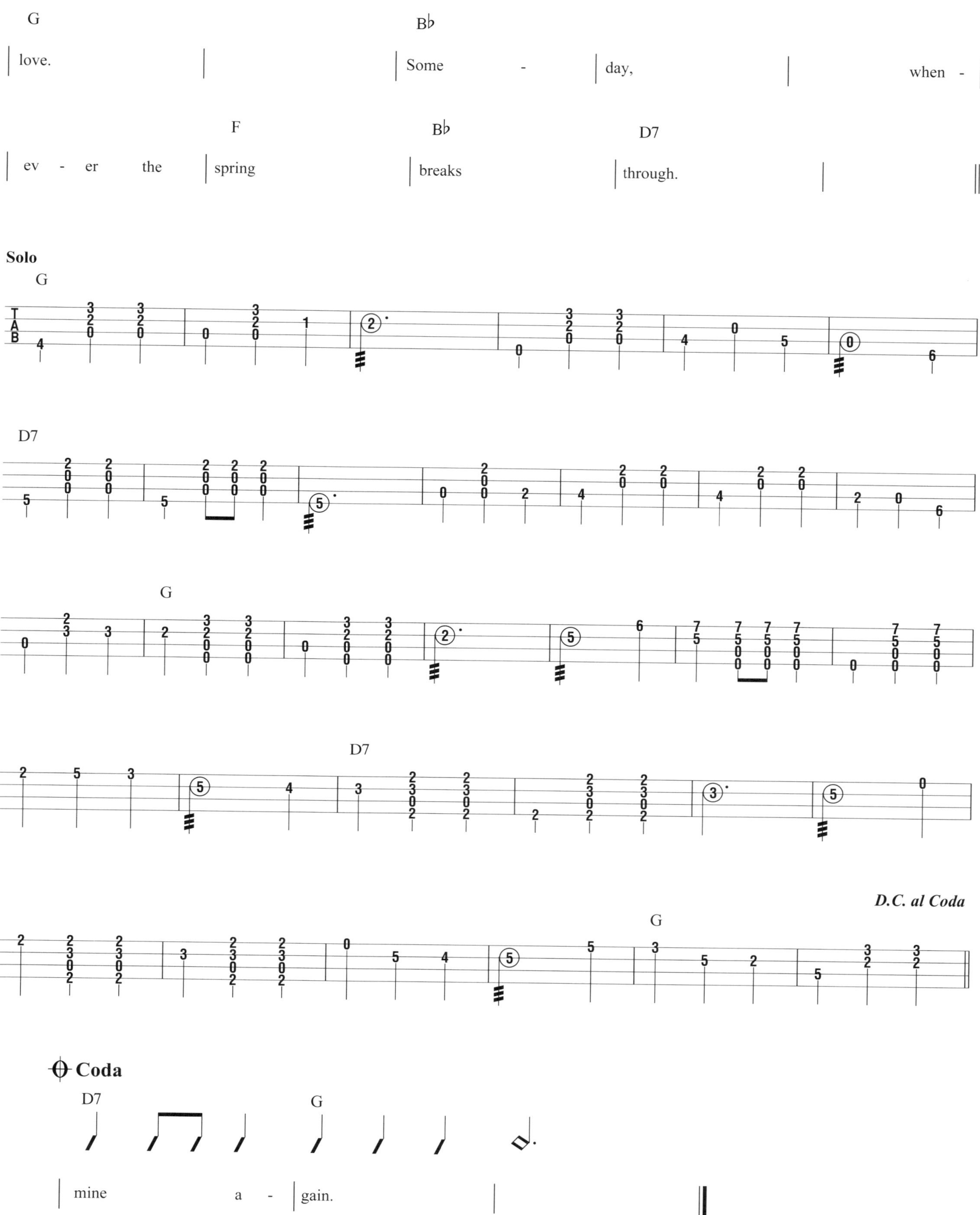
G
B♭
love.
Some - day,
when -
F
B♭
D7
ev - er the spring breaks through.
Solo
G
D7
G
D7
D.C. al Coda
G
Coda
D7
G
mine a - gain.

Additional Lyrics

2. You'll come to me, out of the long ago;
 Warm as the wind, soft as the kiss of snow.
 'Til then, my sweet, think of me now and then.
 Godspeed, my love, 'til you are mine again.

Speak Softly, Love
(Love Theme)

from the Paramount Picture THE GODFATHER

Words by Larry Kusik

Music by Nino Rota

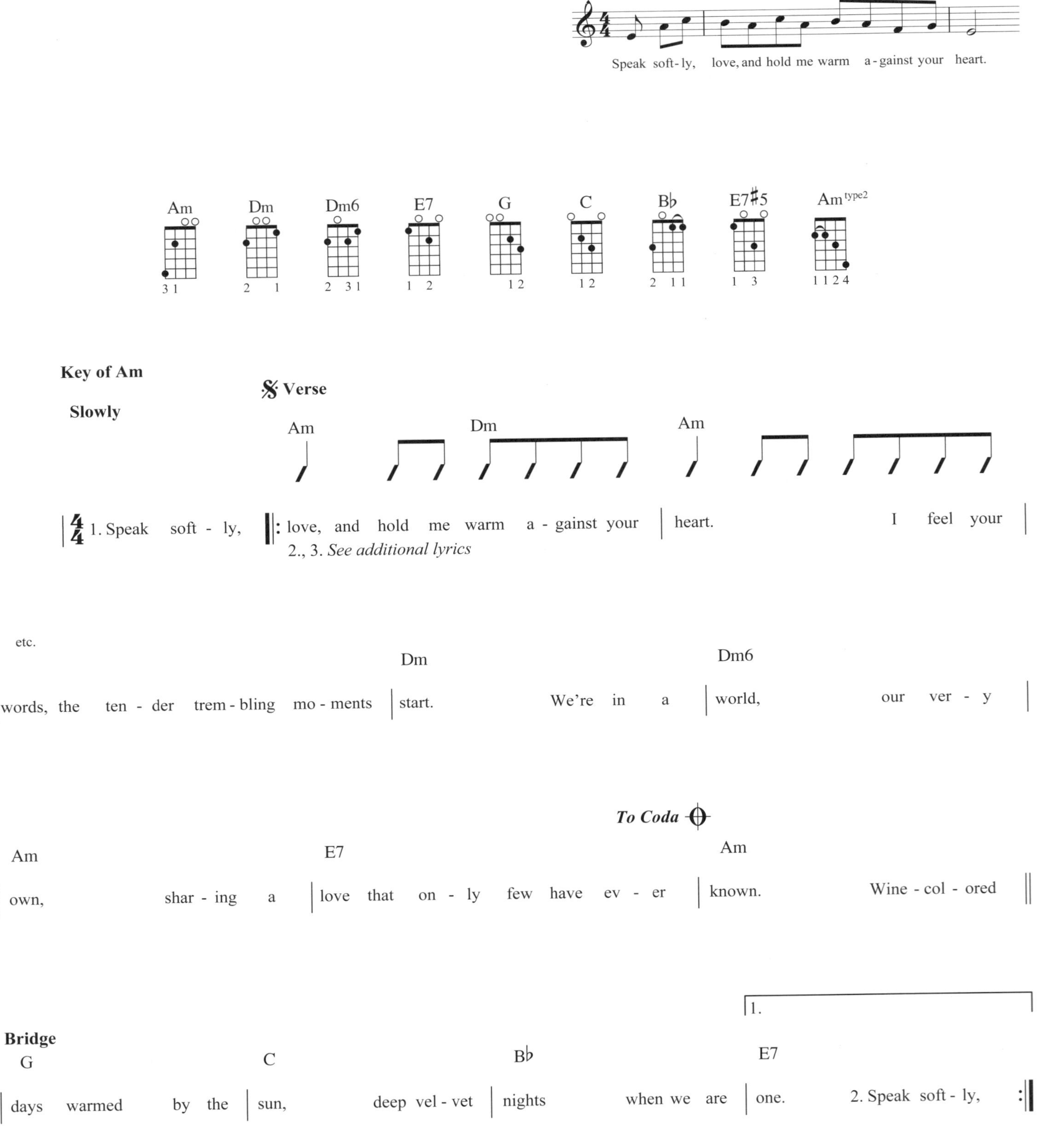

Melody:
Speak soft-ly, love, and hold me warm a-gainst your heart.
Am
Dm
Dm6
E7
G
C
B♭
E7♯5
Am type2
3 1
2 1
2 3 1
1 2
1 2
1 2
2 1 1
1 3
1 1 2 4
Key of Am
Slowly
Verse
Am
Dm
Am
1. Speak soft - ly, love, and hold me warm a - gainst your heart. I feel your
2., 3. See additional lyrics
etc.
Dm
Dm6
words, the ten - der trem - bling mo - ments start. We're in a world, our ver - y
To Coda
Am
E7
Am
own, shar - ing a love that on - ly few have ev - er known. Wine - col - ored
1.
Bridge
G
C
B♭
E7
days warmed by the sun, deep vel - vet nights when we are one. 2. Speak soft - ly,

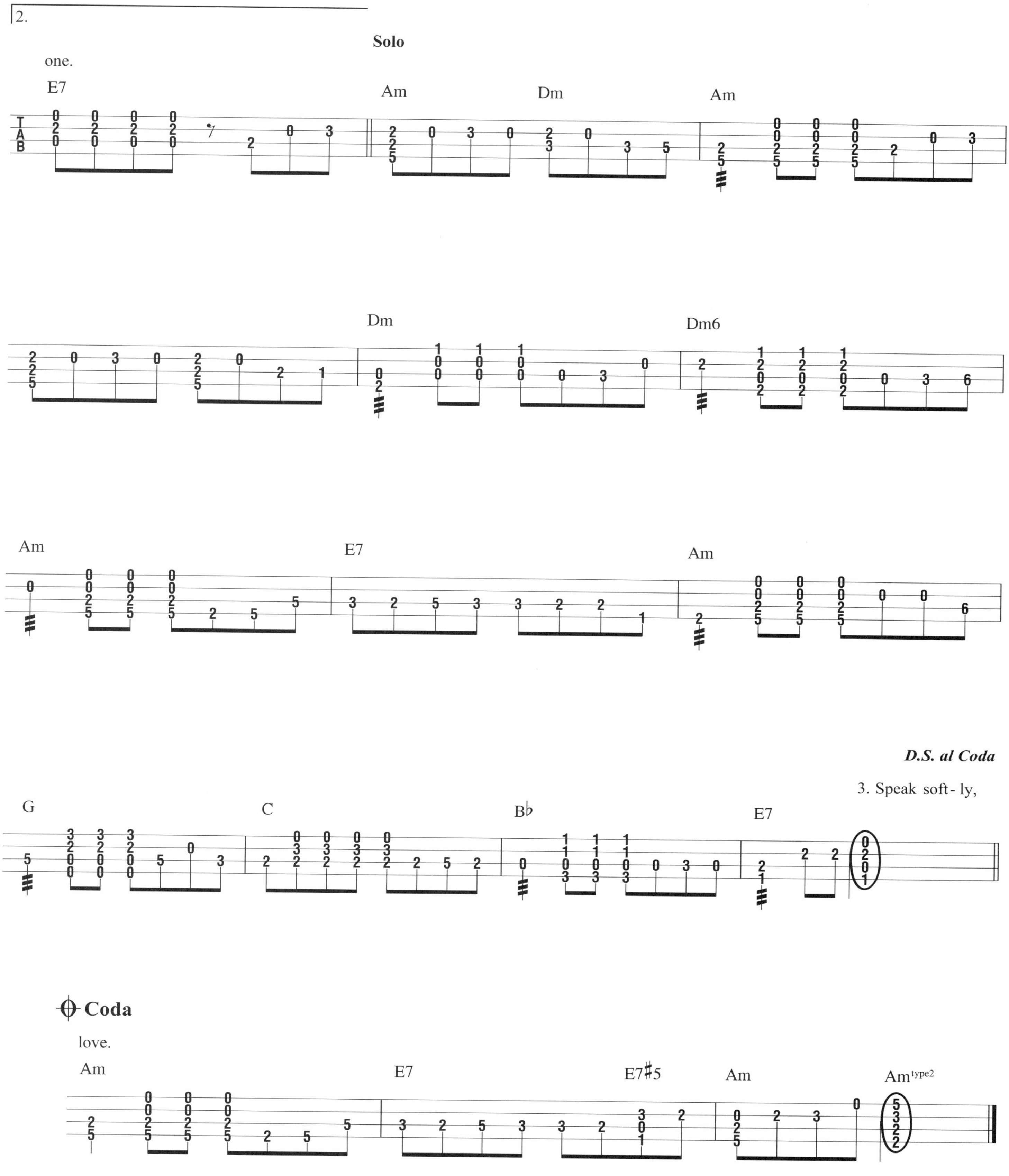

2.

Solo

one.

E7 | Am | Dm | Am

Dm | Dm6

Am | E7 | Am

D.S. al Coda

3. Speak soft- ly,

G | C | B♭ | E7

Coda

love.

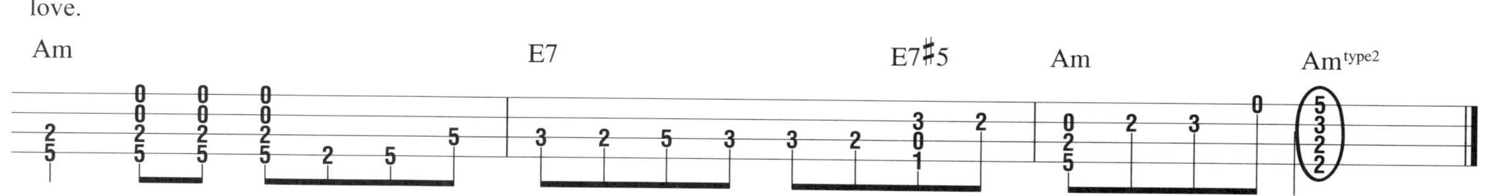

Am
E7
E7♯5
Am
Am type2

Additional Lyrics

2., 3. Speak softly, love, so no one hears us but the sky.
The vows of love we make will live until we die.
My life is yours and all because
You came into my world with love so softly, love.

Take Me Home, Country Roads

Words and Music by John Denver, Bill Danoff and Taffy Nivert

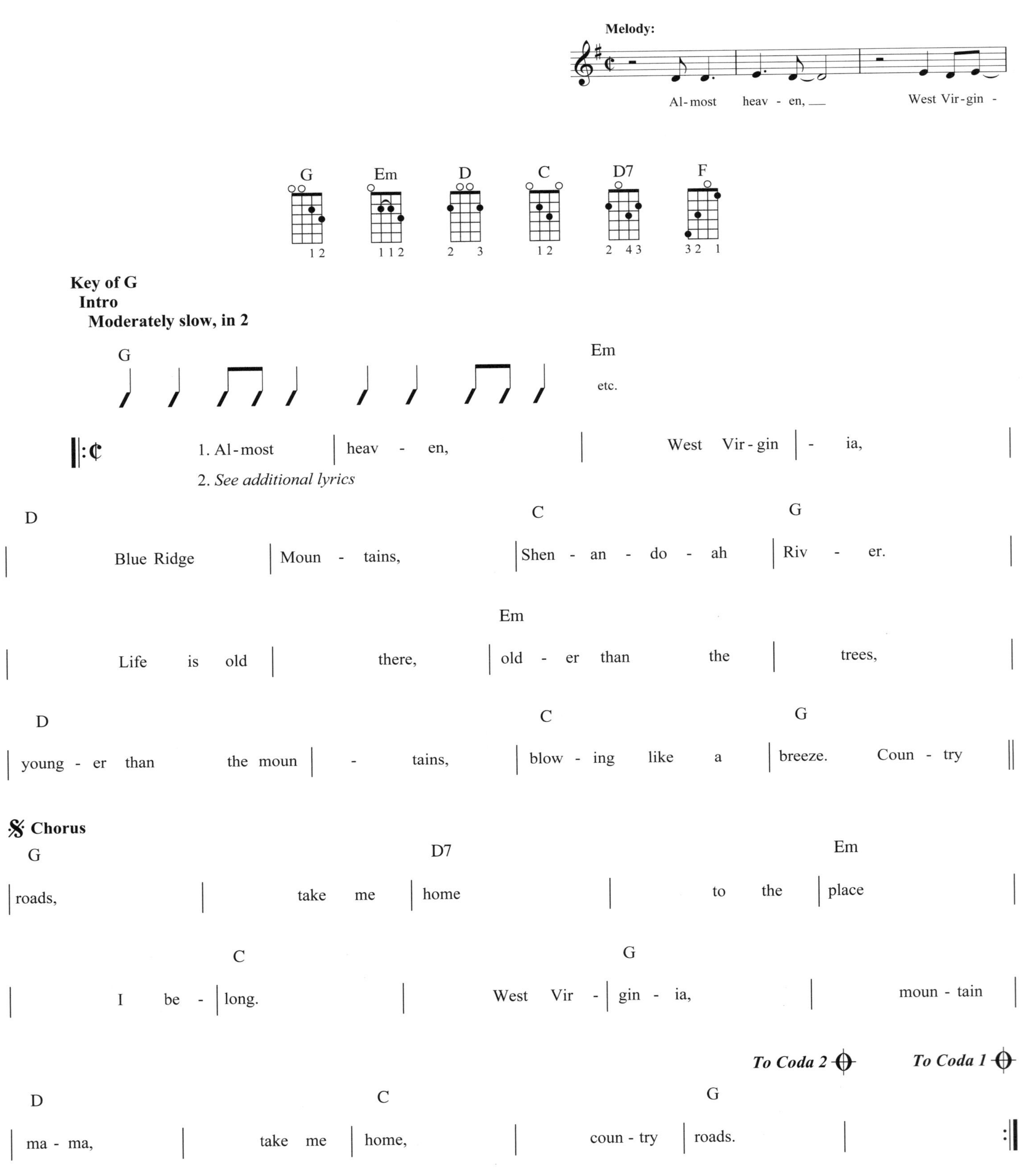
Melody:
Al-most heav - en, West Vir-gin -
G Em D C D7 F
1 2
1 1 2
2 3
1 2
2 4 3
3 2 1
Key of G
Intro
Moderately slow, in 2
G
Em
etc.
1. Al-most heav - en, West Vir-gin - ia,
2. See additional lyrics
D C G
Blue Ridge Moun - tains, Shen - an - do - ah Riv - er.
Em
Life is old there, old - er than the trees,
D C G
young - er than the moun - tains, blow - ing like a breeze. Coun - try
Chorus
G D7 Em
roads, take me home to the place
C G
I be - long. West Vir - gin - ia, moun - tain
To Coda 2
To Coda 1
D C G
ma - ma, take me home, coun - try roads.

Bridge
Em D G
I hear her voice in the morn - ing hour, she calls me. The
C G D
ra - di - o re - minds me of my home far a - way. And
Em F C G
driv - ing down the road I get a feel - ing that I should have been home
D D7
yes - ter - day, yes - ter - day. Coun - try
D.S. al Coda 1
Coda 1
Solo
G Em
D C G
Em
D C G
D.S. al Coda 2
Coun - try
Coda 2
D G
take me home, coun - try roads.

Additional Lyrics

2. All my memories gather 'round her,
   Miner's lady, stranger to blue water.
   Dark and dusty, painted on the sky,
   Misty taste of moonshine, teardrop in my eye.

Tarantella

Traditional

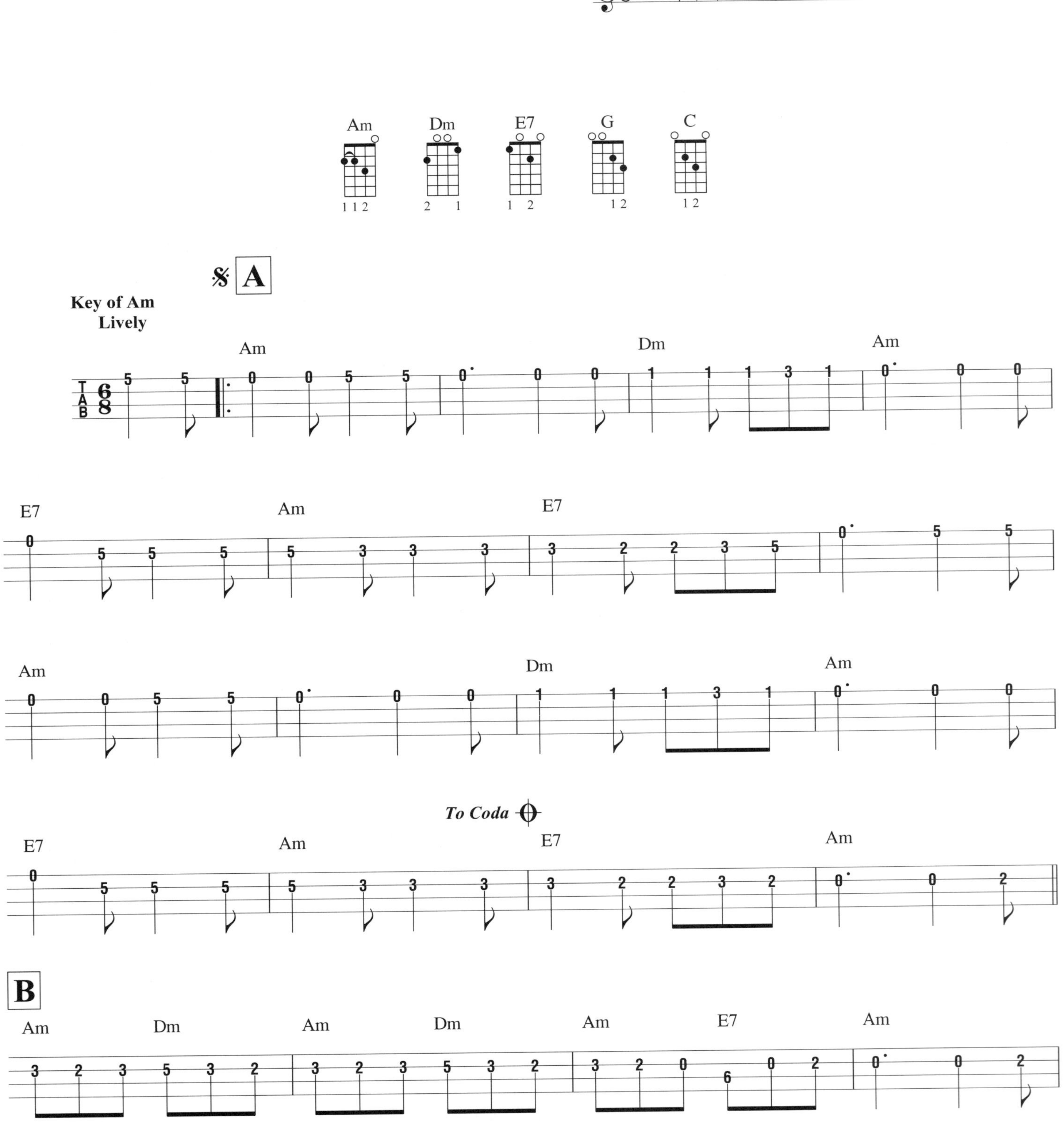

Melody:
Am
Dm
E7
G
C
A
Key of Am
Lively
To Coda
B

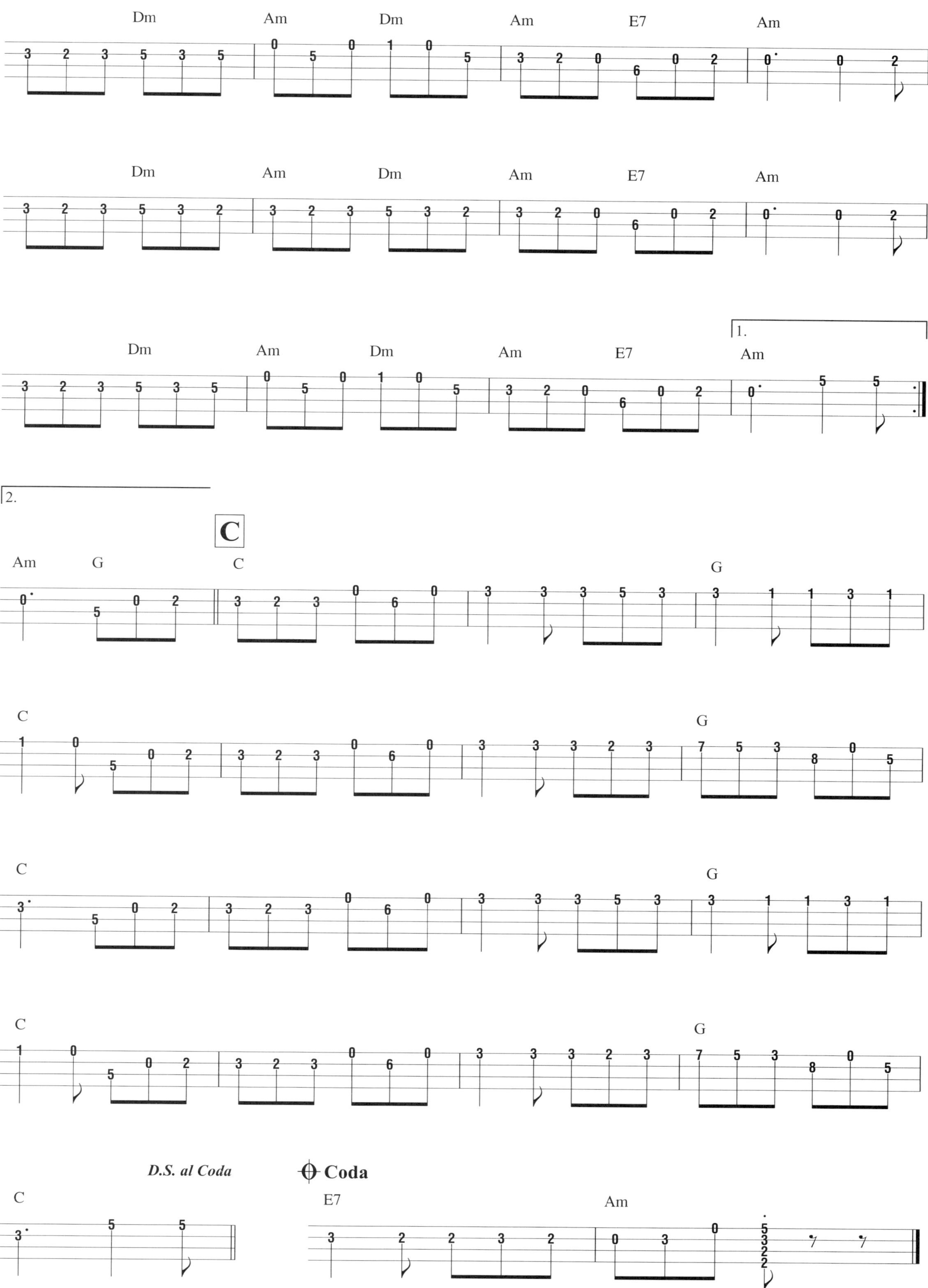
Dm Am Dm Am E7 Am
Dm Am Dm Am E7 Am
1.
Dm Am Dm Am E7 Am
2.
C
Am G C G
C G
C G
C G
D.S. al Coda
Coda
C E7 Am

Tennessee Waltz

Words and Music by Redd Stewart and Pee Wee King

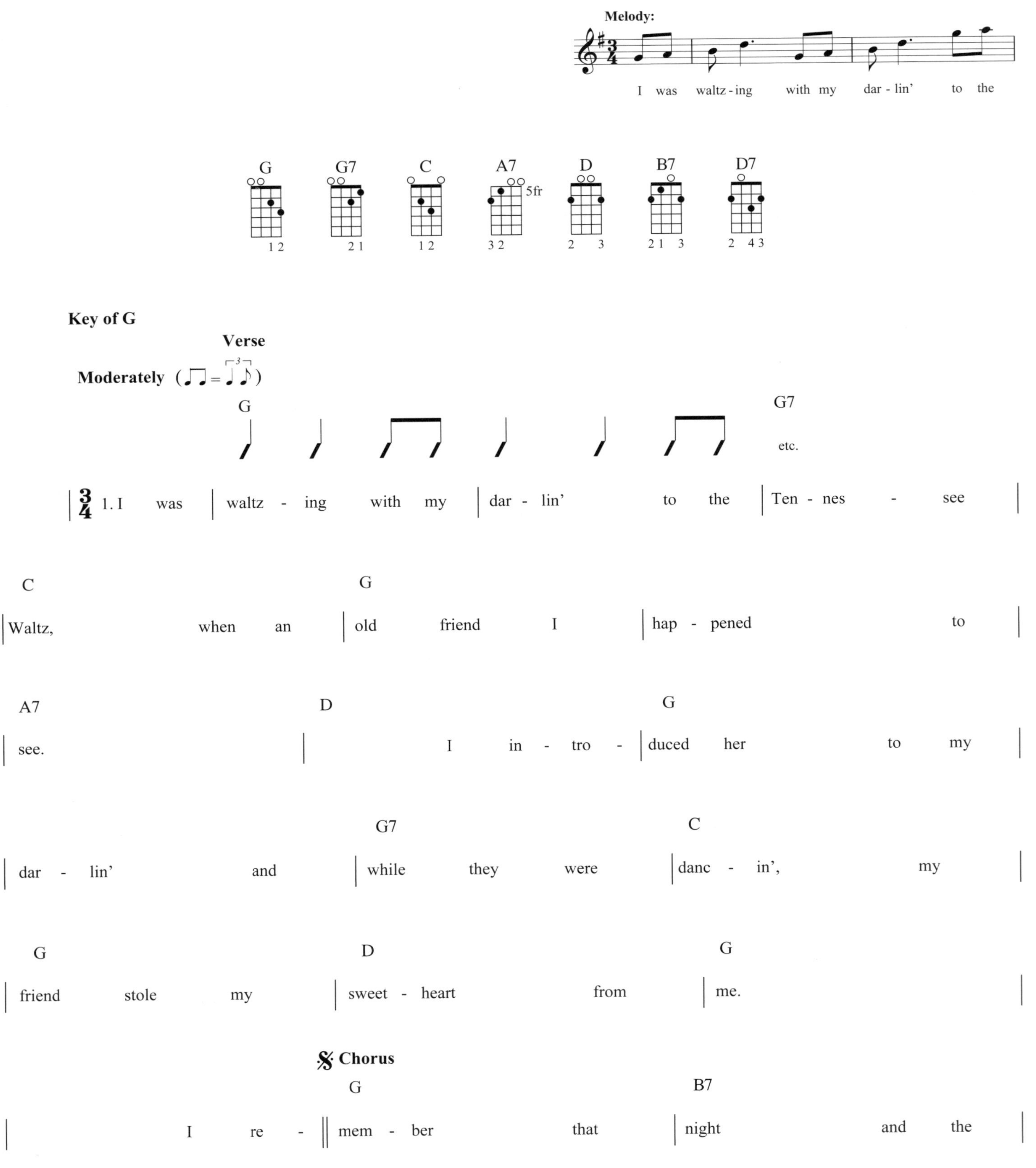

Melody:
I was waltz-ing with my dar-lin' to the
G
G7
C
A7
5fr
D
B7
D7
Key of G
Verse
Moderately
G
G7
etc.
1. I was waltz - ing with my dar - lin' to the Ten - nes - see
C
G
Waltz, when an old friend I hap - pened to
A7
D
G
see. I in - tro - duced her to my
G7
C
dar - lin' and while they were danc - in', my
G
D
G
friend stole my sweet - heart from me.
Chorus
G
B7
I re - mem - ber that night and the

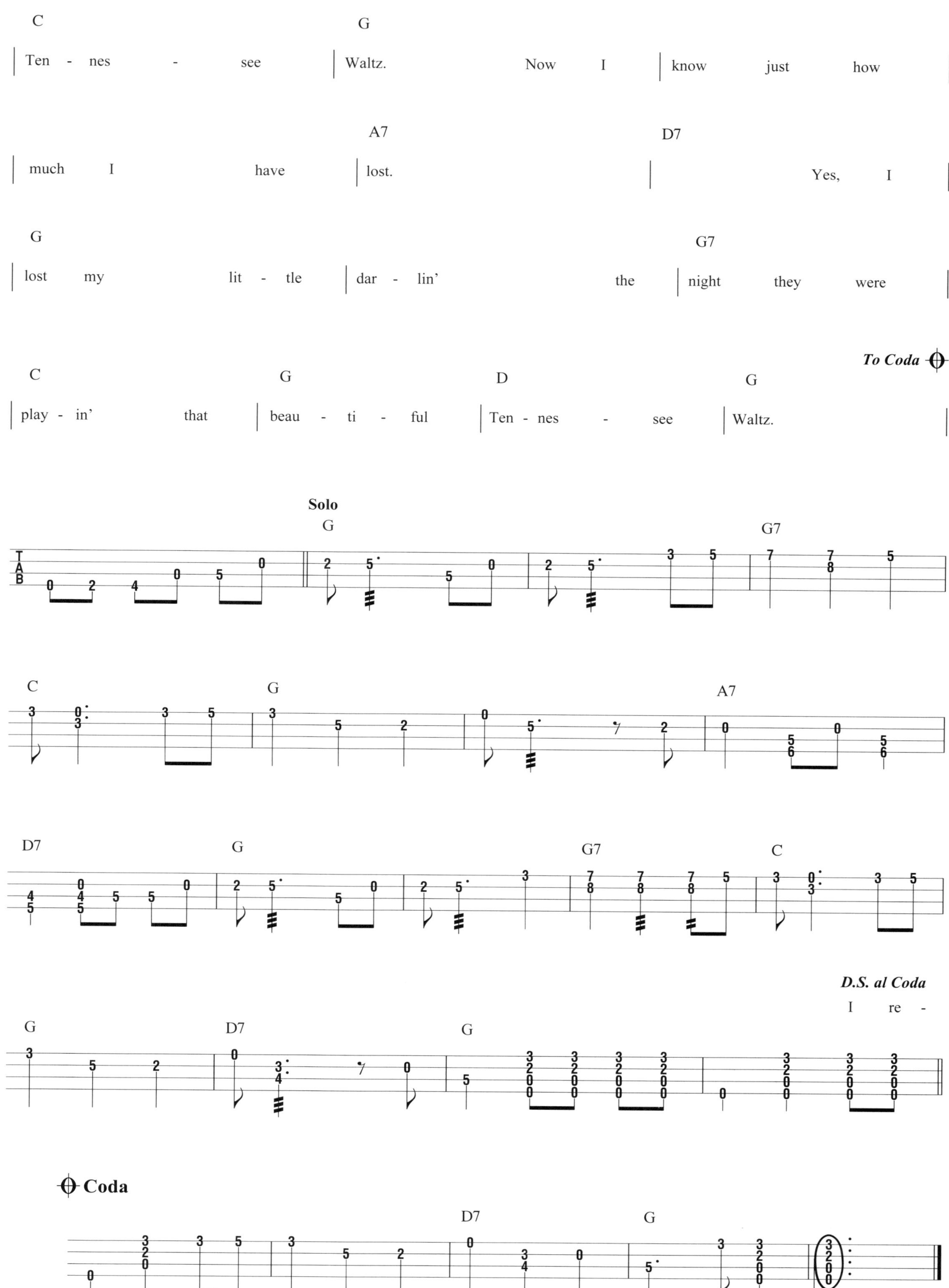

C
G
Ten - nes - see
Waltz.
Now I
know just how
A7
D7
much I have
lost.
Yes, I
G
G7
lost my lit - tle
dar - lin' the
night they were
To Coda
C
G
D
G
play - in' that
beau - ti - ful
Ten - nes - see
Waltz.
Solo
G
G7
T
A
B
C
G
A7
D7
G
G7
C
D.S. al Coda
I re -
G
D7
G
Coda
D7
G

Santa Lucia

By Teodoro Cottrau

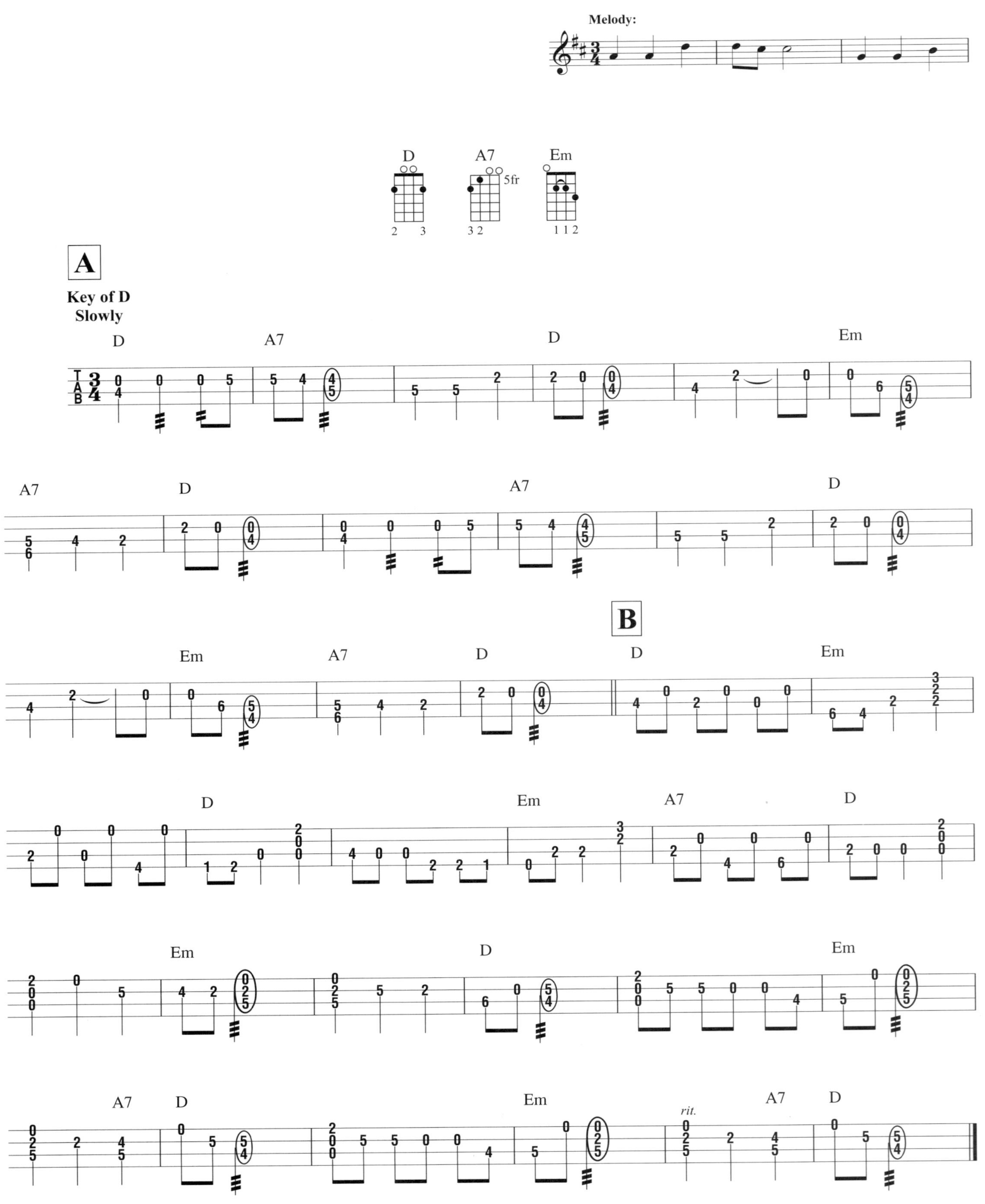
Melody:
D
A7
5fr
Em
A
Key of D
Slowly
B
rit.

That's Amore
(That's Love)

from the Paramount Picture THE CADDY
Words by Jack Brooks
Music by Harry Warren

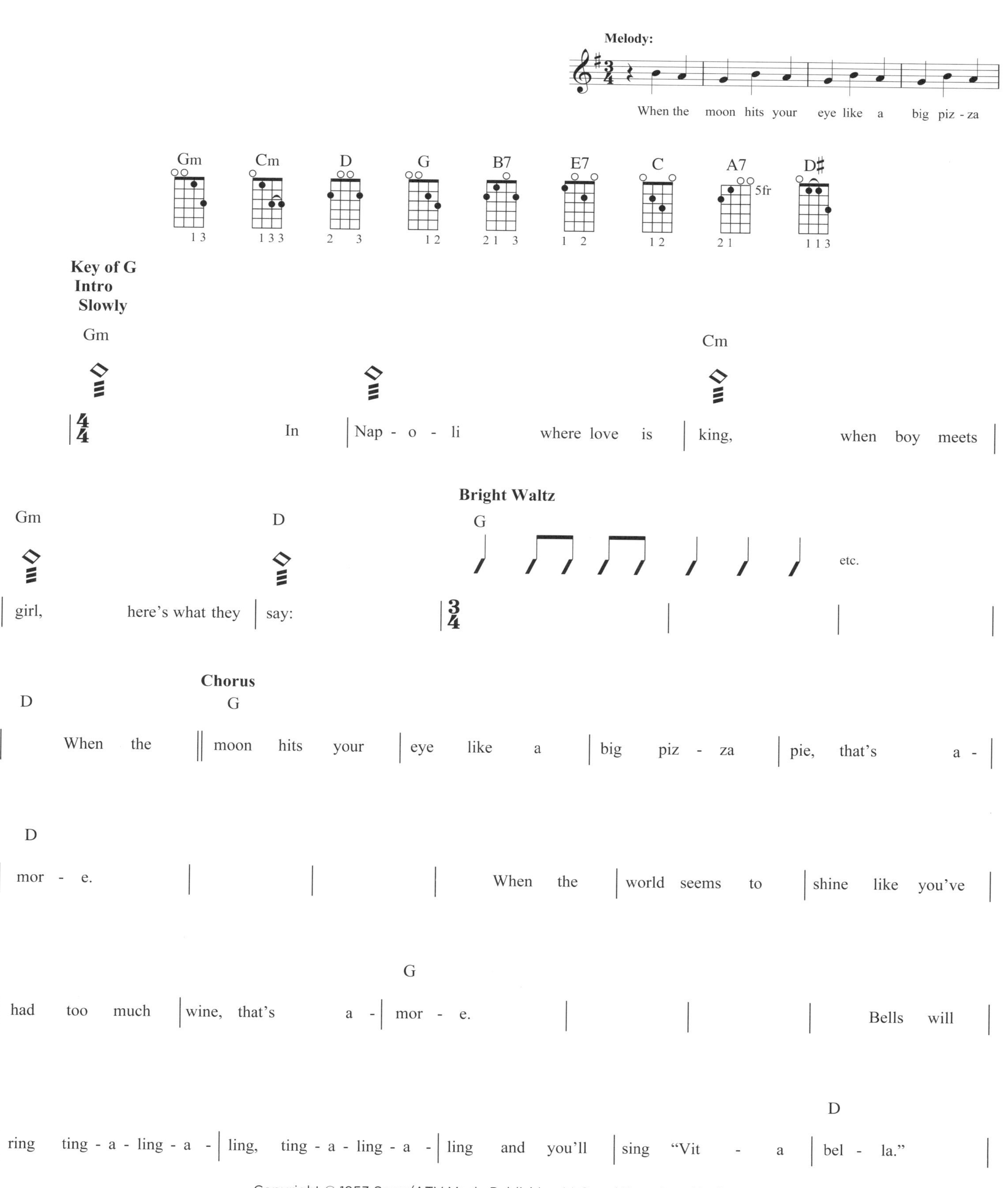

Melody:
When the moon hits your eye like a big piz - za
Gm
Cm
D
G
B7
E7
C
A7
D♯
5fr
Key of G
Intro
Slowly
In Nap - o - li where love is king, when boy meets
girl, here's what they say:
Bright Waltz
etc.
Chorus
When the moon hits your eye like a big piz - za pie, that's a -
more - e. When the world seems to shine like you've
had too much wine, that's a - mor - e. Bells will
ring ting - a - ling - a - ling, ting - a - ling - a - ling and you'll sing "Vit - a bel - la."

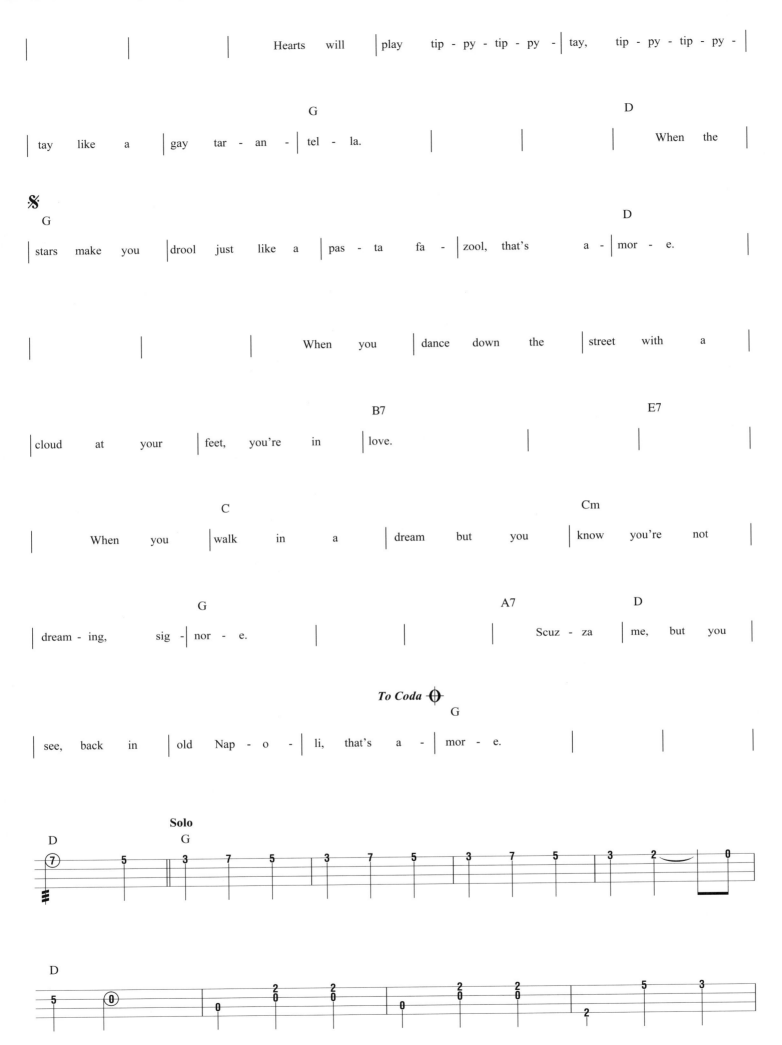

Hearts will | play tip - py - tip - py - | tay, tip - py - tip - py -

G D
| tay like a | gay tar - an - | tel - la. | | | When the

𝄋
G D
| stars make you | drool just like a | pas - ta fa - | zool, that's a - | mor - e. |

| | | When you | dance down the | street with a |

B7 E7
| cloud at your | feet, you're in | love. | | |

C Cm
| When you | walk in a | dream but you | know you're not |

G A7 D
| dream - ing, sig - | nor - e. | | | Scuz - za | me, but you |

To Coda 𝄌
G
| see, back in | old Nap - o - | li, that's a - | mor - e. | | |

Solo
D G
7 5 || 3 7 5 | 3 7 5 | 3 7 5 | 3 2 0 |

D
5 0 | 0 2 0 2 0 | 0 2 0 2 0 | 2 5 3 |

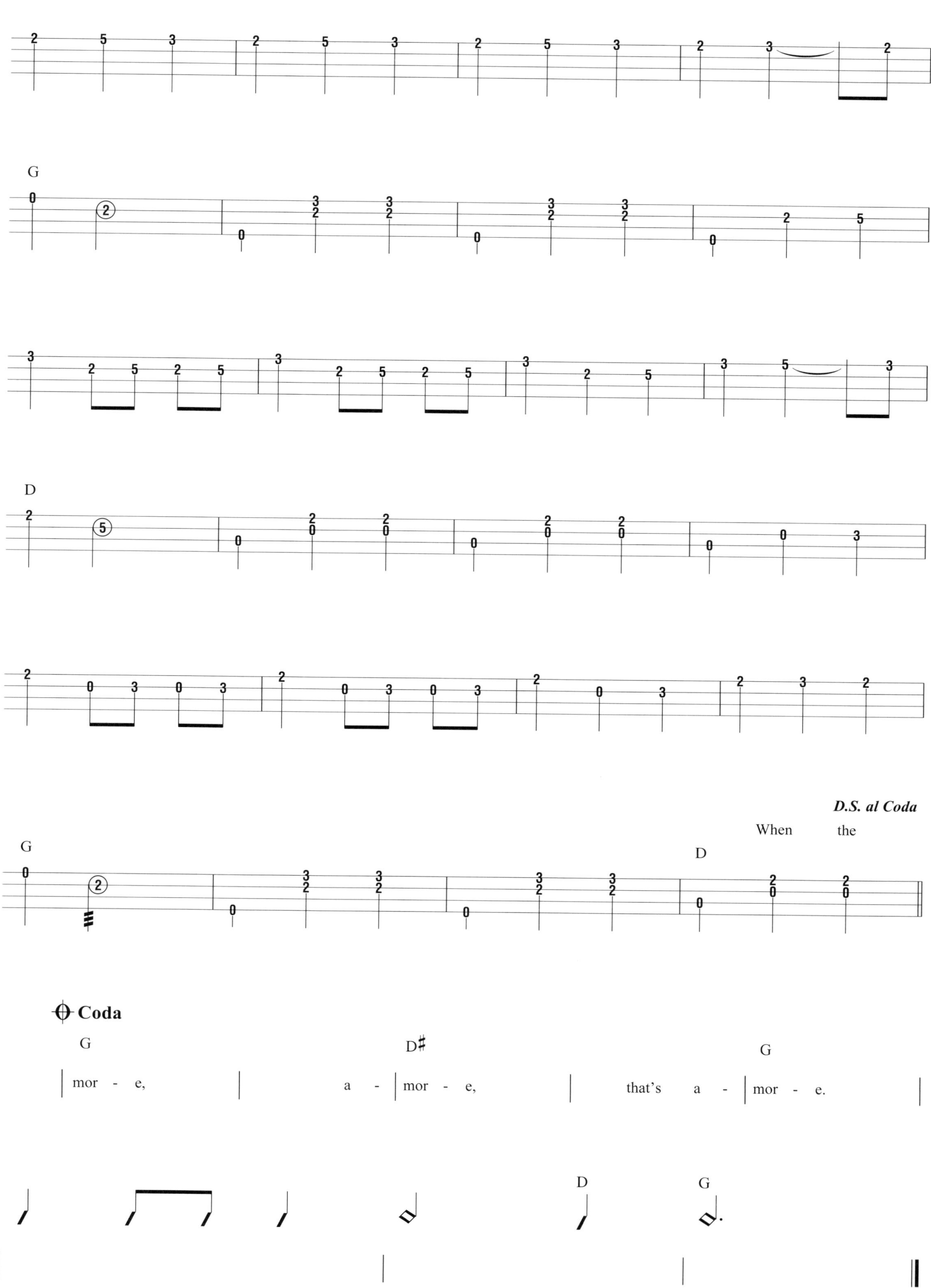
G
D
D.S. al Coda
When the
G
D
Coda
G
D♯
G
mor - e, a - mor - e, that's a - mor - e.
D
G

Turkey in the Straw

American Folksong

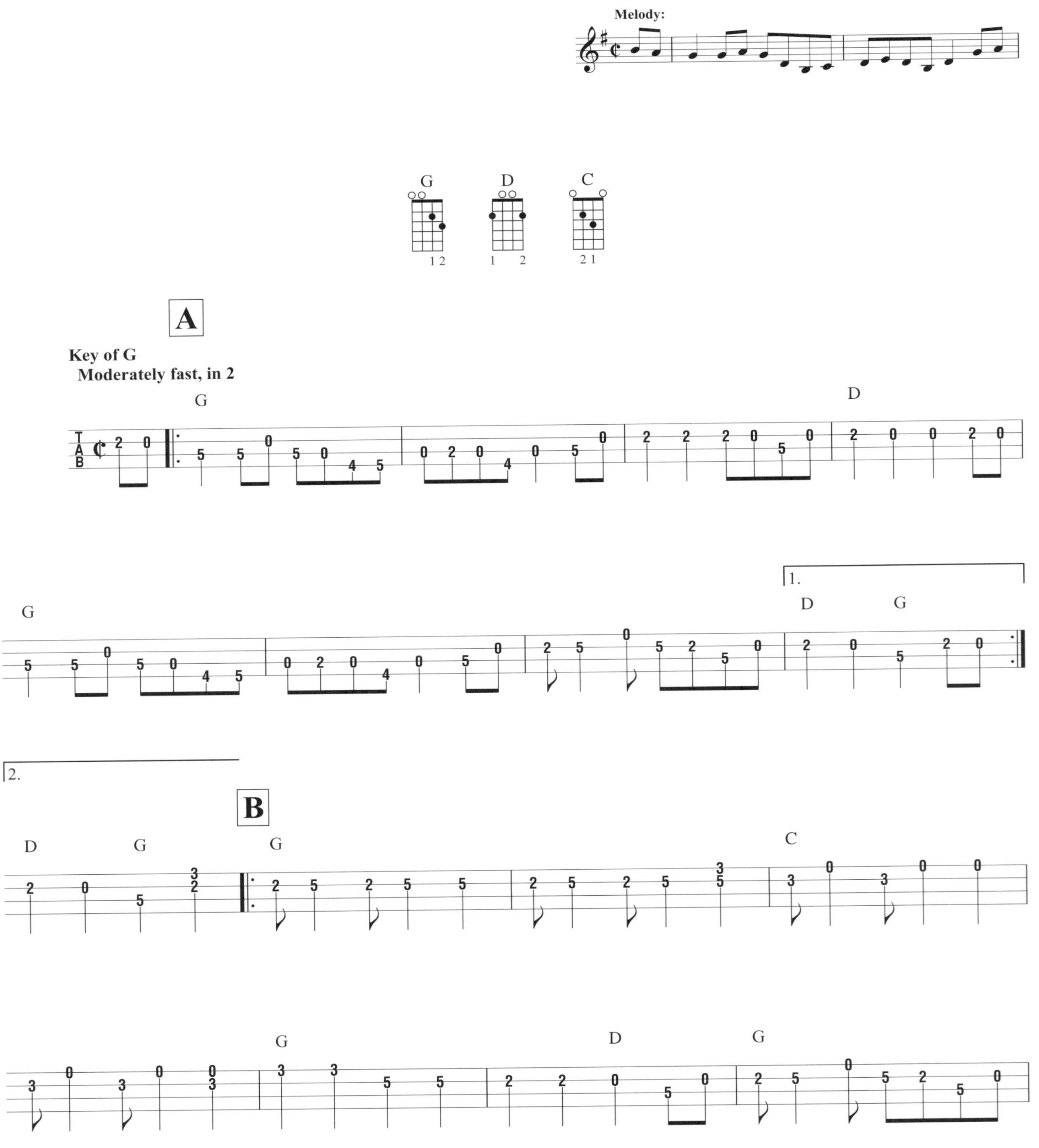

Melody:
G
D
C
A
Key of G
Moderately fast, in 2
1.
2.
B

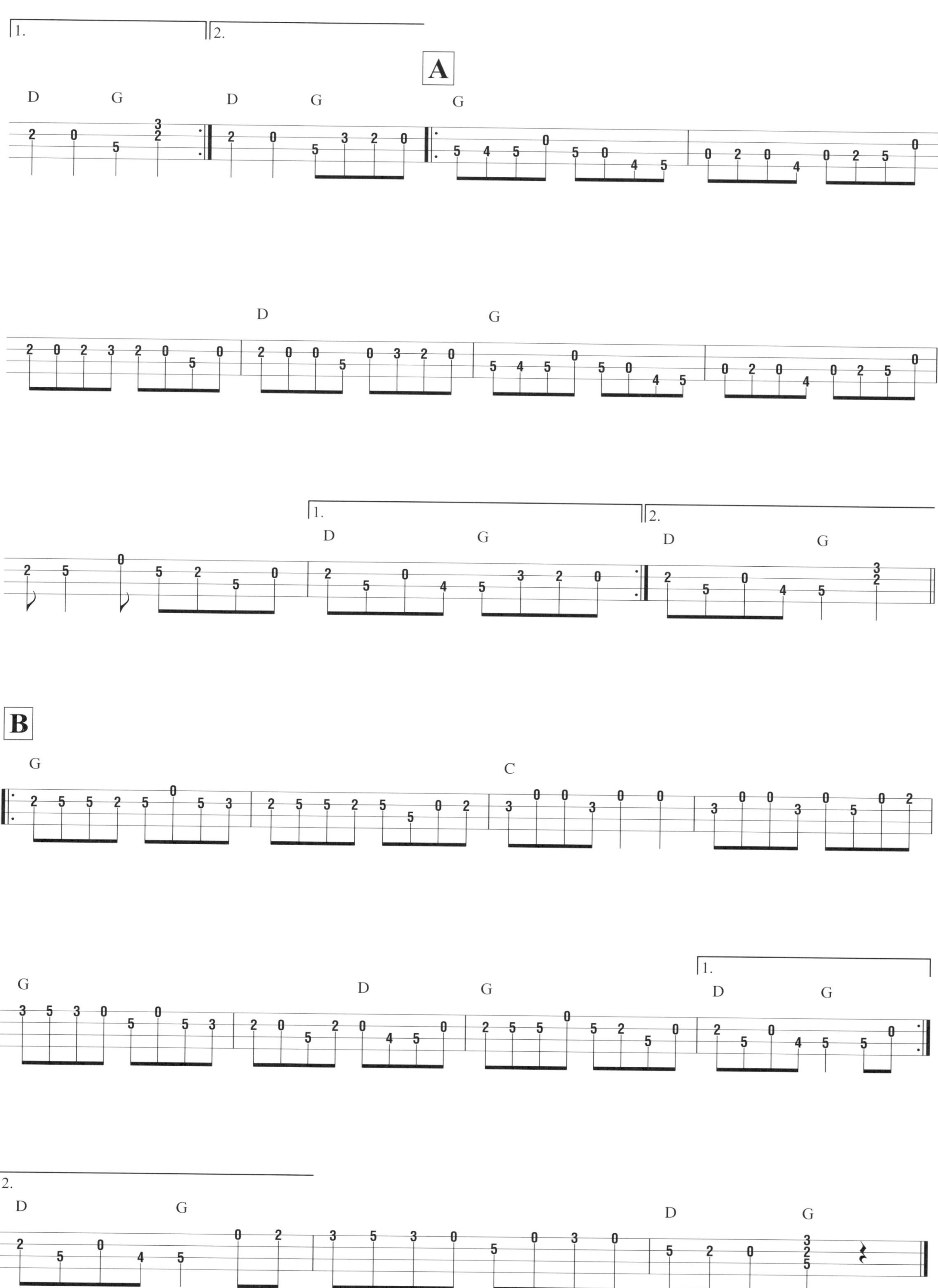
1.
2.
A
D G D G G
D G
1.
D G
2.
D G
B
G C
G D G
1.
D G
2.
D G D G

Volare

Music by Domenico Modugno
English Lyric by Mitchell Parish
Original Italian Text by Domenico Modugno and Francesco Migliacci

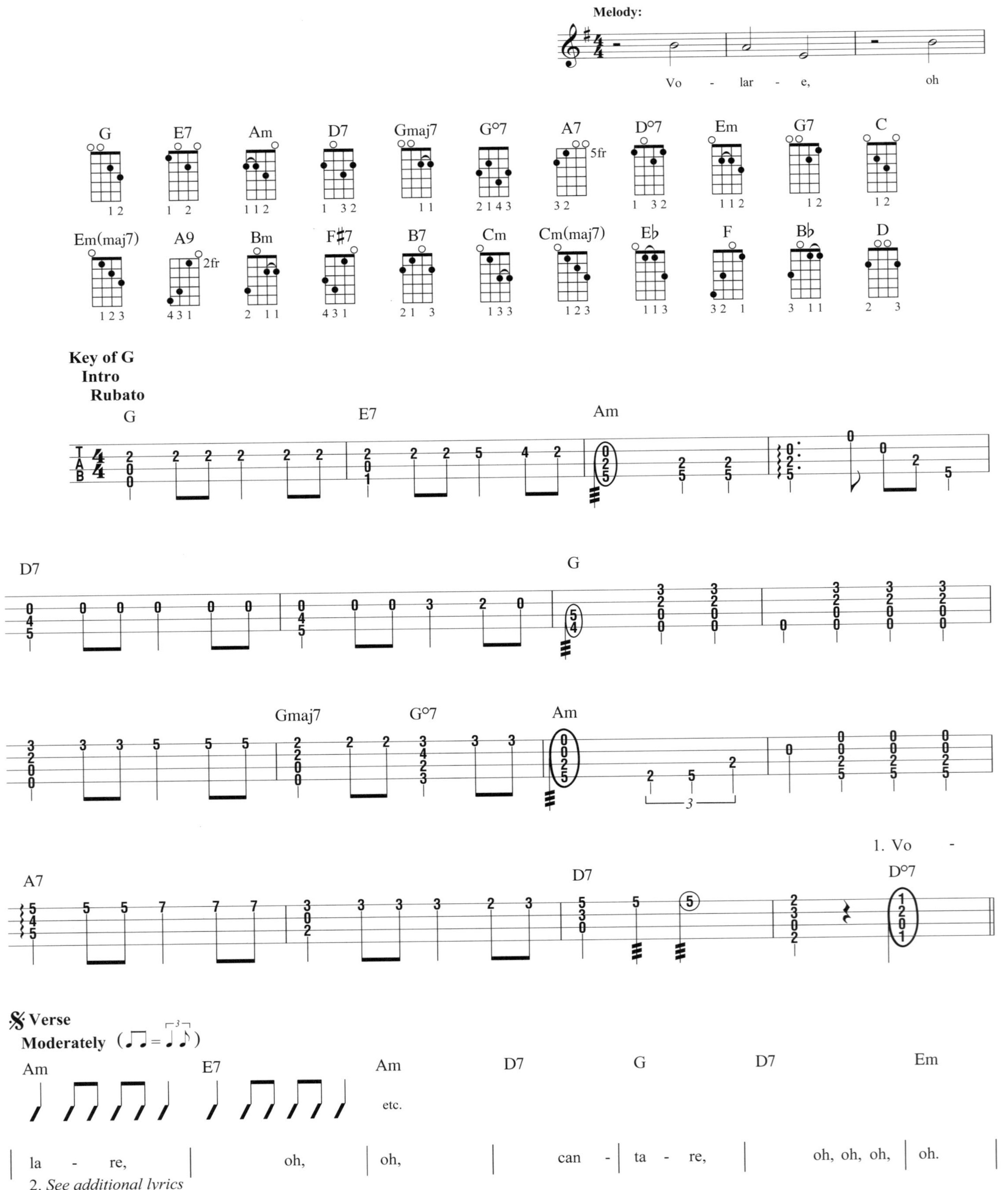

Melody:
Vo - lar - e, oh
G
E7
Am
D7
Gmaj7
G°7
A7
5fr
D°7
Em
G7
C
Em(maj7)
A9
2fr
Bm
F♯7
B7
Cm
Cm(maj7)
E♭
F
B♭
D
Key of G
Intro
Rubato
1. Vo -
Verse
Moderately
etc.
la - re, oh, oh, can - ta - re, oh, oh, oh, oh.
2. *See additional lyrics*

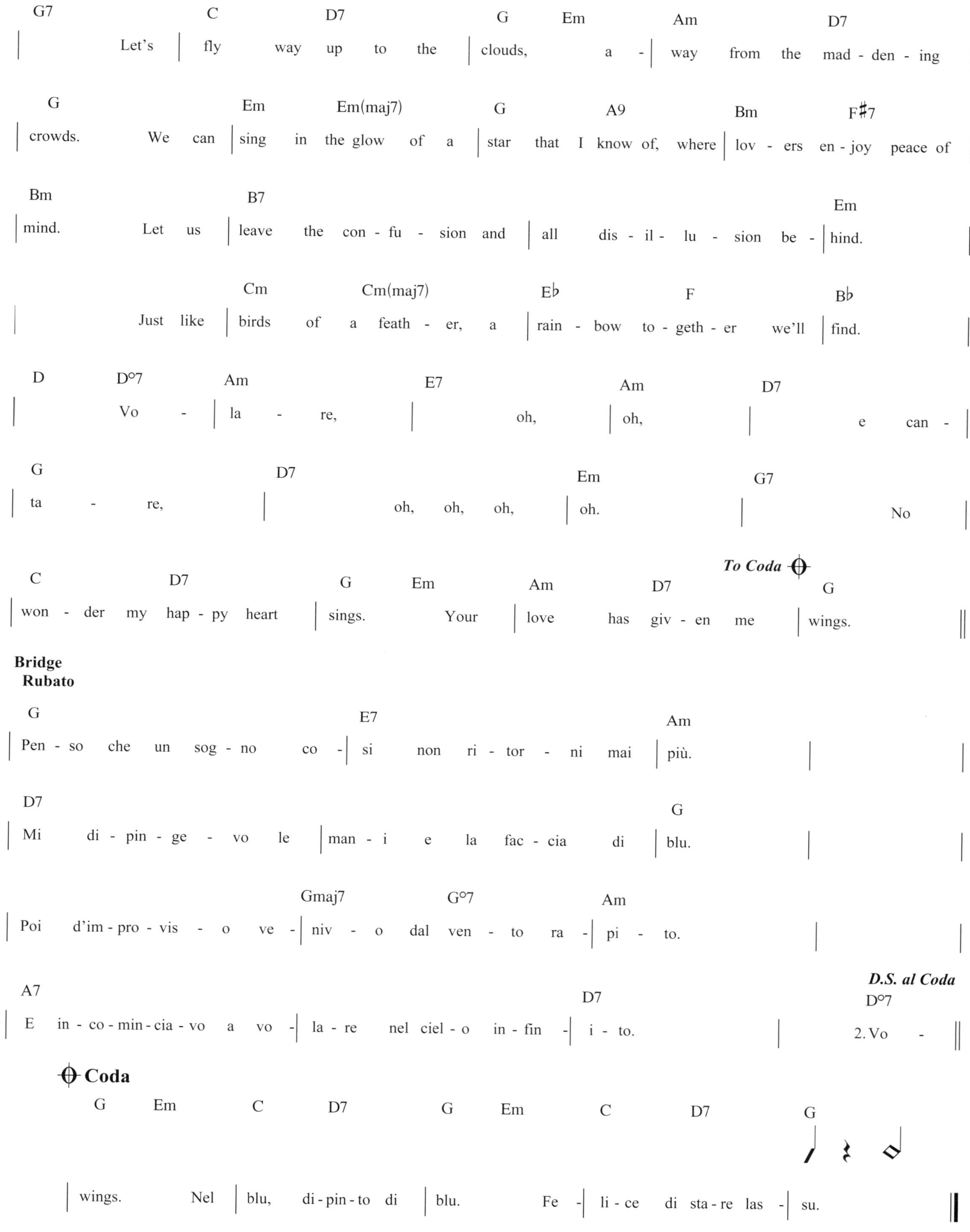
G7 C D7 G Em Am D7
Let's fly way up to the clouds, a - way from the mad - den - ing
G Em Em(maj7) G A9 Bm F♯7
crowds. We can sing in the glow of a star that I know of, where lov - ers en - joy peace of
Bm B7 Em
mind. Let us leave the con - fu - sion and all dis - il - lu - sion be - hind.
Cm Cm(maj7) E♭ F B♭
Just like birds of a feath - er, a rain - bow to - geth - er we'll find.
D D°7 Am E7 Am D7
Vo - la - re, oh, oh, e can -
G D7 Em G7
ta - re, oh, oh, oh, oh. No
To Coda
C D7 G Em Am D7 G
won - der my hap - py heart sings. Your love has giv - en me wings.
Bridge
Rubato
G E7 Am
Pen - so che un sog - no co - si non ri - tor - ni mai più.
D7 G
Mi di - pin - ge - vo le man - i e la fac - cia di blu.
Gmaj7 G°7 Am
Poi d'im - pro - vis - o ve - niv - o dal ven - to ra - pi - to.
D.S. al Coda
A7 D7 D°7
E in - co - min - cia - vo a vo - la - re nel ciel - o in - fin - i - to. 2. Vo -
Coda
G Em C D7 G Em C D7 G
wings. Nel blu, di - pin - to di blu. Fe - li - ce di sta - re las - su.

Additional Lyrics

2. Volare, oh, oh, e contare, oh, oh, oh, oh.
   Nel blu, dipinto di blu. Felice di stare lassu.
   E volavo, volavo felice più in alto del sole ed ancora più su.
   Mentre il mondo pian piano spariva lontano laggiu,
   Una musica dolce suonava soltanto per me.

Wagon Wheel

Words and Music by Bob Dylan and Ketch Secor

Melody:
Head-ed down south to the land of the pines,

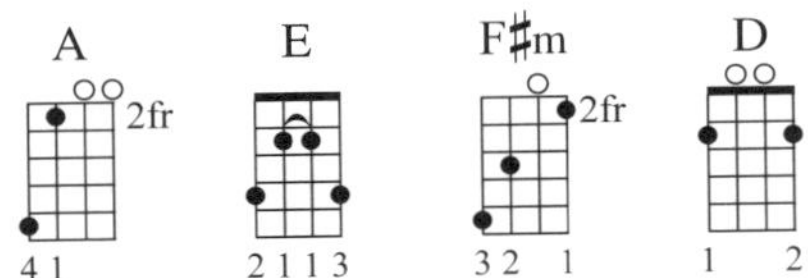
A
2fr
4 1
E
2 1 1 3
F♯m
2fr
3 2 1
D
1 2

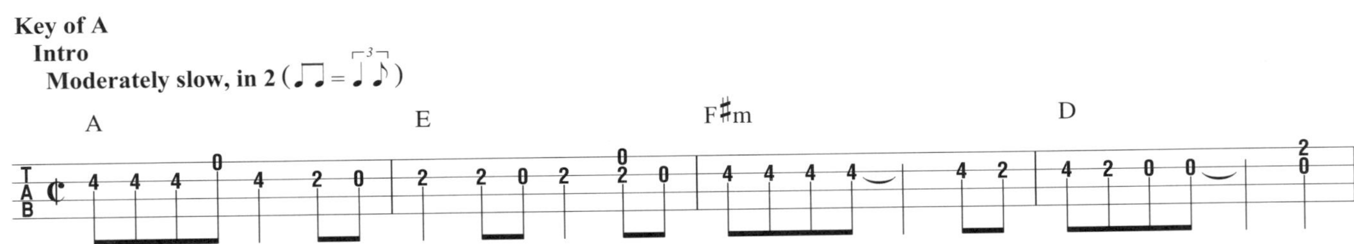
Key of A
Intro
Moderately slow, in 2
A
E
F♯m
D

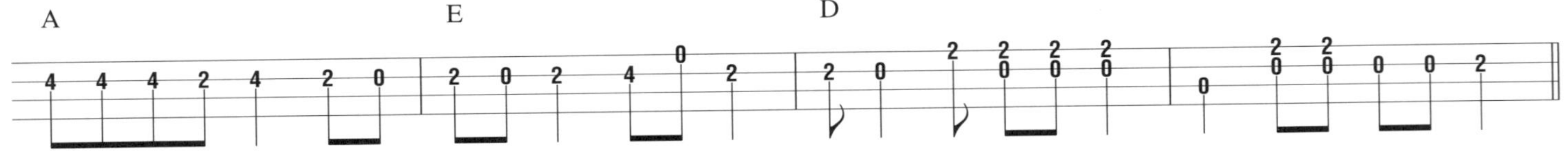
A
E
D

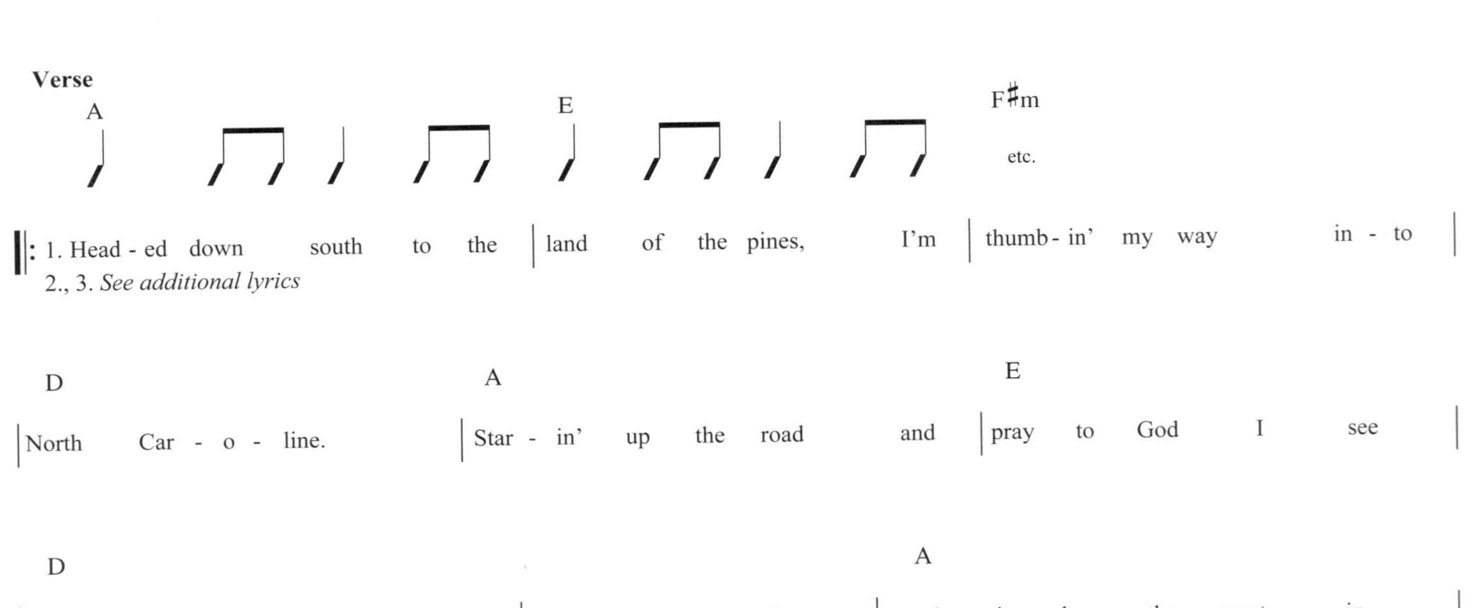
Verse
A
E
F♯m
etc.
1. Head - ed down south to the land of the pines, I'm thumb - in' my way in - to
2., 3. See additional lyrics
D
A
E
North Car - o - line. Star - in' up the road and pray to God I see
D
A
head - lights. I made it down the coast in

E | F♯m | D
| sev - en - teen hours, | pick - in' me a bou - quet of | dog - wood flow'rs, and I'm a - |

A | E | D
| hop - in' for Ra - leigh, I can | see my ba - by to - | night. | So, ||

Chorus

A | E | F♯m
| rock me, ma - ma, like a | wag - on wheel, | rock me, ma - ma, an - y |

D | A | E | D
| way you feel. | Hey, | ma - ma, | rock me. |

A | E | F♯m
| | Rock me, ma - ma, like the | wind and the rain, | rock me, ma - ma, like a |

D | A | E | D | 1.
| south-bound train. | Hey, | ma - ma, | rock me. | :||

2.

A
5 2 0 5 4 0 2
0 0 2 6

Additional Lyrics

2. Runnin' from the cold up in New England,
I was born to be a fiddler in an old-time string band.
My baby plays the guitar, I pick a banjo now.
Oh, the north-country winters keep a-gettin' me down.
Lost my money playin' poker so I had to leave town,
But I ain't turnin' back to livin' that old life no more.

3. Walkin' due south out of Roanoke,
I caught a trucker out of Philly, had a nice long toke.
But he's a-headed west from the Cumberland Gap to Johnson City, Tennessee.
And I gotta get a move on before the sun.
I hear my baby callin' my name and I know that she's the only one,
And if I die in Raleigh, at least I will die free.

Whiskey Before Breakfast

Traditional

Melody:

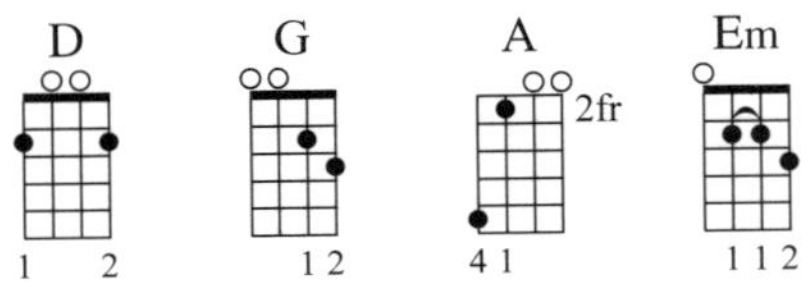
D
G
A
Em
2fr

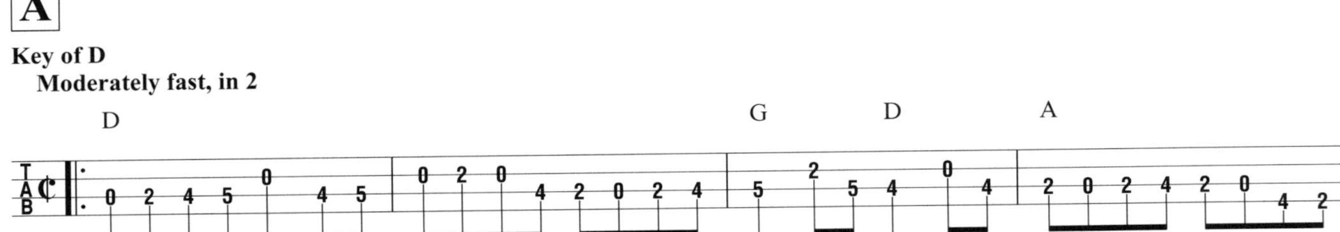
A
Key of D
Moderately fast, in 2
D
G
D
A

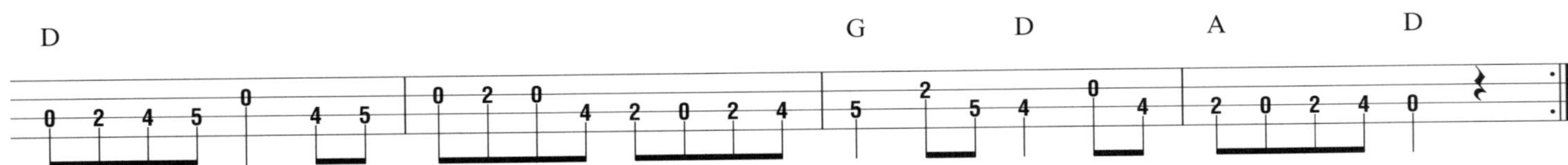
D
G
D
A
D

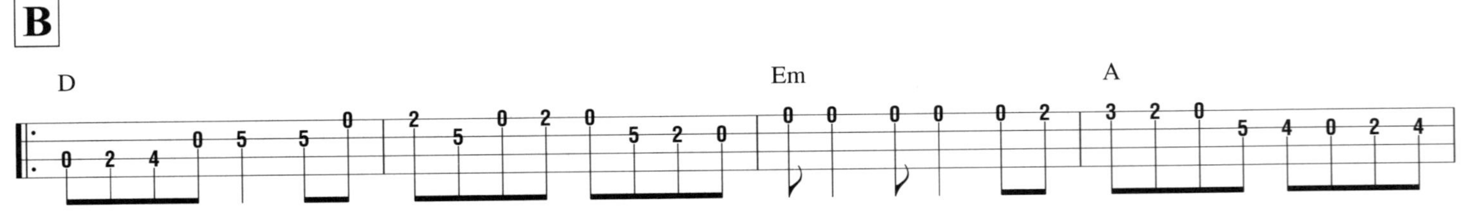
B
D
Em
A

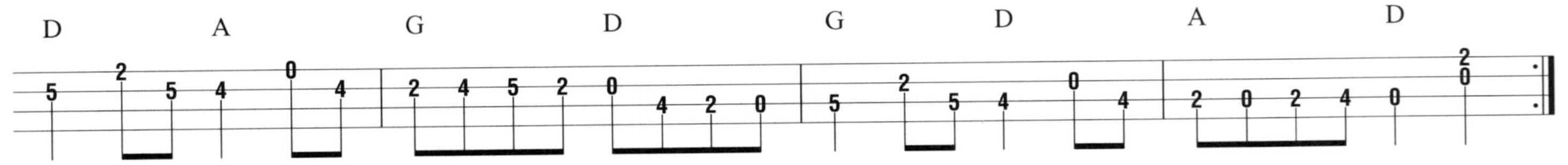
D
A
G
D
G
D
A
D

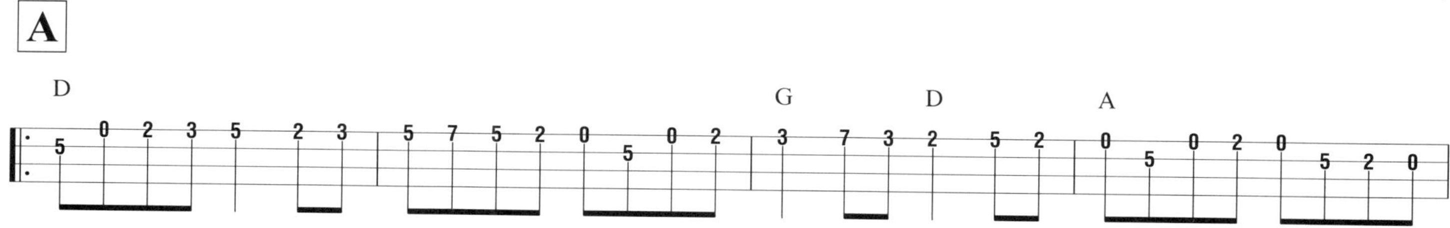
A
D
G
D
A

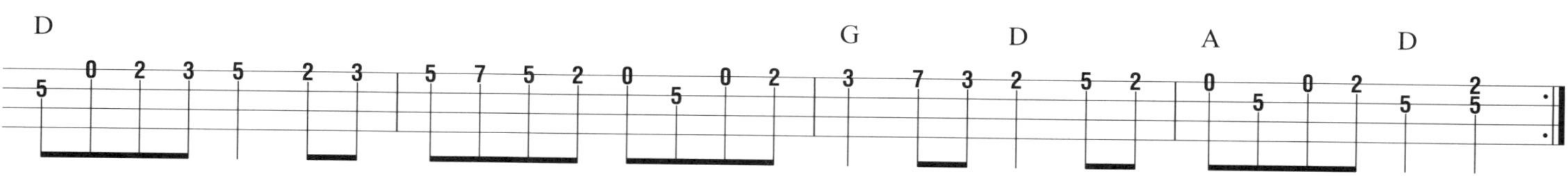
D
G
D
A
D

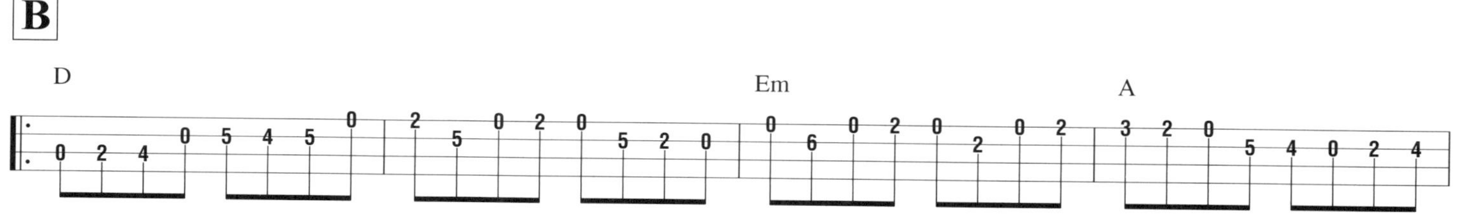
B
D
Em
A

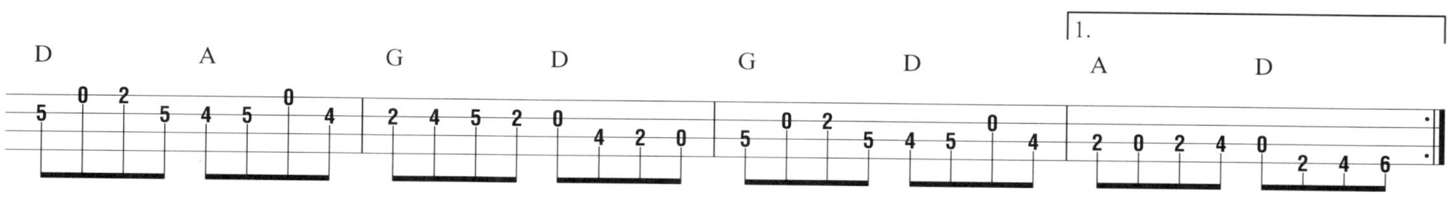
1.
D
A
G
D
G
D
A
D

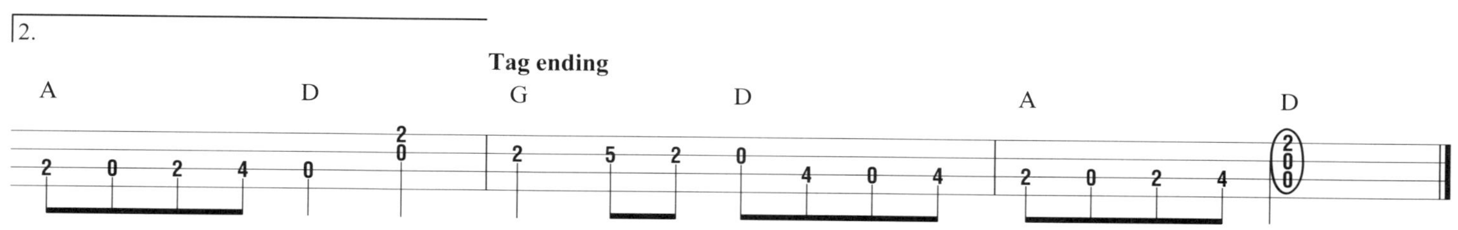
2.
Tag ending
A
D
G
D
A
D

Wildwood Flower

Traditional

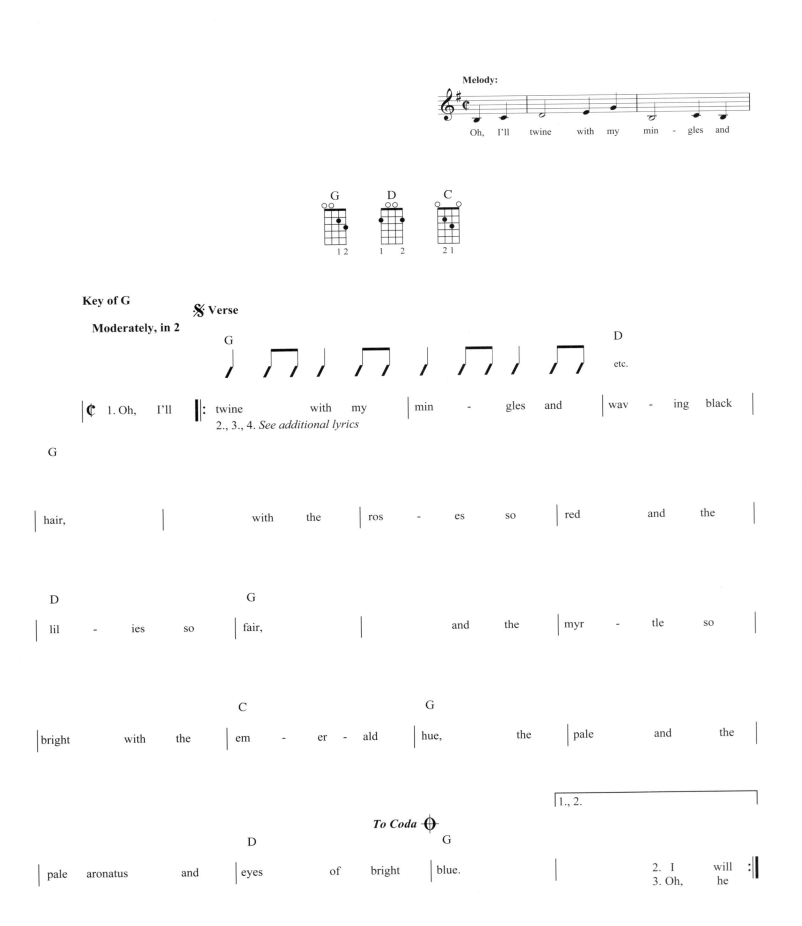

Melody:
Oh, I'll twine with my min - gles and

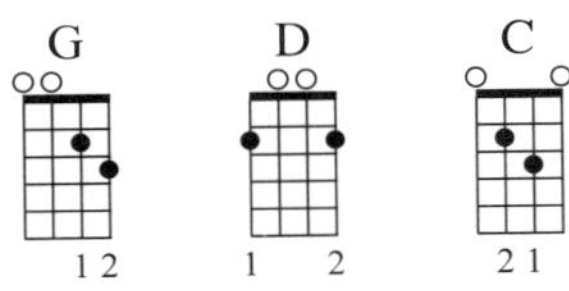
G
D
C
1 2
1 2
2 1

Key of G

Moderately, in 2

Verse

G D etc.

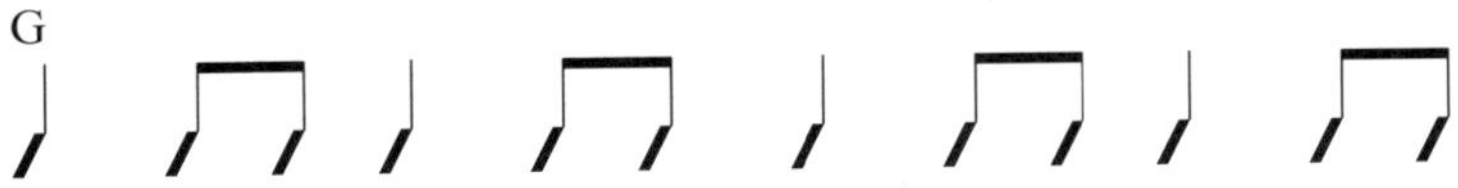

| 1. Oh, I'll |: twine with my | min - gles and | wav - ing black |
2., 3., 4. *See additional lyrics*

G

| hair, | with the | ros - es so | red and the |

D G

| lil - ies so | fair, | and the | myr - tle so |

C G

| bright with the | em - er - ald | hue, the | pale and the |

To Coda

D G 1., 2.

| pale aronatus and | eyes of bright | blue. | 2. I will :|
3. Oh, he

3.

Solo

G D

G

D G

C G

D.S. al Coda

D G

4. Oh, he

𝄌 Coda

G
flow - er.

Additional Lyrics

2. I will dance, I will sing, and my laugh shall be gay.
   I will charm every heart, in his crown I will sway.
   When I woke from my dreaming, my idols was clay.
   All portion of love had all flown away.

3. Oh, he taught me to love him and promised to love
   And to cherish me over all others above.
   How my heart is now wondering, no misery can tell.
   He's left me no warning, no words of farewell.

4. Oh, he taught me to love him and called me his flower,
   That was blooming to cheer him through life's dreary hour.
   Oh, I long to see him and regret the dark hour.
   He's gone and neglected this pale wildwood flower.

Will the Circle Be Broken

Words by Ada R. Habershon
Music by Charles H. Gabriel

Melody:
I was stand - ing by the win - dow

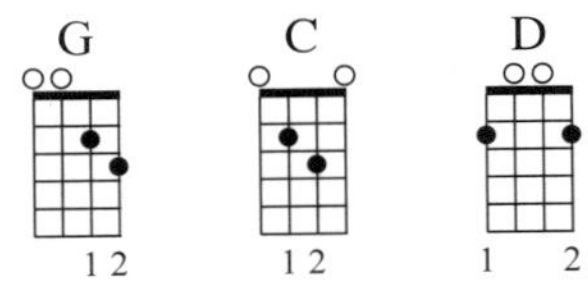
G
C
D

Key of G

Moderately, in 2

Verse

G

etc.

| 1. I was |: stand - ing | by the | win - dow | on one |

C G

| cold and | cloud - y | day, | and I |

| saw the | hearse come | roll - ing | for to |

D G

| car - ry my | moth - er a - | way. | Will the ||

Chorus

G

| cir - cle | be un - | brok - en? | By and |

C G

| by, Lord, | by and | by. | There's a |

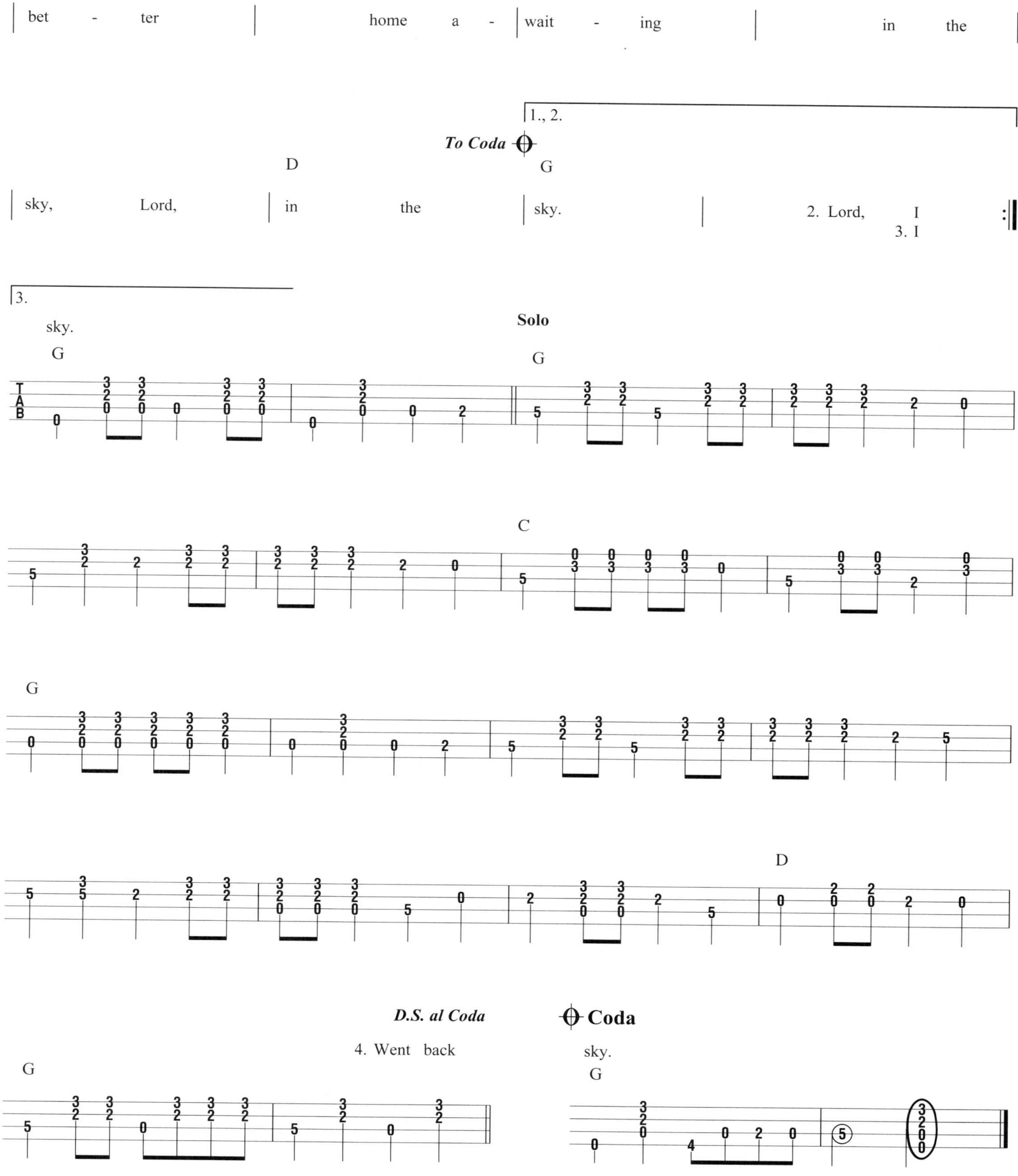
bet - ter home a - wait - ing in the
1., 2.
To Coda
D
G
sky, Lord, in the sky.
2. Lord, I
3. I
3.
sky.
Solo
G
G
C
G
D
D.S. al Coda
4. Went back
Coda
sky.
G
G

Additional Lyrics

2. Lord, I told the undertaker, "Undertaker, please drive slow.
   For this body you are hauling, how I hate to see her go."

3. I followed close behind her, tried to hold up and be brave,
   But I could not hide my sorrow when they laid her in the grave.

4. Went back home, Lord, my home was lonesome since my mother she was gone.
   All my brothers, sisters crying. What a home so sad and lone.

Yesterday

Words and Music by John Lennon and Paul McCartney

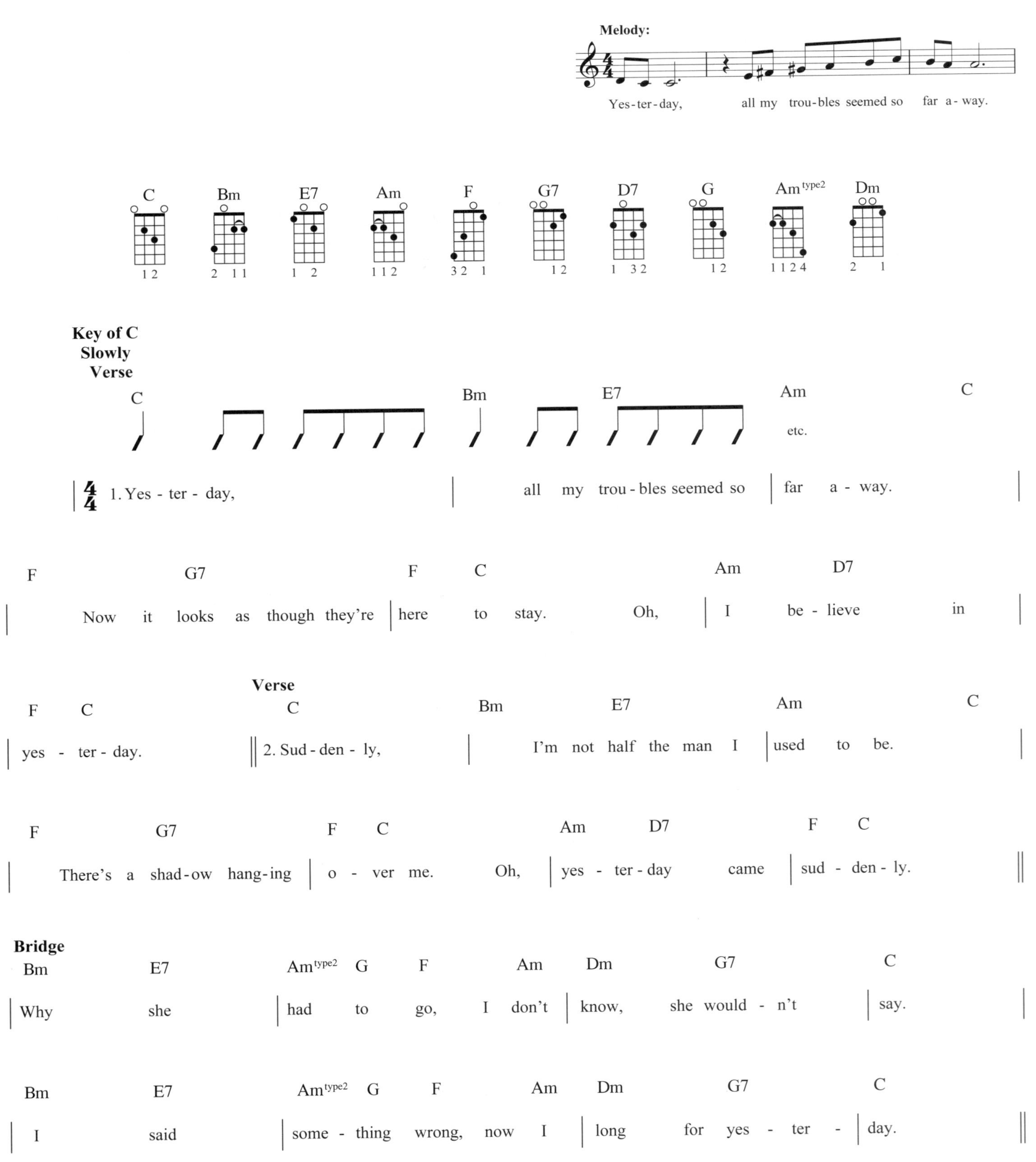
Melody:
Yes-ter-day, all my trou-bles seemed so far a-way.
C Bm E7 Am F G7 D7 G Am type2 Dm
Key of C
Slowly
Verse
C Bm E7 Am C
etc.
1. Yes - ter - day, all my trou - bles seemed so far a - way.
F G7 F C Am D7
Now it looks as though they're here to stay. Oh, I be - lieve in
F C
yes - ter - day.
Verse
C Bm E7 Am C
2. Sud - den - ly, I'm not half the man I used to be.
F G7 F C Am D7 F C
There's a shad - ow hang - ing o - ver me. Oh, yes - ter - day came sud - den - ly.
Bridge
Bm E7 Am type2 G F Am Dm G7 C
Why she had to go, I don't know, she would - n't say.
Bm E7 Am type2 G F Am Dm G7 C
I said some - thing wrong, now I long for yes - ter - day.

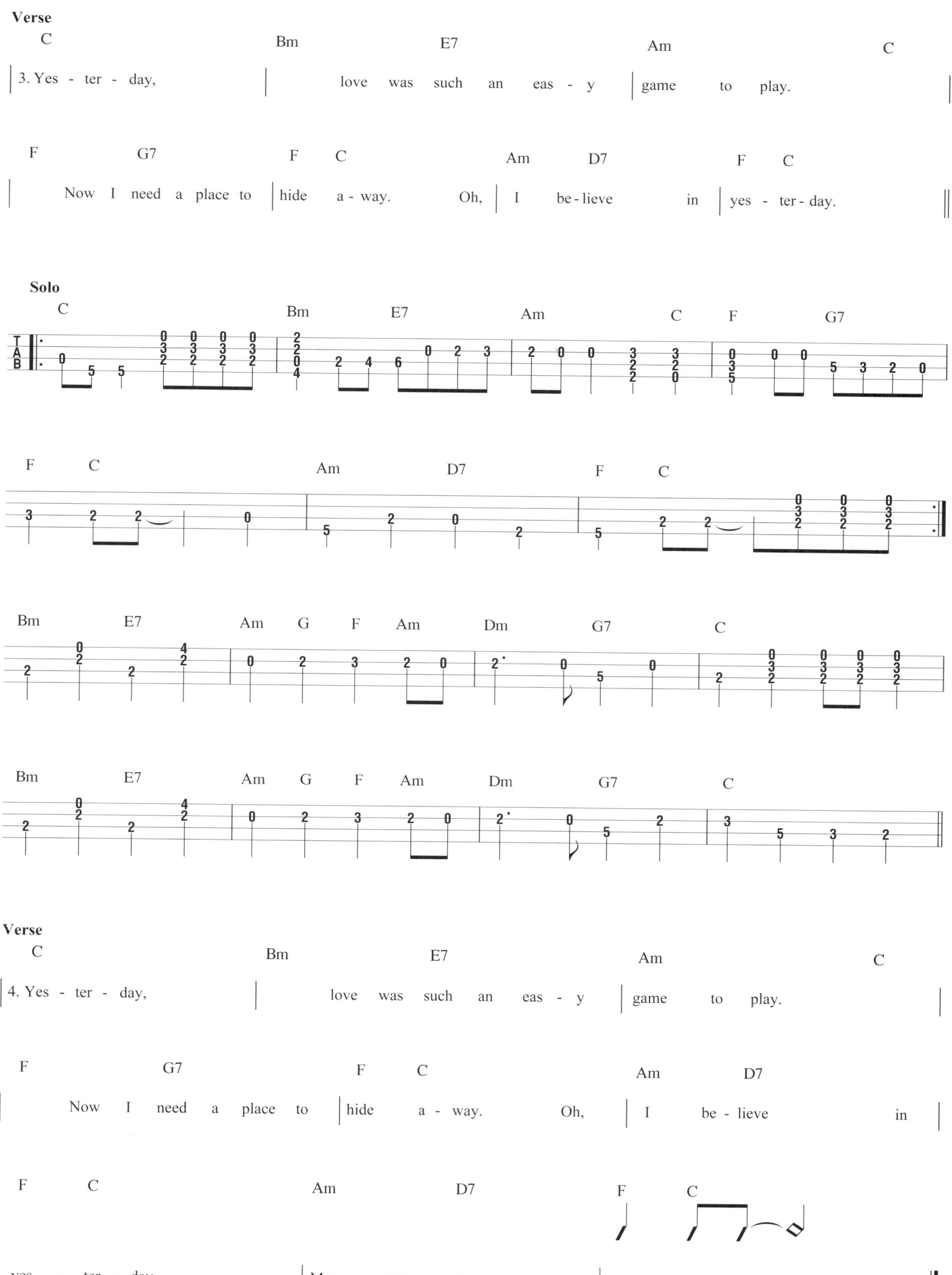
Verse
C Bm E7 Am C
3. Yes - ter - day, love was such an eas - y game to play.
F G7 F C Am D7 F C
Now I need a place to hide a - way. Oh, I be - lieve in yes - ter - day.
Solo
C Bm E7 Am C F G7
T
A
B
F C Am D7 F C
Bm E7 Am G F Am Dm G7 C
Bm E7 Am G F Am Dm G7 C
Verse
C Bm E7 Am C
4. Yes - ter - day, love was such an eas - y game to play.
F G7 F C Am D7
Now I need a place to hide a - way. Oh, I be - lieve in
F C Am D7 F C
yes - ter - day. Mm, mm, mm, mm, mm, mm, mm.

Your Cheatin' Heart

Words and Music by Hank Williams

Melody:

Your cheat - in' heart will make you

C F G D7

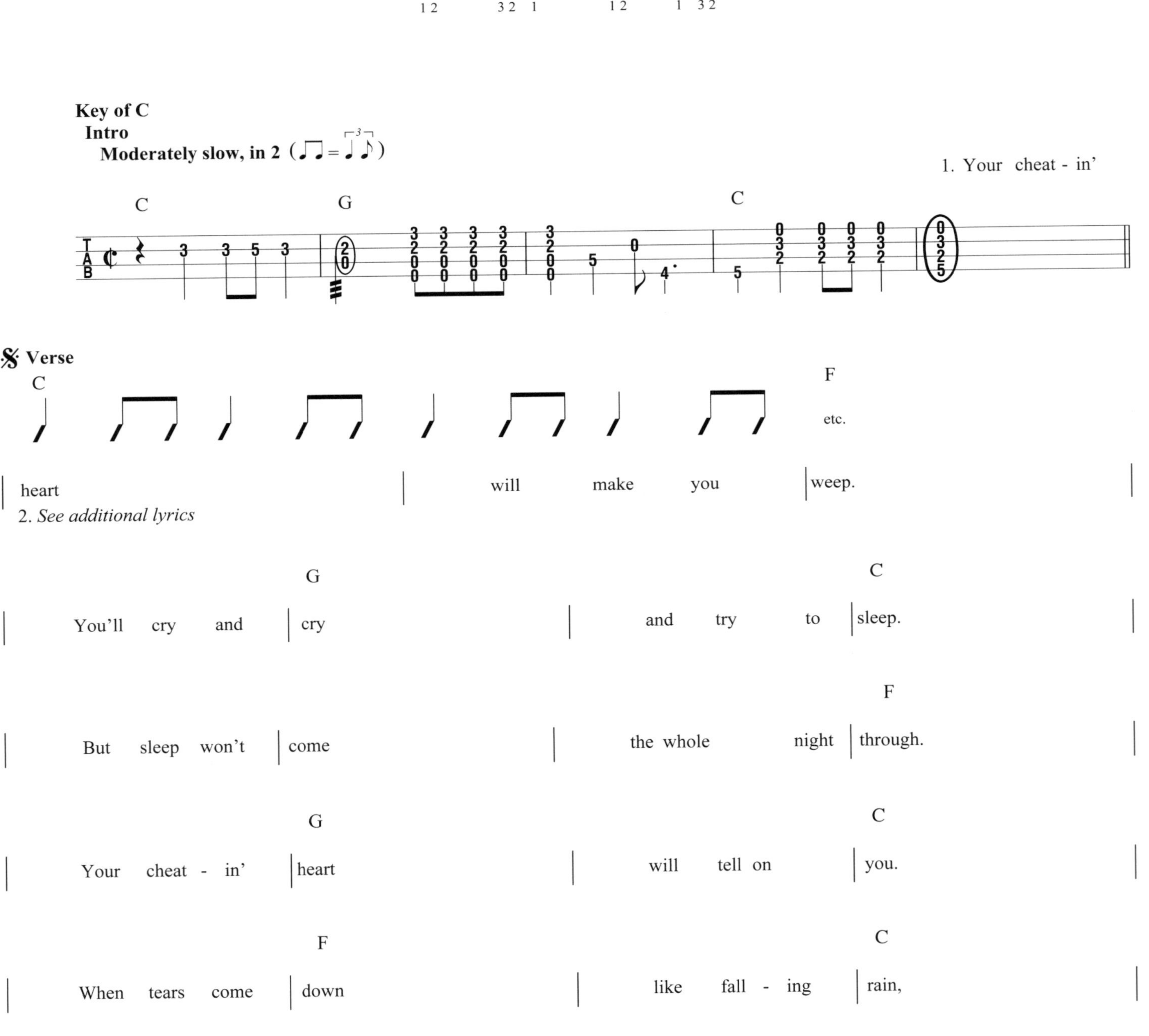

Key of C
Intro
Moderately slow, in 2
C G C
1. Your cheat - in'
Verse
C F
etc.
heart will make you weep.
2. See additional lyrics
G C
You'll cry and cry and try to sleep.
F
But sleep won't come the whole night through.
G C
Your cheat - in' heart will tell on you.
F C
When tears come down like fall - ing rain,

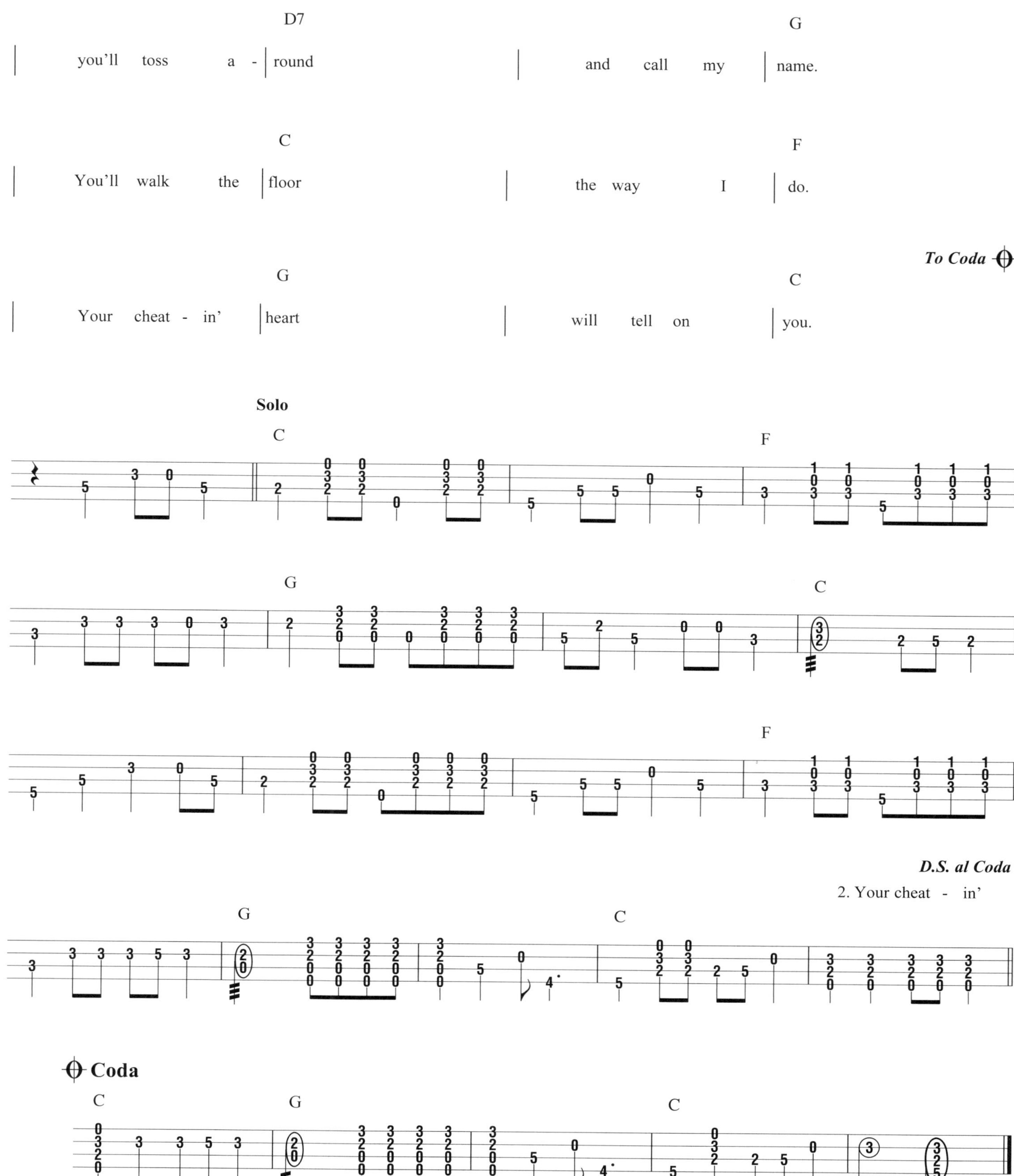
D7
G
you'll toss a - round
and call my name.
C
F
You'll walk the floor
the way I do.
To Coda
G
C
Your cheat - in' heart
will tell on you.
Solo
C
F
G
C
F
D.S. al Coda
2. Your cheat - in'
G
C
Coda
C
G
C

Additional Lyrics

2. Your cheatin' heart will pine some day,
   And crave the love you threw away.
   The time will come when you'll be blue.
   Your cheatin' heart will tell on you.
   When tears come down like falling rain,
   You'll toss around and call my name.
   You'll walk the floor the way I do.
   Your cheatin' heart will tell on you.

Mandolin Rhythm Tab Legend

Rhythm Tab is a form of notation that adds rhythmic values to the traditional tab staff.

TABLATURE graphically represents the mandolin fingerboard. Each horizontal line represents a string course, and each number represents a fret. Rhythmic values are shown using ovals, stems, and dots.

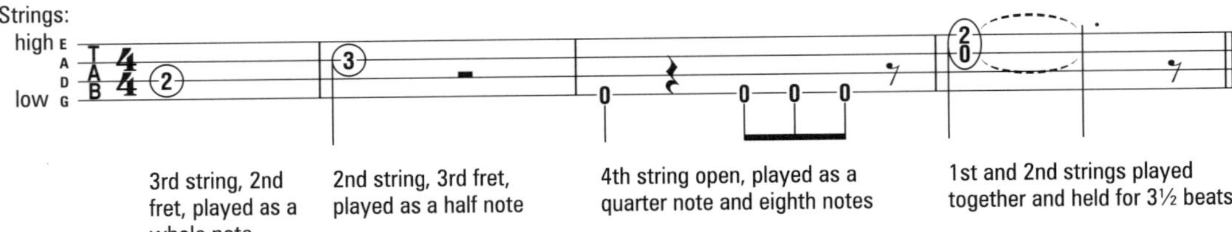

Strings:
high E
A
D
low G

3rd string, 2nd fret, played as a whole note

2nd string, 3rd fret, played as a half note

4th string open, played as a quarter note and eighth notes

1st and 2nd strings played together and held for 3½ beats

Definitions for Special Notation

QUARTER-STEP BEND: Strike the note and bend up 1/4 step.

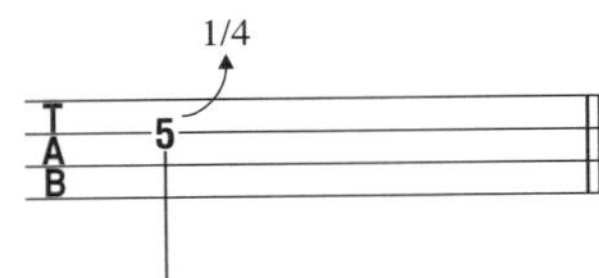

1/4

BEND AND RELEASE: Strike the note and bend up as indicated, then release back to the original note. Only the first note is struck.

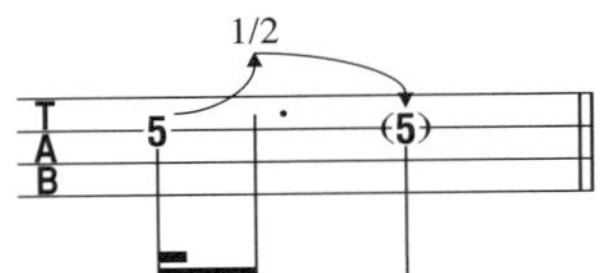

1/2

TREMOLO PICKING: The note is picked rapidly and continuously.

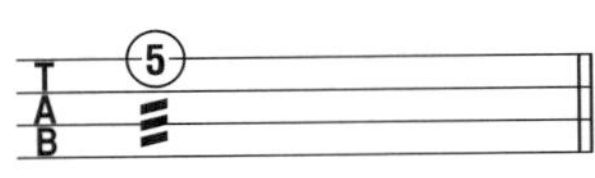

HAMMER-ON: Strike the first (lower) note with one finger, then sound the higher note (on the same string) with another finger by fretting it without picking.

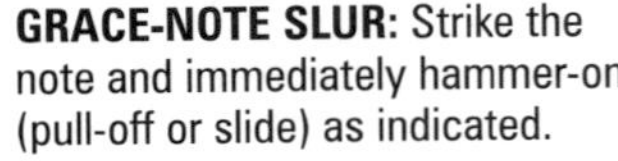

PULL-OFF: Place both fingers on the notes to be sounded. Strike the first note, and without picking, pull the finger off to sound the second (lower) note.

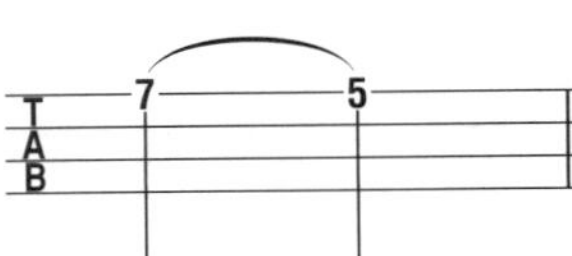

LEGATO SLIDE: Strike the first note and then slide the same fret-hand finger up or down to the second note. The second note is not struck.

SHIFT SLIDE: Same as legato slide, except the second note is struck.

GRACE-NOTE SLUR: Strike the note and immediately hammer-on (pull-off or slide) as indicated.

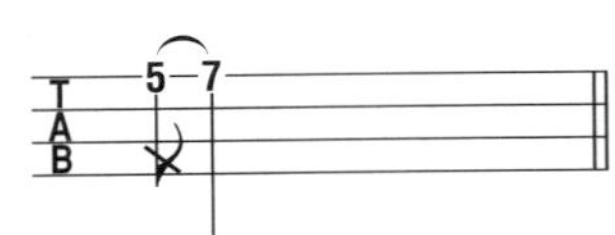

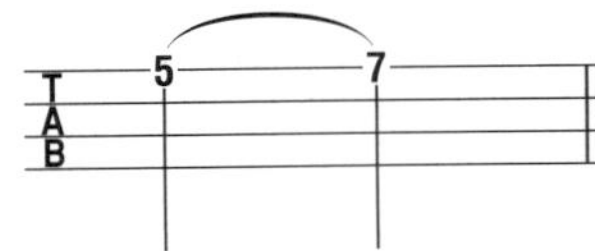

NATURAL HARMONIC: Strike the note while the fret hand lightly touches the string directly over the fret indicated.

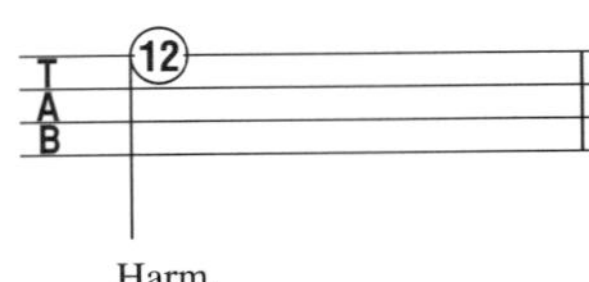

Harm.

MUTED STRING: A percussive sound is produced by laying the fret hand across the string without depressing, and striking it with the pick hand.

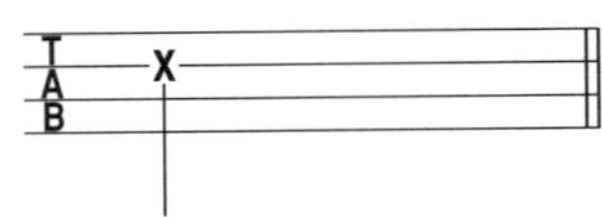

Additional Musical Definitions

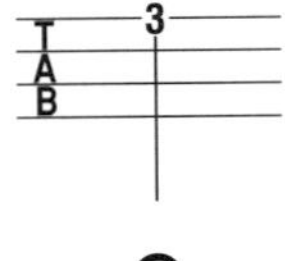

(staccato) • Play the note short

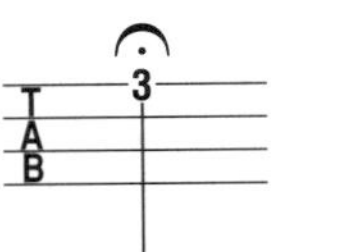

(fermata) • A hold or pause

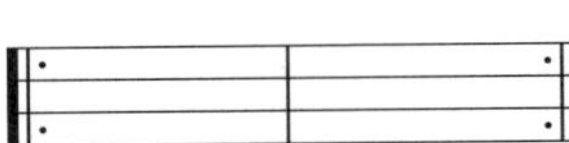

• Repeat measures between signs

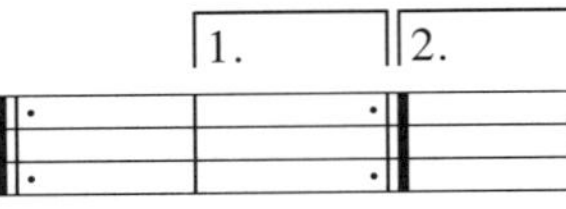

1.
2.

• When a repeated section has different endings, play the first ending only the first time and the second ending only the second time.

D.S. al Coda	• Go back to the sign (𝄋), then play until the measure marked "*To Coda*," then skip to the section labelled "**Coda**."
D.C. al Fine	• Go back to the beginning of the song and play until the measure marked "*Fine*" (end).
N.C.	• No chord
tacet	• Instrument is silent (drops out).

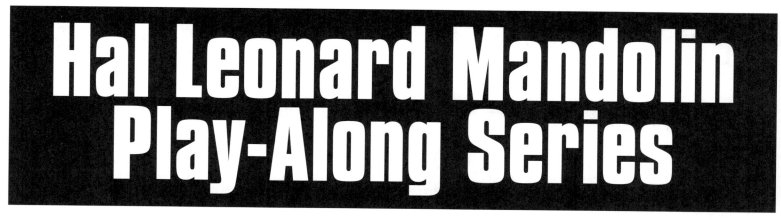

Hal Leonard Mandolin Play-Along Series

HAL•LEONARD®
MANDOLIN PLAY-ALONG

AUDIO
ACCESS
INCLUDED

HAL•LEONARD
MANDOLIN
PLAY-ALONG
VOL. 1
BLUEGRASS

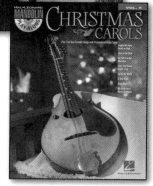

The Mandolin Play-Along Series will help you play your favorite songs quickly and easily. Just follow the written music, listen to the CD or online audio to hear how the mandolin should sound, and then play along using the separate backing tracks. Standard notation and tablature are both included in the book. The audio is enhanced so users can adjust the recording to any tempo without changing the pitch!

INCLUDES TAB

1. BLUEGRASS
Angeline the Baker • Billy in the Low Ground • Blackberry Blossom • Fisher's Hornpipe • Old Joe Clark • Salt Creek • Soldier's Joy • Whiskey Before Breakfast.
00702517 Book/Online Audio $14.99

2. CELTIC
A Fig for a Kiss • The Kesh Jig • Morrison's Jig • The Red Haired Boy • Rights of Man • Star of Munster • The Star of the County Down • Temperence Reel.
00702518 Book/Online Audio $14.99

3. POP HITS
Brown Eyed Girl • I Shot the Sheriff • In My Life • Mrs. Robinson • Stand by Me • Superstition • Tears in Heaven • You Can't Hurry Love.
00702519 Book/CD Pack.............................. $14.99

4. J.S. BACH
Bourree in E Minor • Invention No.1 (Bach) • Invention No.2 (Bach) • Jesu, Joy of Man's Desiring • March in D Major • Minuet in G • Musette in D Major • Sleepers, Awake (Wachet Auf).
00702520 Book/CD Pack.............................. $14.99

5. GYPSY SWING
After You've Gone • Avalon • China Boy • Dark Eyes • Indiana (Back Home Again in Indiana) • Limehouse Blues • The Sheik of Araby • Tiger Rag (Hold That Tiger).
00702521 Book/CD Pack.............................. $14.99

6. ROCK HITS
Back in the High Life Again • Copperhead Road • Going to California • Ho Hey • Iris • Losing My Religion • Maggie May • Sunny Came Home.
00119367 Book/Online Audio $16.99

7. ITALIAN CLASSICS
Come Back to Sorrento • La Spagnola • Mattinata • 'O Sole Mio • Oh Marie • Santa Lucia • Tarantella • Vieni Sul Mar.
00119368 Book/Online Audio $16.99

8. MANDOLIN FAVORITES
Arrivederci Roma (Goodbye to Rome) • The Godfather (Love Theme) • Misirlou • Never on Sunday • Over the Rainbow • Spanish Eyes • That's Amoré (That's Love) • Theme from "Zorba the Greek."
00119494 Book/Online Audio $14.99

9. CHRISTMAS CAROLS
Angels We Have Heard on High • Carol of the Bells • Go, Tell It on the Mountain • Hark! the Herald Angels Sing • Joy to the World • O Holy Night • Silent Night • We Wish You a Merry Christmas.
00119895 Book/CD Pack.............................. $14.99

10. SONGS FOR BEGINNERS
Amazing Grace • Cripple Creek • Devil's Dream • Frankie and Johnny • Frosty Morning • Over the Waterfall • Short'nin' Bread • Stone's Rag.
00156776 Book/Online Audio $14.99

11. CLASSICAL THEMES
Blue Danube Waltz • Eine Kleine Nachtmusik ("Serenade"), First Movement Excerpt • Für Elise • Humoresque • In the Hall of the Mountain King • La donna e mobile • The Merry Widow Waltz • Spring, First Movement.
00156777 Book/Online Audio $14.99

HAL•LEONARD®
www.halleonard.com

Prices, contents, and availability subject to change without notice.

0418

Great Mandolin Songbooks

from Hal Leonard

THE BEATLES FOR SOLO MANDOLIN

20 favorite Beatles tunes in chord melody arrangements for mandolin including: All You Need Is Love • Blackbird • Can't Buy Me Love • Eight Days a Week • Here Comes the Sun • Hey Jude • In My Life • Let It Be • Michelle • Strawberry Fields Forever • Twist and Shout • We Can Work It Out • Yesterday • and more.

00128672 .... $16.99

CHRISTMAS CAROLS FOR MANDOLIN

23 Christmas songs arranged especially for mandolin, including: Away in a Manger • The First Noel • God Rest Ye Merry, Gentlemen • Hark! the Herald Angels Sing • It Came upon the Midnight Clear • Jingle Bells • O Christmas Tree • O Holy Night • Silent Night • Up on the Housetop • We Wish You a Merry Christmas • What Child Is This? • and more.

00699800 .... $10.99

CLASSICAL SOLOS FOR MANDOLIN

This publication contains 20 classical mandolin pieces compiled, edited, and performed by world-renowned virtuoso Carlos Aonzo. The music is arranged in order of difficulty beginning with exercises by Giuseppe Branzoli and finishing with complete concert pieces using the most advanced mandolin techniques. Pieces include: Andante – Pizzicato on the Left Hand (Carlo Munier) • Exercise in A Major (Giuseppe Branzoli) • La Fustemberg (Antonio Riggeiri) • Partita V in G minor Overture (Filippo Sauli) • Theme with Variations in A Major (Bartolomeo Bortolazzi) • and more.

00124955 Book/Online Audio $19.99

DISNEY SONGS FOR MANDOLIN

25 classic melodies from Disney's finest productions over the years presented in arrangements for mandolin. Includes: The Bare Necessities • Be Our Guest • Circle of Life • Colors of the Wind • Go the Distance • Heigh-Ho • It's a Small World • Mickey Mouse March • A Spoonful of Sugar • Under the Sea • When You Wish upon a Star • Zip-A-Dee-Doo-Dah • and more.

00701904 .... $12.99

FIDDLE TUNES FOR FLATPICKERS: MANDOLIN

Now you can learn to play famous fiddle tunes specially arranged for mandolin. Get started flatpickin' now with songs like: Blackberry Blossom • Kentucky Mandolin • Old Joe Clark • Salt Creek • Turkey in the Straw • and more. The accompanying audio features specially mixed tracks that let you hear the mandolin alone, the mandolin with the backing track, or just the backing track so you can play along!

14011276 Book/Online Audio $17.99

FIRST 50 SONGS YOU SHOULD PLAY ON MANDOLIN

INCLUDES TAB

A fantastic collection of 50 accessible, must-know favorites for the beginner who's learned enough to start playing popular songs: Amazing Grace • Crazy • Cripple Creek • Folsom Prison Blues • Friend of the Devil • Hallelujah • Ho Hey • I Am a Man of Constant Sorrow • I Walk the Line • I'll Fly Away • Losing My Religion • Maggie May • Mr. Bojangles • Rocky Top • Take Me Home, Country Roads • Tennessee Waltz • Wagon Wheel • Wildwood Flower • Yesterday • and more.

00155489 Tab, Chords & Lyrics $15.99

FOLK SONGS FOR MANDOLIN

SING, STRUM & PICK ALONG

More than 40 traditional favorites arranged specifically for mandolin: Arkansas Traveler • Buffalo Gals • (I Wish I Was In) Dixie • Home on the Range • I've Been Working on the Railroad • Man of Constant Sorrow • Michael Row the Boat Ashore • My Old Kentucky Home • Oh! Susanna • She'll Be Comin' 'Round the Mountain • Turkey in the Straw • The Wabash Cannon Ball • When the Saints Go Marching In • Yankee Doodle • and more!

00701918 .... $16.99

THE HAL LEONARD MANDOLIN FAKE BOOK

This collection packs 300 songs into one handy songbook: As Time Goes By • Bad, Bad Leroy Brown • Can't Take My Eyes off of You • Daydream Believer • Edelweiss • Fields of Gold • Going to California • Hey, Soul Sister • Ho Hey • I'm Yours • Island in the Sun • King of the Road • Losing My Religion • Maggie May • Over the Rainbow • Peaceful Easy Feeling • Redemption Song • Shenandoah • Toes • Unchained Melody • Wildwood Flower • You Are My Sunshine • and many more.

00141053 Melody, Lyrics & Chords $39.99

MASTERS OF THE MANDOLIN

INCLUDES TAB

This collection of 130 mandolin solos is an invaluable resource for fans of bluegrass music. Each song excerpt has been meticulously transcribed note-for-note in tab from its original recording so you can study and learn these masterful solos by some of the instrument's finest pickers. From the legendary Bill Monroe to more contemporary heroes like Sam Bush and Chris Thile, and even including some non-bluegrass greats like Dave Apollon and Jethro Burns, this book contains a wide variety of music and playing styles to enjoy.

00195621 .... $24.99

THE MIGHTY MANDOLIN CHORD SONGBOOK

Lyrics, chord symbols, and mandolin chord diagrams for 100 pop and rock hits: Blowin' in the Wind • Crazy Little Thing Called Love • Dance with Me • Edelweiss • Georgia on My Mind • Hey Jude • I Feel the Earth Move • Jolene • Lean on Me • Me and Bobby McGee • Mean • No Woman No Cry • Patience • Ring of Fire • Sweet Caroline • This Land Is Your Land • Unchained Melody • Wonderwall • and many more.

00123221 .... $17.99

O BROTHER, WHERE ART THOU?

This collection contains both note-for-note transcribed mandolin solos, as well as mandolin arrangements of the melody lines for 11 songs: Angel Band • The Big Rock Candy Mountain • Down to the River to Pray • I Am a Man of Constant Sorrow • I Am Weary (Let Me Rest) • I'll Fly Away • In the Highways (I'll Be Somewhere Working for My Lord) • In the Jailhouse Now • Indian War Whoop • Keep on the Sunny Side • You Are My Sunshine.

00695762 Tab, Chords & Lyrics $15.99

THE ULTIMATE MANDOLIN SONGBOOK

arr. Janet Davis

The Ultimate Mandolin Songbook contains multiple versions varying in difficulty of 26 of the most popular songs from bluegrass, jazz, ragtime, rock, pop, gospel, swing and other genres, in both standard notation and mandolin tab. Songs: Alabama Jubilee • Autumn Leaves • The Entertainer • Great Balls of Fire • How Great Thou Art • Limehouse Blues • Orange Blossom Special • Rawhide • Stardust • Tennessee Waltz • Yesterday • You Are My Sunshine • and more!

00699913 Book/Online Audio $34.99

HAL•LEONARD®

For more info, songlists, or to purchase these and more books from your favorite music retailer, go to **halleonard.com**

Prices, contents and availability are subject to change without notice.

101 TIPS FROM HAL LEONARD

STUFF ALL THE PROS KNOW AND USE

Ready to take your skills to the next level? These books present valuable how-to insight that musicians of all styles and levels can benefit from. The text, photos, music, diagrams and accompanying audio provide a terrific, easy-to-use resource for a variety of topics.

101 HAMMOND B3 TIPS

101 FLUTE TIPS

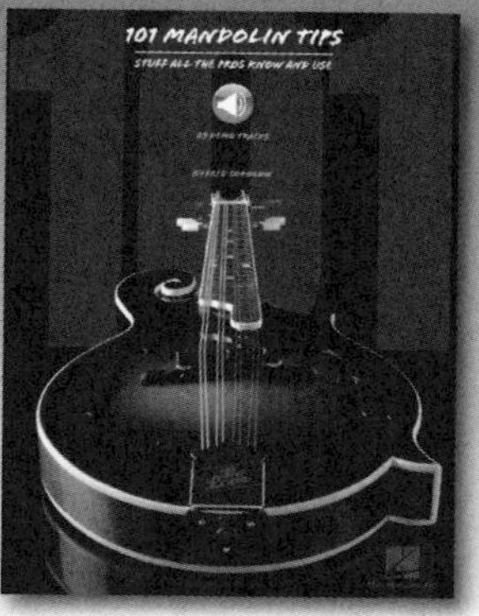
101 MANDOLIN TIPS

101 GUITAR TIPS

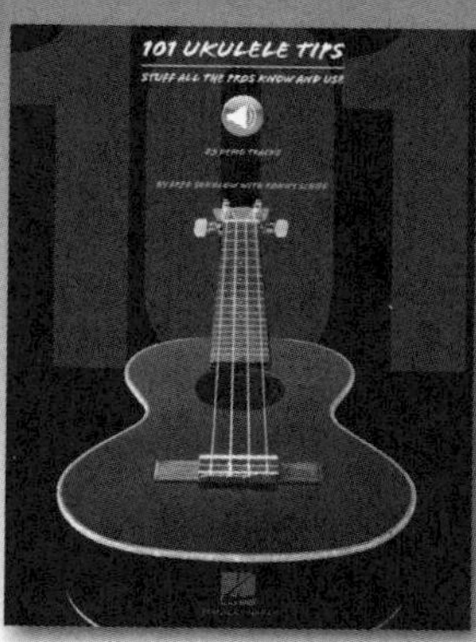
101 UKULELE TIPS

101 HAMMOND B-3 TIPS
by Brian Charette
Topics include: funky scales and modes; unconventional harmonies; creative chord voicings; cool drawbar settings; ear-grabbing special effects; professional gigging advice; practicing effectively; making good use of the pedals; and much more!
00128918 Book/Online Audio $14.99

101 HARMONICA TIPS
by Steve Cohen
Topics include: techniques, position playing, soloing, accompaniment, the blues, equipment, performance, maintenance, and much more!
00821040 Book/Online Audio $17.99

101 CELLO TIPS—2ND EDITION
by Angela Schmidt
Topics include: bowing techniques, non-classical playing, electric cellos, accessories, gig tips, practicing, recording and much more!
00149094 Book/Online Audio $14.99

101 FLUTE TIPS
by Elaine Schmidt
Topics include: selecting the right flute for you, finding the right teacher, warm-up exercises, practicing effectively, taking good care of your flute, gigging advice, staying and playing healthy, and much more.
00119883 Book/CD Pack..................................$14.99

101 SAXOPHONE TIPS
by Eric Morones
Topics include: techniques; maintenance; equipment; practicing; recording; performance; and much more!
00311082 Book/CD Pack..................................$19.99

101 TRUMPET TIPS
by Scott Barnard
Topics include: techniques, articulation, tone production, soloing, exercises, special effects, equipment, performance, maintenance and much more.
00312082 Book/CD Pack..................................$14.99

101 UPRIGHT BASS TIPS
by Andy McKee
Topics include: right- and left-hand technique, improvising and soloing, practicing, proper care of the instrument, ear training, performance, and much more.
00102009 Book/Online Audio $14.99

101 BASS TIPS
by Gary Willis
Topics include: techniques, improvising and soloing, equipment, practicing, ear training, performance, theory, and much more.
00695542 Book/Online Audio $19.99

101 DRUM TIPS—2ND EDITION
Topics include: grooves, practicing, warming up, tuning, gear, performance, and much more!
00151936 Book/Online Audio $14.99

101 FIVE-STRING BANJO TIPS
by Fred Sokolow
Topics include: techniques, ear training, performance, and much more!
00696647 Book/CD Pack..................................$14.99

101 GUITAR TIPS
by Adam St. James
Topics include: scales, music theory, truss rod adjustments, proper recording studio set-ups, and much more. The book also features snippets of advice from some of the most celebrated guitarists and producers in the music business.
00695737 Book/Online Audio $17.99

101 MANDOLIN TIPS
by Fred Sokolow
Topics include: playing tips, practicing tips, accessories, mandolin history and lore, practical music theory, and much more!
00119493 Book/Online Audio $14.99

101 RECORDING TIPS
by Adam St. James
This book contains recording tips, suggestions, and advice learned firsthand from legendary producers, engineers, and artists. These tricks of the trade will improve anyone's home or pro studio recordings.
00311035 Book/CD Pack..................................$14.95

101 UKULELE TIPS
by Fred Sokolow with Ronny Schiff
Topics include: techniques, improvising and soloing, equipment, practicing, ear training, performance, uke history and lore, and much more!
00696596 Book/Online Audio $15.99

101 VIOLIN TIPS
by Angela Schmidt
Topics include: bowing techniques, non-classical playing, electric violins, accessories, gig tips, practicing, recording, and much more!
00842672 Book/CD Pack..................................$14.99

Prices, contents and availability subject to change without notice.

HAL•LEONARD®

www.halleonard.com